STUDY GUIDE TO ACCOMPANY
SOCIOLOGY
AN INTRODUCTION

STUDY GUIDE TO ACCOMPANY
SOCIOLOGY
AN INTRODUCTION • FOURTH EDITION

Michael S. Bassis
Antioch University

Richard J. Gelles
University of Rhode Island

Ann Levine

Craig Calhoun
Consulting Editor
University of North Carolina

Prepared by
Ann Levine
and by
John Maiolo and
Grace Jendrasiak
East Carolina University

McGraw-Hill, Inc.
New York St. Louis San Francisco Auckland Bogotá Caracas Hamburg
Lisbon London Madrid Mexico Milan Montreal New Delhi Paris
San Juan São Paulo Singapore Sydney Tokyo Toronto

STUDY GUIDE TO ACCOMPANY
BASSIS, GELLES, and LEVINE:
SOCIOLOGY: An Introduction

1 2 3 4 5 6 7 8 9 0 DOC DOC 9 5 4 3 2 1 0

ISBN 0-07-004064-8

The editors were Phillip A. Butcher, Katherine Blake,
and Sheila H. Gillams;
the production supervisor was Leroy A. Young;
the designer was Amy E. Becker.
R. R. Donnelley & Sons Company was printer and binder.

STUDY GUIDE

CONTENTS

INTRODUCTION

In some ways, taking a course in sociology is like signing up to watch the evening news. You will be learning about revolutions, crime, unemployment rates, the crisis in education, the trouble with families, and other topics that will frequently appear in the news this semester. There are important differences between sociology and media reports on current events, however. To discover just what they are, you will have to read Chapter One of your textbook. For the moment, let us just say that the way sociologists approach people and events, the kinds of questions they ask, and how they answer them are quite different from that to which you are accustomed. Some of the theories you will find in your study of sociology will challenge commonsense assumptions about how the world works. Many of the findings will surprise you. Be prepared for an intellectual adventure.

This Study Guide is designed to help you on that journey. First, let us tell you what it will not do. It is not a substitute for reading the chapters in your text. Studies that are merely mentioned here are described in detail in the text; concepts that are only defined here are elaborated on in the text; theories outlined here are applied to concrete real world examples in the text. If you read the summaries in this Study Guide and skip the text, you are cheating yourself. It would be like reading the menu in a fine restaurant and leaving without having a meal.

Here is what the Study Guide *can* do. It will tell you how well you have mastered the material in the corresponding chapter of your text. It gives you instant feedback. If you answer all or most of the questions in the Study Guide correctly on your first try, you can sit back and relax. You are prepared for class. If you have not done so well, the Study Guide will tell you which sections of the text you need to read again and which concepts you haven't learned. If, after rereading the discussion in your text you are still uncertain, by all means ask your instructor for an explanation. You can also use the Study Guide to review before exams. The summaries and questions will jog your memory, reminding you of topics and concepts you studied before.

The Study Guide is organized this way. Each chapter begins with a set of Objectives. These objectives are phrased as questions and are arranged in the order in which the material is presented in the corresponding chapter of the text. We suggest that you read each question, flip through the relevant pages in your text, and make a few mental or written notes on the answers.

Next you'll find a list of the Concepts that were introduced in the corresponding chapter of your text. Understanding the terms sociologists use is an important first step toward learning how sociologists think. You are not simply memorizing new words as you did when you memorized vocabulary lists in grade school; you are learning new ideas. Instead of arranging these terms alphabetically, we've grouped related concepts together. If you see a term that you do not remember or do not quite understand, stop right there and go back to reread the section of the text where the term is introduced.

The Chapter Review highlights the main points made in the chapter in your text, following the order in which material was presented there. Read this review carefully before going on to the next sections of the Study Guide chapter.

The Concept Review asks you to match terms with the correct definition. The correct answers follow. If you have trouble with some of the terms, you may find it helpful to review groups of related concepts. Circle the ones you missed and return to them when you have completed the Study Guide chapter.

The Review Questions are a list of twenty to twenty-five multiple-choice questions based on theories and research in the corresponding chapter of the text. These questions do not follow the order of topics in the text. They are scrambled to make things a little harder for you. Answer all the questions first, then turn to the answer section. We've included a brief explanation of each correct answer and a reference to the relevant pages in the text. To get the most of out this section, look at the question, read the explanation, then think about why the other choices are wrong.

The next section, Myth or Fact?, is intended as a tease. The answers to these true or false questions are found in your text. By now you know most of the answers. But before you studied the chapter in your text you probably would have answered many of these questions incorrectly. The answers violate many of our unquestioned assumptions. If you want to have some fun, and if you enjoy a good argument, try them on someone who isn't studying sociology--for example, your parents or a friend. But before you do this, make sure you have your facts straight.

The Critical Thinking section consists of information and questions designed to show how you can apply sociological concepts to discussions of social issues or personal concerns. These materials, some of which will include summaries or excerpts from new studies, bring concepts to life by asking you to imagine participating in experiments or real-life situations that illustrate those concepts.

In a few chapters we have added an Exercise, a questionnaire that allows you to evaluate your own behavior from a sociological point of view. These questionnaires have been included for your enjoyment.

Given these materials, in combination with your text, you will find that studying sociology can be a very pleasant journey from start to finish.

We wish to express our appreciation and sincere thanks to Donna Evans of East Carolina University for her untiring assistance and patience in typing this manuscript. Betty Lou White, also of East Carolina, provided valuable assistance in keeping the necessary equipment, software, and supplies available. She and Alise Rowan, of Greenville, North Carolina, were invaluable in helping to untangle the mysteries of word processing programs.

Ann Levine
John Maiolo
Grace Jendrasiak

PART ONE: THE SOCIOLOGICAL PERSPECTIVE

Chapter One
SOCIOLOGICAL REALITIES

OBJECTIVES

After reading Chapter One you should be able to give in-depth answers to the following questions:

1. What is sociology?
2. How does what you learn about the "real world" from studying sociology differ from conventional wisdom (common sense) and what you learn from the TV news?
3. What is the relationship between sociology and common sense?
4. What is the sociological imagination?
5. How does the sociological explanation of suicide differ from commonsense explanations?
6. What is the promise of sociology in regard to individual and public enlightenment? identification of social problems? solutions to problems?

CONCEPTS

You should also understand the following sociological concepts:

anomie
altruistic suicide
anomic suicide
egoistic suicide
copycat suicide
social forces
social facts
sociological imagination
bad news bias
sociology

CHAPTER REVIEW

I. What is sociology?

Sociology is one of the family of social sciences that seeks to explain patterns of human behavior. Specifically, sociology is the study of the groups and societies people create and of how these, in turn, affect the people who create and maintain them.

Your text explains sociology by comparing it with other social sciences, especially psychology. Psychology focuses on internal traits and personality--the behavior and attitudes that characterize Jim, whomever he is, with whatever he is doing. In contrast, sociology is interested in the behavior and attitudes that characterize all college students (or all criminals or all female executives) regardless of their individual personalities. Why are all college students in some ways alike? The sociological approach is that the kind of society in which you live and your position in that society in part determine the kind of person you are. Thus, the emphasis in sociology is on how external forces shape behavior.

II. How does what you learn about the "real world" from studying sociology differ from "commonsense" impressions and what you learn from TV news?

Many Americans acquire most of their information about the world from the groups within which they interact, and the mass media, especially the TV news. Your text discusses how our perceptions of the social world are determined in large part by our position in that world, and how something as seemingly simple as what we physically see is affected by our interactions with others. Then, the text identifies three ways by which the image of the real world presented on the TV news differs from that offered by sociology.

A. The TV news focuses on dramatic events and famous people. What the President did today is news; what you did today is not--unless you were caught robbing a bank, participated in a protest march, or died in a disco fire. Sociologists are as interested in ordinary people and commonplace events as they are in exceptional people and behavior.

B. Much of what you see on the TV news is bad news--violent crime, natural disasters, international conflict. For example, the news may report statistics on the millions of Americans who are unemployed and interview a family that is about to lose its home. The millions of Americans who are employed and are making their mortgage payments are not *news*. Sociological research often shows that things are not as bad as they seem on the news.

C. On TV newscasts, complex events must be squeezed into two- or three-minute slots. You learn the *who, what, when, and where* but seldom the *why*. Sociology is concerned with establishing connections between events, tracing patterns, and thus making sense out of current events.

III. What are the public and private uses of sociology?

Like all sciences, sociology is based on the belief that a better understanding of the world will lay the foundation for improving the quality of both public and private life.

C. Wright Mills' concept of sociological imagination illustrates the private uses of sociology. The imagination is the ability to grasp the connections between public issues and private troubles (for example, in divorce and unemployment). The questions in this and later chapters of this Study Guide will test your sociological imagination, as well as your grasp of material in the text.

IV. How does the sociological explanation of suicide differ from other types of explanations?

Suicide is an act that cries out for explanation. Why did the victim do it? Commonsense explanations and news reports tend to be individualistic, focusing on why a particular person committed suicide. But individualistic explanations cannot explain variations in suicide rates--why, for example, the suicide rate for young Americans rose in recent years. It was this puzzle that drew the French sociologist Emile Durkheim to the study of suicide. Although published almost a century ago (1897), Durkheim's classic work on suicide challenges assumptions about suicide that are still popular today. Painstaking analysis of statistics convinced Durkheim that variations in suicide rates among different groups could not be explained by mental illness, ethnic or racial background, or climate. He concluded that there was something about the group itself that encouraged or discouraged suicide.

Your text traces Durkheim's intellectual journey to show how he came to identify three different types of suicide:

A. Egoistic suicide occurs under conditions of *excessive individualism,* when people have become detached from groups that might have inspired their loyalty and participation.

B. Altruistic suicide, in contrast, occurs under conditions of *excessive attachment,* when individuals so identify with a group or community that their own life has no independent value.

C. Anomic suicide occurs under conditions of anomie, or "lawlessness" in the broad sense, when traditional values and guidelines for behavior have broken down.

Note that in each case Durkheim explained suicide rates in terms of the characteristics of the groups and communities in which people lived--not in terms of psychological or biological factors. He argued that one can no more explain patterns of social behavior in terms of individual motives than one can explain the human body by describing individual cells. Society is more than the sum of its individual members. Durkheim chose suicide as a subject because it illustrates how social forces are social facts, and influence a form of behavior that most of us consider intensely private. That social forces influence such behavior is a key point in the chapter and one of the basic lessons of sociology.

V.   What is the promise of sociology?

Society is changing rapidly. A most immediate task of sociology is to provide a framework for understanding such changes, in both our public affairs and private lives.
   A. Sociology can make people aware of the different ways in which social arrangements shape their lives. It can enlighten the general public to the nature and the effects of such social arrangements.
   B. Sociology has the ability to examine the assumptions underlying conventional wisdom, and to correct popular ideas that are wrong.
   C. Sociology can identify problems that the public has not recognized.
   D. Sociologists can design and evaluate alternative solutions to social problems. This includes problems in the private sector as illustrated by Rosabeth Kanter's work with Indsco.

CONCEPT REVIEW

Match each of the following terms with the correct definition.

   a. social forces
   b. anomic suicide
   c. commonsense impressions of the social world
   d. sociological imagination
   e. altruistic suicide
   f. sociology
   g. anomie
   h. egoistic suicide

   1. _B H_   Suicide that results from lack of attachment to social groups or a community, as opposed to suicide resulting from *too much* of an attachment.
   2. _a_   Influences on people's perceptions, attitudes, and behavior that derive from social institutions and social change.
   3. _d_   The ability to see the interplay of biography and history and the connections between public issues and private troubles.

4. _g_ A breakdown in social guidelines at the societal, or group, level for behavior and the social definitions of right and wrong.

5. _AB_ Suicide that results from a major disruption of the social order.

6. _f_ The systematic study of the groups and societies human beings create, how they influence our behavior, and how they change over time.

7. _E_ Suicide that results from excessive attachment to a group or community.

8. _C_ Often incorrect perceptions, based on everyday interaction.

Answers

1. h	5. b
2. a	6. f
3. d	7. e
4. g	8. c

REVIEW QUESTIONS

These questions test your overall grasp of the material in Chapter One. The correct answers, with a short explanation, are printed at the end of the section.

1. Which of the following is one of the concerns that distinguishes sociology from TV journalism?
   a. its emphasis on *knowns*
   b. its insistence on the hard facts
   c. its focus on social contexts
   d. its interest in current events

2. The Soviet occupation of Afghanistan during the 1970s and 1980s is comparable to which of the following experiences in U.S. history, according to the text?
   a. the Civil War
   b. the Vietnam war
   c. World War I
   d. our involvement with the Nicaraguan Contras

3. Emile Durkheim was the first sociologist to systematically examine a number of different types of suicide. Which of the following did Durkheim cite as an example of altruistic suicide?

    a.   the high rate of suicide in Protestant nations
    b.   the high suicide rate during economic booms
    c.   the high suicide rate among soldiers
    d.   the high suicide rate among single people

4.   What we think we physically see can be affected by our interactions with others, according to the text. This was illustrated by a discussion of which of the following research efforts?
    a.   the experiment with lines by Solomon Asch
    b.   Kanter's research with Indsco
    c.   Erikson's study of Buffalo Creek
    d.   Phillips' study of copycat suicides

5.   As used in your text, the phrase *bad news bias* refers to:
    a.   the *great man theory* of history
    b.   inaccurate reporting of the facts
    c.   the misrepresentation of white-collar crime
    d.   the overreporting of conflict, hardship, and disasters

6.   The term *sociological imagination* refers to:
    a.   a strategy for reducing wars, unemployment, and divorce
    b.   what sociologists have and nonsociologists lack
    c.   an interest in biographies
    d.   C. Wright Mills' theory of history
    e.   the ability to see personal problems within a social perspective

7.   Durkheim's classic work *Suicide* was based on:
    a.   interviews with families of individuals who had committed suicide
    b.   logical analysis of the possible motives for suicide
    c.   systematic analysis of official statistics on suicide
    d.   biological and environmental theories of the day
    e.   all of the above

8.   A journal article reports that anorexia nervosa (chronic, self-imposed starvation) is most likely to occur among young, middle-class women whose families set high standards of achievement. This is an example of:
    a.   psychological analysis
    b.   biomedical research
    c.   sociological findings
    d.   the bad news bias

9. Sociology is distinguished from other social sciences by its concern with:
   - a. the way groups and societies shape behavior ← *What is Sociology?*
   - b. the historical origins of current events
   - c. patterns of behavior
   - d. people's motives
   - e. the real world

10. Sociology has the ability to:
    - a. identify heretofore unrecognized problems
    - b. design solutions to social problems
    - c. enlighten the general public
    - d. all of the above

11. The fact that suicide rates are higher for single than for married people, and higher for childless couples than for couples with children, illustrates:
    - a. egoistic suicide
    - b. altruistic suicide
    - c. anomic suicide

12. The comparatively high suicide rate at the beginning of the Great Depression in the United States was an example of:
    - a. egoistic suicide
    - b. altruistic suicide
    - c. anomic suicide

13. Which of the following studies might you be likely to find in a sociological journal?
    - a. a case history of a teenage suicide
    - b. an analysis of the effects of family size on student achievement
    - c. a biomedical study of drug dependency
    - d. a history of the Industrial Revolution
    - e. a discussion of symbolic logic

14. Durkheim argued that variations in the suicide rate must be explained in terms of:
    - a. individual motives
    - b. social forces
    - c. altruism
    - d. egoism

Answers

1. c: Sociologists do insist on the facts, analyze current events, and on occasion, interview famous people--but so do TV newscasters. Analysis of social contexts, however, is unlikely to appear on the evening news. News broadcasts emphasize events that are spectacular, and will draw advertising. (See section entitled Sociology versus TV News.)

2. b: Villages were burned to the ground in both cases, and many civilians were killed. The difference was that Americans saw news coverage of the war in Vietnam every day which aroused public opinion. Soviet citizens did not see coverage of the war in Afghanistan because the government banned TV crews from filming events there. (News as the Dramatic Picture)

3. c: Altruistic behavior is associated with *excessive loyalty.* The best-known example of this is the tradition of hara-kiri among Japanese soldiers. (Speculation versus Fact)

4. a: According to the text, the subjects of the experiments were given incorrect answers during the trials by others in the groups. Most subjects went along with the majority opinion. (The Social Definition of Reality)

5. d: The phrase *bad news bias* is used, not to condemn news reporting, but to point out a dramatic flair in broadcasting that may create false impressions. (News as the Unique Event)

6. e: Mills was advocating a way of looking at personal troubles within a larger perspective, often outside the control of the individual. The sociological imagination allows one to see that his or her problems may not be his or her own doing. Such an understanding permits one to see that a private problem may not be due to an individual failing. So often, social forces are at work over which individuals have no control whatsoever. (Sociological Imagination)

7. c: Durkheim's objective was to show that scientific examination of the social facts is more valuable than philosophical, psychological, or any approach(es) which emphasize(s) suicide as an act in individual terms, or speculation. (Explaining Suicide: Two Approaches)

8. c: The information in this article is based on social (not psychological or biological) data and reflects the scientific search for general patterns. It is important to focus on social forces for the explanation. (Explaining Suicide: Two Approaches)

9. a: To some extent, sociology is concerned with all of these phenomena (answers a--e). What sets sociology apart, however, is its emphasis on groups and societies. (What Is Sociology?)

10. d: These represent the promise of sociology, and distinguish the discipline from conventional wisdom and most other social sciences. (The Promise of Sociology)

11. a: Parents (especially of large families) are active participants in a group that commands their loyalty, reducing chances for suicide. (The Case of Suicide--Egoistic Suicide)

12. c: Durkheim linked anomic suicide to sudden changes in the social environment, such as the stock market crash of 1929, that make people feel that the way they organized their lives no longer works. (The Case of Suicide--Anomic Suicide)

13. b: Sociologists study the effects of groups on behavior. Case studies are used in psychology; biomedical research is the province of physical science; history is the business of historians; and logic is a question for philosophers. (What Is Sociology?)

14. b: Durkheim held that social facts (such as the suicide rate) can only be explained in terms of social forces--in this case, the success or failure of accepted rules and reasons for living in linking people to a community. (The Case of Suicide)

MYTH OR FACT?

One of the aims of sociology is to challenge common sense. The following questions are designed to test your ability to distinguish popular myths from social facts, based on the material in the chapter you have just read. Think carefully before you answer.

1. Media coverage of current events may not always accurately portray a situation due to time, budget constraints, and personal biases.   t/f
2. Suicide rates tend to go up during economic booms.   t/f
3. Sociology is not useful in helping one cope with everyday individual problems.   t/f
4. Sociology can be helpful in solving social problems.   t/f

Answers

1. *True.* Standards vary, and in general journalists aim for a high degree of accuracy. However, what your text suggests is this: In the effort to capture your attention and keep you tuned in, the TV news focuses on the exotic, overreports bad news, and oversimplifies complex events.
2. *True.* Durkheim found that any sudden change in people's way of life, for better or worse, tends to increase the suicide rate.

3. *False.* Sociological analysis of social problems can help one locate his or her problems within larger societal forces.

4. *True.* Sociologists are often called upon to help legislators and regulators form social policies.

CRITICAL THINKING

When you have mastered the basic material in this chapter, you are ready to use what you have learned--in conversations about current events or local gossip; in discussions and papers for some of your other courses; in late-night musings about what it all *means.* These questions are designed to exercise your sociological imagination.

1. You are a reporter on a local newspaper and are asked to cover a rock concert. How might you exercise sociological imagination in your story?

2. Let us assume that you are an assertive person who stands up for your beliefs. Let us assume, further, that you feel women are discriminated against in the athletic programs at your college. You are asked to defend this belief before one of the following groups:

   a group of six female undergraduates who agree with you
   a group of six male undergraduates who have mixed opinions
   a group of six undergraduates who strongly disagree with you
   a group of six professors whom you do not know
   a group of six professors you do know, one of whom gave you a C minus (or worse) on your last paper

Would you present your argument in the same way before all of these groups? Would you feel equally comfortable (or uncomfortable) in all of these situations? What does this tell you about social pressure?

3. The suicide rate among elderly Americans steadily increased in the 1980s, according to government records. The nation experienced a 25% increase between 1981 and 1986 alone (to 21.6 people per 100,000 for the elderly, as against an overall national rate of 12.8).

   In attempting to explain this phenomenon social scientists have proposed a new type, *rational suicide.* Medical technology has made it possible for people to live longer lives, but has not improved the quality of life for the elderly. Science cannot protect older people from an accumulation of losses (loss of a spouse, friends, health, the status of being a worker, a meaningful role in life). A rational examination of their lives may convince some elderly that life is no longer worth living. Health experts also point out that it is relatively easy for the elderly to commit suicide--by not eating, not taking life-sustaining medications, or by taking an overdose of prescribed medications.

What are some of the moral and ethical problems the nation faces in dealing with this matter? Are new laws necessary to define the respon- sibilities of those involved (e.g. doctors, family)? What should the nation do to improve the quality of life to prevent rational-type sui- cides? Are we prepared to pay the enormous costs of doing so?

Chapter Two

THE SCIENCE OF SOCIOLOGY:
THEORY AND RESEARCH

OBJECTIVES

After reading Chapter Two you should be able to give in-depth answers to the following questions:

1. What makes sociology a science?
2. What are the basic steps in scientific research?
3. What are the ethical standards sociologists use?
4. What are the leading theoretical orientations in sociology today?
5. How do sociologists conduct an experiment, a survey, a field study, or a historical study?
6. How are theory and research connected?

CONCEPTS

You should also understand the following sociological concepts:

science
variable
dependent variable
independent variable
experiment
experimental group
control group
experiment
subject
field study
survey
simulation
sample
random assignment
self-fulfilling prophecy

dysfunctional
means of production
theory
Protestant Ethic and *Spirit of Capitalism*
theoretical orientation
structural perspective
symbolic interactionism
informed consent
conflict theory
functionalism
action theory

CHAPTER REVIEW

I. What makes sociology a science?

Why should you consider a sociological study of the reasons people get divorced (to pick one topic) more reliable than a journalist's observations or the insights of a friend who has just gone through a divorce? The answer lies in the scientific method. Like all scientists, sociologists follow five basic rules for establishing and explaining facts. You should try very hard to remember these throughout the course. It should also be noted that these simple steps will serve you well in other courses involving science, whether they are social or natural sciences.

A. Sociologists demand proof. In everday conversation we often rely on hearsay (second- or third-hand observations) and beliefs (ideas that we accept on faith, because they seem obvious or logical). Scientists are pro-fessional skeptics: They demand empirical, or factual, evidence.

B. Scientists are human beings and as susceptible as anyone else to seeing what they want to see. (As pointed out in Chapter One, our percep-tions are not mental photographs of reality; they are filtered through our expectations and wishes.) But--a critical *but*--scientists have developed a number of procedures for minimizing bias and error. These must be followed religiously if one wants to claim to be a scientist.

C. Sociology, like all sciences, is communal and self-critical. Public debate and the testing and retesting of ideas function as a self-correcting mechanism in science. No theory or finding, however famous, is accepted uncritically.

D. In everyday discussions, we often use a single, vivid illustra-tion to make a point. But a single case may be the exception to the rule. Sociologists search for general patterns that apply to many cases. (Recall Durkheim's study of suicide, described in Chapter One.)

E. Sociologists seek not only to describe social behavior, but also to explain social behavior with theories.

II. What are the basic steps in scientific research?

Your text outlines seven steps that all scientists take in their research. Don't forget that they conduct their research within a framework of a
Code of Ethics. Once a team of sociologists has selected a topic (step 1),
they review the literature (step 2); formulate one or more hypotheses (step
3); decide on a research method, sampling procedures, and measurements (step
4); collect data that may prove or disprove their hypotheses (step 5); analyze the data, keeping an eye open for unanticipated findings (step 6); then
publish their findings and/or present them at a meeting (step 7). Scientific
research requires equal amounts of imagination and hard labor!

III. What are the leading theoretical orientations in sociology today?

Without a lens, a camera will only record a blur of light. Without
theory, science would be a random collection of meaningless facts. Theories
enable sociologists to generate relevant questions and findings, guide
research, and then organize the results in a meaningful and coherent fashion.
There are several main theoretical orientations in sociology today. Your
text explains these theories.
A. Functionalism is based on the view that a society is made up of
specialized structures (the family, religion, the economy, and so on) and
that each of these structures performs a vital function in maintaining the
whole. These specialized structures are interdependent. Under normal conditions they work together to promote harmony and stability. Functionalists
emphasize the importance of consensus among members of a society and the
potentially harmful effects of sudden change on groups or society, which has
been criticized as supporting the status quo.
Functionalists hold that to understand why a behavior pattern exists in a
society, one must examine the consequences of that pattern. This means analyzing the latent (unintended) functions as well as the manifest (intended)
functions.
B. Conflict theory is based on the view that the structure of society
is the result of competition for scarce resources, especially the means of
production. Marx held that capitalism divides society into two opposing
classes: those who control capital and those who must sell their labor. Contemporary conflict theorists have broadened this scenario to account for the
cross-cutting interests of diverse groups in society today and for the emergence of a world capitalist system.
Conflict theorists maintain that to understand why a behavior pattern
exists in society, one must determine who benefits from that pattern and how
such persons maintain their position of power.
C. Symbolic interactionism, the third classic theoretical perspec-

tive in sociology, focuses on the cumulative effects of individual actions and interpersonal relationships in everyday behavior. It is premised on the idea that everyday interaction is determined by the way people interpret events and relationships. The emphasis is on the symbolic meanings people attach to social encounters.

Whereas functionalists and conflict theorists focus on the roles a society creates for people and how that society distributes people among those roles, symbolic interactionists focus on the way people interpret their roles.

D. In part, as a result of a reexamination of the classics, contemporary sociologists have begun to attach importance to the function of both structure and action in society. One new area of interest is in the ways in which the structure or shape of society influences, or even determines, everyday behavior. The second sees people's ideas and beliefs, goals, and intentions as the key to understanding society and emphasizes the role individual social actors play in creating, maintaining, or changing social structure.

IV. How do sociologists conduct an experiment, survey, field study, or historical study?

The four research methods that sociologists employ most often are: (1) experiments (controlled examination of cause and effect); (2) surveys (collecting data on a large population with standardized questionnaires and/or interviews); (3) field studies (observation of behavior in its natural setting); and (4) historical studies (collecting data from records and statistics over time).

Your text describes four classic studies of education in detail, identifying the problem the researcher chose to study, the method he or she employed, the findings, and the strengths and weaknesses of each method.

A. *Pygmalion in the Classroom*: Rosenthal and Jacobson set up an experiment to test the effects of teachers' expectations on student achievement. They gave children a standard intelligence test at the beginning of the year, then told teachers that the tests had identified some of the children as *bloomers* who would show great improvement over the coming year. In fact, the children on the *bloomer* list (the experimental group) were chosen at random and showed no more promise than youngsters not on the list (the control group). At the end of the year, Rosenthal and Jacobson found that the *bloomers* had indeed made progress, especially those in the lower grades. They concluded that teacher expectations function as a self-fulfilling prophecy: If teachers expect certain students to do well, they devote much more time to them and praise their efforts, and as a result, the students do improve.

The main advantage of an experiment is that it allows researchers to control outside influences and isolate cause and effect. The main drawbacks are that the setting may be artificial (most experiments are conducted in laboratories) and the scope of the study is limited to one or two variables.

   B. *The Adolescent Society*: Coleman set out to study cultural differences among high school students. Using the survey method, he administered questionnaires and interviews to students, parents, and teachers at ten Illinois high schools. Analyzing the data was the most difficult--and rewarding--part of his study. Students from different ethnic backgrounds did not show differences in values and attitudes, as he anticipated they would. After puzzling over this for some time, Coleman concluded that adolescents had developed a society and subculture of their own. He attributed this to the fact that young people are *segregated* from the adult world during their school years.

   The major advantages of a survey are that it allows a researcher to collect data on a large population and to compare the responses of different pop- ulations. The main disadvantage is that the responses to questions may be superficial.

   C. *Making the Grade*: Becker, Geer, and colleagues found that virtually all studies of education dealt with results; little was known about students' attitudes toward higher education. They decided to conduct a field study at the University of Kansas. To their relief, they found students were happy to cooperate. After many hours of observation and interviewing, the researchers concluded that most students had developed a GPA (grade point average) perspective. Making the grade came first. On the whole, students were more serious, and more willing to assist one another in making the grade, than the researchers had anticipated.

   The chief advantage of a field study is that it allows researchers to observe subtleties in behavior first hand. The main disadvantages are that researchers can study only a small population and that their relationship with the subjects may influence their findings.

   D. Katznelson and Weir demonstrate the historical study method to examine the current *crisis* in America's public education system. They reviewed the work of other scholars, documents, records, and changes in the law, etc. They found that public education was a useful accompaniment to industrialization. Comparisons are made between the rise of public education in Europe and the United States. In the latter, schools are more egalitarian and locally controlled. That same local control has created differences in financing and control.

   The main advantage of the historical method is that it allows for the examination of rare events over time. The main drawback is the limit on available data which the researcher may need for an accurate portrayal.

V. How are theory and research connected?

Theory and research are connected through the research cycle (illustrated in Figure 2-3 of your text). Theories generate hypotheses; hypotheses guide researchers in the collection of data; analysis of data yields empirical generalizations; these generalizations may support existing theories or generate new or revised theories; this leads to new hypotheses--and so on, around the circle. In sociology, as in all sciences, the cycle is continuous. Actually, the work is never complete, as new findings emerge. This is what makes the research enterprise difficult and exciting at the same time.

CONCEPT REVIEW

Match each of the following terms with the correct definition.

a. sample
b. manifest function
c. field study
d. action perspective
e. experiment
f. control group
g. historical research
h. dependent variable
i. experimental group
j. independent variable
k. content analysis

l. hypothesis
m. variable
n. ethical standards
o. subject
p. random assignment
q. theoretical orientation
r. survey
s. latent function
t. theory
u. means of production
v. science

1. _E_   A systematic, controlled examination of cause and effect, and the preferred research protocol if possible.
2. _S_   The unintended, and often unrecognized, consequence of a behavior pattern or social arrangement.
3. _O_   A person studied under social science research.
4. _D_   The perspective that recognizes that individuals produce society and culture through their interactions with one another.
5. _L_   A testable statement about a possible cause-and-effect relationship.
6. _F_   The subjects in an experiment who are not exposed to the experimental treatment.
7. _I_   The subjects in an experiment who are exposed to the experimental treatment, as opposed to a group which is not.

8. _b_   The intended and recognized consequence of a behavior pattern or social arrangement.

9. _n_   Guidelines for researchers who use human subjects in order to assure that they treat the subjects with dignity and protect their rights to privacy.

10. _p_   The random division of subjects into control and experimental groups.

11. _r_   A research method involving the use of standardized question-naires, interviews, or both to gather data on a large population.

12. _t_   A set of relatively general, abstract statements that explains some aspect of the real world.

13. _H_   A change in the subject's behavior that is due to the factor whose effects the researcher is studying.

14. _c_   A research method involving direct observation of social behavior in its natural setting.

15. _m_   Any condition that can change.

16. _A_   That portion of the population under investigation that the researcher actually studies.

17. _g_   A theory that attempts to explain all (or the most important) aspects of social life.

18. _u_   Marx's term for the means by which wealth for the powerful is created (raw materials, factories, technical knowledge, etc.), and the masses are exploited.

19. _K_   A research method for discovering patterns in communication based on the analysis of written texts, conversations, and other sources.

20. _q_   A research method that studies events over time, and uses data gathered by others.

21. _j_   The factor whose effects the researcher studies by control or manipulation in an experiment.

22. _V_   A set of agreed-upon procedures for establishing and explaining facts.

Answers

1. e	6. f	11. r
2. s	7. i	12. t
3. o	8. b	13. h
4. d	9. n	14. c
5. l	10. p	15. m

16. a   19. k   22. v
17. q   20. g
18. u   21. j

REVIEW QUESTIONS

1. One of the key differences between sociology and the physical sciences is:
    a. In sociology, theory and research are linked in a continuous cycle.
    b. When sociologists study individual cases and specific events, they are looking for evidence of general principles.
    c. Research findings are never taken as *the first word* in sociology, but are always open to question.
    d. Ultimately sociologists aim to explain and predict.
    e. The subjects of sociological studies may intentionally or unintentionally deceive a researcher.

2. The view that modern societies are divided into many competing groups whose interests crisscross one another, preventing a division into hostile camps, is associated with which of the following schools of thought or famous sociologists:
    a. structural functionalism
    b. Karl Marx
    c. Emile Durkheim
    d. symbolic interactionism
    e. modern conflict theory

3. The experimental method is often the preference of sociologists. The main advantage of the experimental method is:
    a. flexibility
    b. economy
    c. control
    d. depth
    e. comparative data

4. A researcher wants to know whether the average American college student thinks alcohol, marijuana, and nicotine are dangerous drugs. He or she wants to do research on the topic, and can choose from a number of research strategies. The best strategy would be to:

a. conduct an experiment
b. design a survey
c. carry out a field study
d. conduct a historical study
e. any one of the above

5. Which of the following statements best reflects the action-oriented view?
    a. Change is an inevitable, even desirable, part of social life.
    b. If people define situations as real, the situations are real in their consequences.
    c. Societies are like organisms.
    d. From each according to one's ability; to each according to one's need.
    e. The function of the family is to bear and raise children.

6. In his survey of high school students conducted in the late 1950s, Coleman found that young people were:
    a. eager to live up to their parents' expectations
    b. uninterested in any activities related to school
    c. achievement oriented
    d. people oriented
    e. concerned with *making the grade*

7. A team of researchers is conducting an experiment on the effects of TV violence on children's behavior. They show children in Group A a typical cops and robbers program with ten violent confrontations and show children in Group B a film on a sailing crew, and then observe the youngsters in a playground. The children in Group A are:
    a. the dependent variable
    b. the independent variable
    c. the control group
    d. the experimental group
    e. the *bloomers*

8. Once a sociologist has selected a research topic and surveyed the literature, the next step is:
    a. choosing a research design
    b. formulating hypotheses
    c. collecting data
    d. analyzing data
    e. publishing findings

9. The historical study of free public education found similarities between the European system and the U.S. system. A major difference, however, was found to be:
   a. in the U.S., public education was found to predate voting rights
   b. in Europe public education was found to be under the control of local governments
   c. American schools tend to be more egalitarian than European schools
   d. the percentage of European students who attend college is more than double of that in the U.S.
   e. European schools tend to be more racially segregated than schools in the U.S.

10. Rosenthal and Jacobson's experiment focused on:
    a. the effect of teachers' high expectations on student achievement
    b. the random assignment of children to experimental and control groups
    c. the independent variable
    d. the possibility that researchers influence the behavior of the people they are studying
    e. the *nonbloomers* in the experiment

11. Which of the following is a latent function of the U.S. educational system?
    a. providing a baby-sitter
    b. teaching students skills, values, and attitudes
    c. awarding students credentials that they can use as bargaining chips in the job market
    d. teaching young people to follow rules
    e. producing more Ph.D.'s than there are jobs requiring advanced education

12. Your college newspaper has given you the assignment of predicting the results of an upcoming campus election. There are 3,500 students on your campus. Your prediction is most likely to be accurate if you:
    a. interview fifty students who are coming down the library steps
    b. mail questionnaires to all 3,500 students and report on the 200 who reply
    c. divide a list of students into freshmen, sophomores, juniors, and seniors; males and females; liberal arts, business, nursing, and engineering majors; commuters and residents--and then pick twenty names at random from each category for interviews

    d.   conduct intensive interviews with everyone in your sociology class

    e.   interview the candidates' campaign managers

13. One disadvantage of the survey as a research tool is:
    a.   reliance on self-reports
    b.   limited scope
    c.   the observer effect
    d.   flexibility
    e.   all of the above

14. The foundations of conflict theory live in the writings of:
    a.   Emile Durkheim
    b.   Herbert Spencer
    c.   Robert Merton
    d.   Karl Marx

15. Which of the four research methods described in this chapter is the most subjective (that is, the most dependent on the researcher's impressions)?
    a.   an experiment
    b.   a survey
    c.   a field study *depends on observations & relationship c̄ subjects*
    d.   a historical study

16. Which of the following statements about the science of sociology is false?
    a.   Sociology is an empirical science.
    b.   Hunches and speculation have no role in sociology.
    c.   Sociologists are concerned with techniques for minimizing bias and error.
    d.   Sociology is a public venture.
    e.   Sociologists seek generalizations that explain and predict social behavior.

17. The view that society is held together by consensus and interdependence is associated with one of the following theoretical orientations. Which is it?
    a.   functionalism
    b.   conflict theory
    c.   symbolic interactionism
    d.   none of the above
    e.   all of the above

18. Professor Jones has analyzed the results of a series of confidential interviews with female college seniors and their mothers. He found that most of the mothers had had one or two affairs before they got married. Although most of their daughters said they had a more liberated attitude toward sex than their mothers had, most had had sex with only one or two partners--in most cases, a man they seriously considered marrying. Professor Jones concludes that the *theory* of the sexual revolution is a myth. At what point did he enter the research cycle?
    a. theory building
    b. construction of hypotheses
    c. data collection
    d. empirical generalizations/data analysis

19. Professor Jones theorizes that there has been a revolution in perceptions of sexual activity in the past twenty-five years, but comparatively little change in behavior. He decided to test this theory by asking college women how sexually active they think their mother's generation was before marriage and how many partners they think other women their own age have before marriage. At what point in the research cycle is Professor Jones now?
    a. theory building
    b. construction of hypotheses
    c. data collection
    d. empirical generalizations/data analysis

20. The basic question symbolic interactionists ask is:
    a. What are the consequences of a social pattern?
    b. Who benefits from a social arrangement?
    c. How are the different elements of society integrated?
    d. How does everyday behavior support or modify social definitions of reality?
    e. How do privileged groups within a society *maintain* positions of power and privilege?

21. Which of the following statements would a structural sociologist be most likely to support?
    a. The spread of computers is reinforcing class differences, making it even easier for the elite to control the masses.
    b. Computers are changing the way people think and behave; already it is possible to shop, deposit and withdraw money, and obtain information without speaking to a salesperson, bank teller, or librarian.

   c.   People make computers conform to their own personal styles of working, rather than the reverse.

   d.   How people use computers depends on the meaning they attach to working with new, sophisticated equipment.

22. A researcher wishes to study patterns of divorce rates in the nineteenth century, and uses court statistics, searches archival records, examines novels, and examines divorce laws as they have come into existence. This is an example of

   a.   an experiment
   b.   a survey
   c.   a historical study
   d.   simulation

23. The *Protestant Ethic* and the *Spirit of Capitalism*, written by Max Weber, held that the defining feature of modern society was

   a.   the shift from a traditional to a rational orientation toward social action
   b.   industrialization
   c.   urbanization
   d.   capitalism

Answers

1. e: All of the other answers apply to the physical as well as the social sciences. (See section entitled Sociology as a Science.)

2. e: This view is most closely associated with the contemporary conflict theorist Lewis Coser, whose work can be seen as a revision of Marxist theory in light of the conditions in society today. (The Role of Theory)

3. c: An experiment that includes control groups is the best technique for isolating, and hence controlling, variables. (Methods)

4. b: When a researcher is interested in making generalizations about a large population (e.g., all college students), a survey is most appropriate. (The Strengths and Weaknesses of Surveys)

5. b: This statement by W. I. Thomas captures the view that social behavior is determined in large part by the meanings that people attach to social encounters. (Explaining Everyday Social Behavior: Symbolic Interactionism)

6. d: Coleman found that high school students were most concerned with being accepted by their peers. For boys in the 1950s, this meant

being a star athlete; for girls, a leader in other activities. (The Adolescent Society)

7. d: In this experiment, exposure to TV violence is the experimental treatment; the children in Group A are the experimental group and the children in Group B are the controls. (The Research Procedure)

8. b: This step in the research procedure involves translating hunches into testable statements about cause and effect. (The Research Procedure)

9. c: While our system tends to make some distinctions between *vocational* and *college preparatory* courses, this difference is not as deeply entrenched as in Europe. (A Historical Study: Schooling for All)

10. a: They found that teacher expectations functioned as a self-fulfilling prophecy. Others have disputed this finding, however. (An Experiment: Pygmalion in the Classroom)

11. a: A person who declared that schools were little more than expensive baby-sitting services would be considered a cynic. Answers b-d describe manifest (intended and recognized) functions; answer e could be described as a dysfunction. (Explaining Society: The Functionalist and Conflict Perspectives)

12. c: This approach would give you a representative sample and the best chance of predicting the election. (The Research Procedure)

13. a: Participants in a survey may tell a researcher what they think he or she wants to hear. The same is true in interviews conducted as part of field studies, but the latter method allows the researcher to compare people's self-reports with actual behavior. (The Research Procedure)

14. d: Although not strictly speaking a sociologist, Marx had a profound influence on the field. Many conflict theorists today would describe their thinking as *Marxist,* though not communist in the political sense. (Explaining Society: The Functionalist and Conflict Perspectives)

15. c: Whereas a survey turns respondents' answers into quantifiable data (e.g., 6.72 percent said *yes*) and an experiment has built in controls, a field study depends on the researcher's observations and relationships with subjects. This is why it is most useful for exploratory research. (The Research Procedure)

16. b: Sociologists do demand empirical evidence. Nevertheless, imagination (often in the form of speculation and hunches) plays a role in the early stages of research. (Sociology as a Science)

17. a: Where traditional functionalists stressed the need for harmony in a society, contemporary functionalists emphasize the delicate balance

among different groups in a society. (Explaining Society: The Functionalist and Conflict Perspectives)

18. d: Analysis of the data exposed an unexpected pattern: Mothers and daughters were more alike than they realized. (Note that we are using the term *theory* loosely here.) (The Research Procedure)

19. b: Professor Jones is translating his *theory* into testable statements. He hypothesizes that if the main change is in perceptions and not sexual activity, young women will believe that their mothers' generation was less active than they are but that other women their age are more active than they are. (The Research Procedure)

20. d: Answers a and c are the main concerns of functionalists; answers b and e, the main concerns of conflict theorists. (Explaining Society: The Functionalist and Conflict Perspectives)

21. b: Structural sociologists emphasize the impact of external forces on choices and behavior. Conflict theorists would be more likely to agree with choice a; action theorists, with choice c; and symbolic interactionists, with choice d. (The Role of Theory)

22. c: The aim of a historical study is to research a past event, and/or an event over time. The research has to rely on information gathered by others, or reported in books, newspapers, archives, etc. (A Historical Study: Schooling for All)

23. a: Weber was trying to emphasize the importance of the actions of individuals and how these impact societal structure. This was his attempt to infuse sociology with the value of the subjective dimension of human behavior. (The Role of Theory)

MYTH OR FACT?

1. The sole aim of scientific research is to confirm hypotheses. t/(f)

2. The main difference between sociology and journalism is that, as an empirical science, sociology relies heavily on statistical analysis. t/(f)

3. The study of free public education showed that public education in the U.S. is more locally controlled than in Europe. (t)/f

4. All or the majority of social research has proven that teacher expectations function as a self-fulfilling prophecy. t/(f)

Answers

1. *False.* A hypothesis is only a tentative statement about cause and effect. The aim of research is to confirm, refute, or modify hypotheses.
2. *False.* Sociology is an empirical science, and many sociological studies are based on sophisticated statistical analysis. But this is only one part of the research cycle. The main difference between sociology and journalism is that sociologists are concerned not only with reporting behavior, but also with testing and retesting theories that explain and predict behavior.
3. *True.* But, this is also a problem. Local financing and control often work to the disadvantage of working class and minority children.
4. *False.* Rosenthal and Jacobson did find that student achievement reflects teacher expectations. But other social scientists have questioned their methods, and attempts to repeat the experiment have not always yielded the same results. This illustrates two of the self-correcting mechanisms in science: public debate and the testing and retesting of hypotheses.

CRITICAL THINKING

1. Your sociology instructor sets up a debate on education. One debating team will be assigned the functional point of view; a second team, conflict theory; a third team, the action perspective. Each team will be asked to explain the GPA perspective among college students. Which team would you join? Why?

2. In reviewing this chapter, you began thinking like a scientist and questioned other scientists' conclusions. Coleman suggested that whereas adults think school is learning, adolescents see school as a social event. You suspect that parents and teenagers are more alike; that parents are as concerned about their children's popularity as they are about grades. How would you go about translating this hunch into a research design?

3. A team of sociologists is conducting a field study, similar to that described in the text, on your campus. One of the researchers approaches you in the student lounge, explains the study, and asks for an hour interview. You agree. It is an intensive interview: She asks about your parents' expectations, whether you consider yourself a dedicated student, how you think your friends see you, and countless other questions. Would

you answer truthfully?

Next, suppose you are called into the dean's office, introduced to a researcher, and asked to participate in the study. Would you agree? Would you give the same answers as you gave under the first procedure? Why? What does this tell you about field studies?

Now imagine that a year later you learn that the real purpose of the study was to determine whether extracurricular activities interfere with school performance. You were chosen because you are captain of the basketball team, an editor on the school paper, and the leader of an antinuclear protest. How would you feel about the study now?

PART TWO: SOCIAL BEHAVIOR

Chapter Three

CULTURE

OBJECTIVES

After reading Chapter Three you should be able to give in-depth answers to the following questions:

1. Why is the study of culture important?
2. What are the basic elements of culture?
3. What is the difference between ethnocentrism and cultural relativism?
4. Does everyday behavior conform to cultural standards?
5. How and why do cultures change?

CONCEPTS

You should also understand the following sociological concepts:

culture
beliefs
values
norms
folkways
mores
laws
sanctions
symbols
language
Sapir-Whorf hypothesis
enculturation
culture shock
ethnocentrism
cultural relativism
ideal culture
counterculture

subculture
cultural lag

CHAPTER REVIEW

I.   Why is the study of culture important?

Your text cites two major reasons for studying culture. First, cross-cultural contacts are becoming an everyday event. The United States continues to be a magnet for people around the world. Moreover, most major U.S. corporations have operations on other continents. The people next door, the local grocer, the physician in the hospital emergency room--any of them might have come from another culture. This is one, very practical, reason to study culture.

Second, human beings depend on their cultural roots. Other species are born with a repertoire of instincts (or genetic programs) for adapting to the environment. With very few instincts, humans have to learn to adapt. The term *culture* refers to an overall plan for coping with the environment that is based on tradition and learning. In everyday conversation, we use the word *culture* to refer to an appreciation of the finer things in life--good music, good wine, and so on. Social scientists use the word to describe a people's entire design for living. The study of culture is pivotal in sociology and anthropology, as well. Study this concept very carefully. A good understanding of it will serve you well throughout this course, and others as well.

Your text uses variations in sexual behavior to illustrate that much of what we take for granted, as part of *human nature*, turns out to be the result of enculturation. This is why the move from one culture to another is so unsettling.

II. What are the basic elements of culture?

Although the contents differ, all cultures consist of six basic elements: beliefs, values, norms and sanctions, technology, symbols, and language. Your text uses examples from American and Vietnamese culture to illustrate these concepts.

A. All cultures are grounded in a set of beliefs, or shared knowledge and ideas about the nature of life. Whereas Americans think of time as marching on (you can't go back again), the Vietnamese conceive of time in cycles (things come around again). This difference is crucial in understanding the Vietnamese culture.

B. Technology sets the tone for culture, influencing not only how people work, but also how they socialize and think about the world. Despite global marketing, significant differences in the material environment remain. To rural Vietnamese immigrants, the United States probably seems as fantastic as Disneyland does to children.

C. All cultures set values, or shared standards for what is right and desirable. The Vietnamese value family loyalty, adaptability, and propriety. In contrast, Americans value individualism, sticking to one's principles, and assertiveness. This value translates into every aspect of life.

D. Norms translate beliefs and values into specific rules for behavior--a set of *Thou shalt* and *Thou shalt nots*. Traditionally, Vietnamese girls were not allowed to leave their homes without a chaperone. Their parents arranged their marriages. In contrast, American girls are expected to date when they reach adolescence (and are thought odd if they do not). Parents advise but are not supposed to dictate their choice of husband. Norms vary in intensity from sacred taboos to everyday habits (or folkways). Norms also vary according to the actor and the situation. There are different rules for children and adults, funerals and disco dances. Sanctions are the punishments and rewards people use to enforce norms.

E. Symbols are designs or objects that have acquired special cultural meaning (such as a red hexagon for *Stop*). The same object may symbolize different feelings in different cultures. We see dogs as pets, for example; rural Southeast Asians are more likely to consider dogs livestock. The most important set of cultural symbols is language.

F. Language is a key element of culture. Whereas other animals communicate via signs (sounds and gestures whose meaning is fixed), humans communicate by means of symbols (sounds and gestures whose meaning depends on shared understandings). Words can be combined in different ways to convey an unlimited number of messages, not only about the here and now, but also about the past and the future, to symbolize that which is absent, and to permit one to examine the impossible as well as possible.

A people's language provides clues to the way they view the world. Whereas English provides only one term for addressing another person (*you*), Vietnamese provides numerous terms indicating degrees of respect (and illustrating their concern with propriety). But there is little evidence that language determines the way people think (review the Sapir-Whorf hypothesis).

III. What is the difference between ethnocentrism and cultural relativism?

Even anthropologists experience culture shock in unfamiliar cultural settings. It is not easy to transplant oneself into another cultural setting and feel comfortable all at once. In fact, adjustment takes a great deal of time and patience. One reason for this lies in an understanding of the term *ethnocentrism*. (This is the feeling of cultural superiority.) Most, if not all, peoples have a high opinion of their own design for living, compared with those of other peoples. Our own culture becomes so much a part of us that we think of our own way of doing things as the only way. Taken out of context, any custom seems peculiar. Your text illustrates this by describing the body ritual of the Nacirema (American spelled backward). Cultural relativism--the view that behavior must be understood in terms of its own cultural context--is the opposite of ethnocentrism.

IV. Does everyday behavior conform to cultural standards?

The answer to this question is yes and no. There may be more internal cultural inconsistencies in a large, heterogeneous, rapidly changing society like the United States than there are in small, isolated societies. But people everywhere devote considerable thought and energy to evading the rules. What is most interesting about this is that people tend to bend the norms in the same ways. Thus, every group of people which qualifies as a culture has an ideal culture, consisting of the ways they believe people ought to (must) *behave,* and a real culture, consisting of the ways in which they think it is OK to *deviate.*

A subculture exists when a group of people has developed a set of variations on cultural norms and values that set these people apart from other members of their society. Subcultures may develop around ethnic identity, occupation, special interests, or even sexual preferences. When a group opposes a number of widely held norms and values, it is known as a counter-culture.

V. How do social scientists explain the similarities and differences among cultures?

Human beings are all members of the same species. How, then, do social scientists explain the wide range of variations in designs for living? Your text examines four theoretical orientations to the study of culture.

A. Functionalists view culture as a highly integrated system, each element of which contributes something to the whole. In analyzing cultures, they focus on the ways in which beliefs and practices function to satisfy basic human needs and to reinforce commitment to a social system. Put another way, functionalists examine the social consequences of different elements of culture. Erikson, for example, holds that the public punishment of deviants (as in the Salem witch trials) reinforces cultural boundaries.

B. Cultural ecologists view culture as a means of adapting to the environment. Although they resemble functionalists in some respects, they focus on the ecological consequences of different beliefs and practices. Viewed from this perspective, the riddle of *cow love* in India can be explained as an efficient way of securing fuel and muscle power in a land overcrowded with people.

C. Conflict theorists see culture as part of the struggle for economic dominance and power in a society. Culture may enhance the power of the elite in some situations and provide a springboard for revolutionary change in others.

D. Some theorists stress the dynamic, purposeful role individuals and groups play in creating and maintaining culture. According to this view, culture is not something people acquire passively, but something they actively create. (See the discussions about the Individual and Culture.) Further, an enduring problem for sociologists is to strike a balance between determining how cultural patterns are socially constructed and recognizing individual creativity. *In fact, how this is done has been the subject of considerable controversy in sociology from the beginning.*

VI. How and why do cultures change?

Major changes in a people's design for living may come from outside (the result of changes in the natural environment or contacts with other cultures) or from the inside (the result of discovery and invention). Whatever the source, change may produce cultural lag and problems of adjustment. Your text cites the cargo cults of New Guinea as an extreme example of cultural dislocation.

CONCEPT REVIEW

Match each of the following terms with the correct definition.

a. folkways	l. symbol
b. beliefs	m. ideal culture
c. sanctions	n. enculturation
d. ethnocentrism	o. culture shock
e. instincts	p. norms
f. language	q. real culture
g. subculture	r. cultural relativism
h. counterculture	s. law
i. Sapir-Whorf hypothesis	t. culture
j. values	u. mores
k. cultural lag	v. technology

1. _b_   Shared ideas about how the world operates.
2. _r_   The view that a culture must be viewed in terms of its own meanings.
3. _d_   The tendency to judge other cultures in terms of one's own.
4. _e_   Genetically programmed behavior patterns.
5. _u_   Norms that are so sacred that violation is unthinkable.

6. _c_ The socially imposed rewards and punishments that are used to encourage conformity to cultural norms.

7. _g_ Symbols, norms, values, and language which distinguish members of a group from other societal members.

8. _j_ Abstract, shared standards of what is right.

9. _l_ Something (e.g., an object) that evokes meaning.

10. _p_ Specific set of rules about what people should or should not do, say, or think in a given situation.

11. _m_ Norms and values to which people openly adhere.

12. _H_ A subculture that actively opposes the values and practices of the larger society.

13. _o_ The feelings of disorientation, bewilderment, and stress that people experience when they enter an unfamiliar cultural setting.

Folkways 14. _a_ Norms that are not sacred but are so ingrained that people conform to them automatically, out of habit, in everday interaction.

15. _s_ A norm that has been established as a formal code by officials of the state.

16. _K_ A delay between changes in technological advancements or physical conditions and, the subsequent adjustments in norms and values.

17. _i_ The idea that our language causes us to pay attention to certain things and to ignore others.

18. _q_ Norms and values that people may not formally admit to, but follow nonetheless.

19. _n_ Immersion in a culture to the point where that particular design for living seems _only natural._

20. _t_ A people's entire design for living.

21. _f_ A set of shared symbols (spoken and written words) and rules (grammar or syntax) for combining symbols in meaningful ways.

22. _V_ The knowledge and techniques a people use to create the material objects of their culture.

Answers

1. b	9. l	17. i
2. r	10. p	18. q
3. d	11. m	19. n
4. e	12. h	20. t
5. u	13. o	21. f
6. c	14. a	22. v
7. g	15. s	
8. j	16. k	

REVIEW QUESTIONS

1. A major difference between human cultures and other animals' *designs for living* is:
    a. Culture is based on instincts.
    b. Culture is a form of adaptation.
    c. Culture is transmitted through learning.
    d. Culture depends on communication.
    e. Culture provides *instructions* for courtship, child-rearing, and other distinctively human behavior.

2. The cargo cults of New Guinea are an example of cultural innovation resulting from:
    a. changes in the natural environment
    b. cultural contact
    c. discovery
    d. invention

3. Which of the following is a core value in Vietnamese culture?
    a. reckoning time in sixty-year cycles
    b. the notion that family honor is more important than individual goals or even moral principles
    c. the notion that one should stick to one's principles
    d. the celebration of death days
    e. the use of different pronouns to indicate degrees of respect

4. Cultural ecologists see the protection of cattle in India as:
    a. a riddle
    b. providing a living symbol of social solidarity
    c. benefiting the wealthier members of Indian society at the expense of the poor
    d. providing a cheap and reliable source of energy/labor
    e. an example of cultural lag

5. The Supreme Court has ruled that the use of peyote (a natural hallucinogenic drug) by the Native American Church is not illegal, on the grounds that the Constitution grants freedom of religion. This is an example of:
    a. positive sanctions
    b. negative sanctions
    c. ethnocentrism
    d. cultural relativism

6. The belief that sex is a powerful biological drive that plays a central role in every adult's life is an example of:

    a.   real culture
    b.   ideal culture
    c.   cultural relativism
    d.   biological destiny
    e.   enculturation

7. Countless popular songs tell Americans that for every person there is one, and only one, true love. This is an example of:
    a.   real culture
    b.   ideal culture
    c.   subculture
    d.   patterned evasion

8. A co-worker stops you in the hall. He has noticed you tucking stationery, stamps, paper clips, and other office supplies into your briefcase before you leave work. He says he won't say anything to your boss, but he wants you to know he thinks that is wrong. This is an example of:
    a.   an informal positive sanction
    b.   a formal positive sanction
    c.   an informal negative sanction
    d.   a formal negative sanction

9. Which of the following groups does not constitute a subculture?
    a.   Italian-Americans
    b.   the Moonies
    c.   jazz musicians
    d.   gay men
    e.   women

10. Which of the following is a value?
    a.   Students should not throw spitballs during class.
    b.   Students who cheat on exams should be suspended.
    c.   All young people have a right to education.
    d.   College instructors shouldn't date their students.

11. In the not-too-distant past, the Bureau of Indian Affairs created boarding schools for Native American children. The idea was to help youngsters enter the mainstream of U.S. society by separating them from their past and from other members of their tribes. This policy was an example of:
    a.   positive sanctions
    b.   negative sanctions
    c.   ethnocentrism
    d.   cultural relativism

12. The difference between values and norms is that:
    a.   Values are shared.
    b.   Norms are shared.
    c.   Values apply to specific situations.
    d.   Norms apply to specific situations.
    e.   Norms may be violated in everyday life.

13. The notion that men are stronger than women is a:
    a.   belief
    b.   norm
    c.   value
    d.   sanction
    e.   superstition

14. Which theoretical view best explains the manufacture of culture?
    a.   cultural ecology
    b.   production of culture
    c.   conflict theory
    d.   functionalism

15. What is the main difference between traditional functionalism and cultural ecology?
    a.   Cultural ecologists stress human physical or survival needs.
    b.   Functionalists view culture as essential to human survival.
    c.   Cultural ecologists explain cultural practices by analyzing the consequences of behavior.
    d.   Functionalists do not explain the origins of particular cultural practices.

16. On which of the following points would conflict theorists and cultural ecologists agree?
    a.   Cultural patterns are the product of evolution.
    b.   Cultural patterns are the product of economic relationships.
    c.   Cultural patterns are best illuminated through materialistic patterns.
    d.   None of the above.

17. According to the Sapir-Whorf hypothesis:
    a.   Language shapes our perceptions and thoughts.
    b.   Language is the storehouse of culture.
    c.   Language is a set of shared symbols.
    d.   Eskimo languages are more precise than English.
    e.   Language enables people to transmit culture from generation to generation.

18. The so-called cultural revolution of the late 1960s and early 1970s, the *hippie* years, was short-lived. Which of the countercultural values developed then seems to have survived?
   a. the ethic of self-fulfillment
   b. the ethic of self-sacrifice
   c. the idea that success should be defined in terms of community involvement, adventure, and love
   d. the idea that success in a career (measured largely in terms of earnings) is a prerequisite for happiness in other areas

19. Americans believe that it is wrong to take another human life, yet many Americans support the death penalty. This is an example of:
   a. real culture
   b. ideal culture
   c. a subculture
   d. patterned evasion
   e. internal inconsistency

20. The rule about putting your napkin in your lap before you start eating is an example of:
   a. a more
   b. ethnocentrism
   c. a folkway
   d. a law

21. Which of the following is an example of mores?
   a. the incest taboo
   b. refusing to salute the flag
   c. driving above the speed limit
   d. forgetting to attend a cousin's wedding

22. The major difference between animal signs and human language is:
   a. The meaning of words and phrases is fixed.
   b. The meaning of signs is flexible.
   c. With language, humans can communicate with one another.
   d. With language, humans can communicate information about people and events which are far removed in time and space.
   e. Animals cannot lie.

Answers

1. c: No other species is as dependent on learning as humans. The different ways we adapt to the environment, communicate, select mates, and rear young depend on cultural learning, not instinct. (See section entitled Culture: An Overview.)

2. b: Viewing the wealth and power of Westerners through the lens of their own technology, Melanesians could not but conclude that the newcomers had powerful magic. (Cultural Inconsistencies and Diversities)

3. b: Answers a, d, and e are drawn from Vietnamese culture, but they describe beliefs and practices, not values. Answer c is an American value. (The Elements of Culture)

4. d: Cultural ecologists maintain that many customs that seem anachronistic (left over from earlier times) in fact help people to adapt to their environment, even if they themselves are not conscious of this. (Culture: An Overview)

5. d: The Court treated the custom of using peyote in religious services as a valid part of a cultural whole. (Norms and Sanctions)

6. e: Human sexual beliefs and practices are highly variable. This particular belief is a product of modern American culture and hence an example of enculturation. The Dani view sex quite differently. (Culture: An Overview)

7. b: Judging by the numbers of Americans who delay marriage to *play the field,* seek divorces, and engage in extramarital flirtations, if not affairs, this is an ideal we honor in the breech. (The Elements of Culture)

8. c: The man was criticizing you in a way likely to make you feel embarrassed (a negative sanction) but did not pursue the matter through official channels (a formal negative sanction). (Norms and Sanctions)

9. e: Subcultures and countercultures may be based on ethnic identity, religion, occupation, life style (gay men), or political commitments. If we had listed *feminists* instead of women, the correct answer would have been *none of the above* since all would be subcultures. (Subcultures and Countercultures)

10. c: Values are abstract standards or ideals. The other answers describe specific guidelines for behavior, or norms. (The Elements of Culture)

11. c: This policy was based on the unquestioned assumption that mainstream American culture is superior to Hopi, Navajo, and other Native American cultures. (Ethnocentrism and Cultural Relativism)

12. d: Both norms and values are shared standards; both may be routinely ignored in everyday behavior. The difference between them is that values are abstract standards whereas norms are concrete rules. (The Elements of Culture)

13. a: Beliefs are shared ideas about cause and effect--in this case, the idea that male genes promote strength. The notion that men should, therefore, carry heavy packages for women is a norm derived from this belief. (Not all cultures share this view: in some, women are expected to perform most heavy labor.) (The Elements of Culture)

14. b: This approach is based on the idea that living people produce culture in an active way, within a framework of influences such as technology,

social structure, and economics. The other theories discussed in your text tend to view culture as a given (functionalism), as unconscious adaptation to environmental conditions (cultural ecology), or as a reflection of power struggles (conflict theory). (Explaining Culture)

15. a: Functionalists see culture as satisfying a collection of social, psychological, and physical needs; cultural ecologists emphasize the last. (All other answers apply to both theoretical schools.)

16. c: Conflict theorists and cultural ecologists agree that cultural patterns are best explained in terms of material or physical factors. But the former see these patterns as resulting from the struggle for wealth and power whereas the latter see them as resulting from the struggle for survival. (Explaining Culture)

17. a: Sapir and Whorf argued that language in part determines how we see the world. (Language)

18. a: In the shift from hippies to yuppies, the idea of self-fulfillment has remained, though the approved means to achieve this goal may have changed. (The Elements of Culture)

19. e: The simultaneous belief in the rule *Thou shalt not kill* and the rule *an eye for an eye* are examples of internal contradictions in culture. (Cultural Inconsistencies and Diversities)

20. c: Folkways are conventions or habits that people follow without giving much thought to what they are doing or why. (The Elements of Culture)

21. a: Mores are rules for behavior that people consider sacred. Although all of the other answers describe violations of norms or laws, none of these actions is considered *unthinkable* except incest. (The Elements of Culture)

22. b: The main advantage of language is flexibility. Whereas the meaning of signs is fixed, words and phrases can be combined in different ways to send different messages. (Language)

MYTH OR FACT?

1. The capacity for language is genetically programmed.   t/f
2. Europeans and their American cousins are the most ethnocentric people in the world. Witness the colonization of most of Latin America, Africa, and Asia; the enslavement of Africans; the dislocation and slaughter of Native Americans.   t/f
3. American society is becoming more and more *homogenized*; the number and influence of ethnic subcultures is declining.   t/f
4. Every adult has a natural heterosexual destiny; long periods of abstinence are unhealthy.   t/f

Answers

1. *True.* The capacity for language is a product of natural selection and the evolution of large brains and vocal apparatus in the human species. Although apes have been taught to use sign language, they do not do so in the wild. The rapidity with which all normal children learn to speak suggests that they are somehow *wired* for language. What language people speak and how they use the language is not genetically fixed, however.
2. *False.* Most peoples have a cultural *superiority complex.* Indeed, most languages include derogatory terms for outsiders that suggest they are something less than human. The Greeks considered all foreigners *barbarians*; the Arabs were slave traders long before Europeans entered this business. Nevertheless, Europeans had the technology and social organization to force their cultural standards on much of the world in the nineteenth and early twentieth centuries, so that European ethnocentrism had a major impact on modern history.
3. *False.* Although not all sociologists would agree on this point, there is evidence that ethnic subcultures are *here to stay.* Moreover, new immigrants are contributing to the diversity of the American population, and new subcultures based on occupation or life style are also adding to the chorus. (The gay subculture and unconventional religious groups like the Hare Krishna are familiar examples.)
4. *False.* It would be absurd to claim that genes and hormones play no role in human sexual behavior. But wide variations in sexual activities and preferences demonstrate that enculturation is at least as powerful as the sex drive. In Victorian England, for example, conventional wisdom held that women did not enjoy sex. The Dani consider long periods of sexual inactivity normal--and a Western anthropologist's interest in sex unnatural.

CRITICAL THINKING

1. In many places, members of small, preliterate tribes are struggling to prevent their ancestral lands from falling into the hands of developers. Organizations such as Cultural Survival and Survival International are lobbying against plans to resettle and enculturate such tribes, on the grounds that it is morally wrong to strip people of their culture. Others would argue that maintaining these tribes is equivalent to maintaining a living museum, and that it is wrong not to give all of the other benefits of modern society. Which side would you take in this debate? Why?

2. Your text cites the gay subculture as one of the newer subcultures in the United States. Stop to think for a moment. Why would homosexuals (but not heterosexuals) develop their own newspapers and gathering places, an in-

siders' language that outsiders do not understand, and other distinctive patterns? Is this an example of self-segregation, a response to discrimination, or both? What does this tell you about the formation of subcultures? How would your answers to these questions apply to the singles subculture also found in most cities today?

3. You are interested in the production of culture. In particular, you are interested in the production of textbooks. Who decides which textbooks get published? Who decides which topics and studies find their way into a sociology text? What are the consequences of such decisions? How would you go about studying the production of textbooks? (Suggested Reading: Lewis A. Coser, Charles Kadushkin, and Walter W. Powell, *Books: The Culture and Commerce of Publishing,* New York: Basic Books, 1982.)

4. Given the many cultural differences between the Vietnamese and Americans, how are Vietnamese-Americans doing today? Adjustment to life in the United States has not been easy for the refugees of 1975. Within a year or two, most left their American sponsors to resettle near other Vietnamese, especially in California and Texas. Many also helped other relatives to gain admission to this country and get started here. Although the establishment of ethnic communities may have slowed the process of *Americanization*, it also eased feelings of isolation and enabled the Vietnamese to form a variety of self-help groups. The great majority of Vietnamese refugees (nine in ten) are employed, but few have been able to find jobs equal to those they held in Vietnam. This is especially true for those in high-level occupations. Former doctors are working as lab technicians; former engineers, as artisans; former managers, as clerks and salespeople; and the like. A relatively high percentage suffered from psychological and family problems, especially in their first years in this country. How does the term *culture shock* apply here? How transferable are the skills of the Vietnamese to American society? What would be some impediments to a full adjustment?

EXERCISE: New Rules for Americans--Where Do You Stand?

Announcements that the 1960s and 1970s were a period of *cultural revolution* in America were probably exaggerated. The much publicized anti-establishment, anti-materialist norms of the hippie counterculture have given way to a renewed interest in conventional careers and material success among so-called yuppies. But this does not mean Americans are going back to the old rules. At the beginning of the 1980s, Yankelovich, Skelly, and White conducted a national survey of 3,000 working Americans. Some of the questions they asked are listed below. Answer the questions yourself, then read the discussion that follows to see how your responses compare with the survey.

1. I spend a great deal of time thinking about myself. yes/no
2. Satisfaction comes from shaping oneself, rather than from home and family life. agree/disagree
3. I feel a strong need for *new experiences.* yes/no
4. I believe people should be free to look, dress, and live the way they want. agree/disagree
5. I feel the need to find more excitement and sensation. yes/no
6. I prefer to spend dollars for travel rather than on possessions. yes/no
7. I want to be outstanding in my field of work. yes/no
8. I want something meaningful to work toward. yes/no
9. I want time and energy left over after work and family to pursue personal interests. yes/no
10. Self-improvement is important to me and I work hard at it. yes/no

If you answered *yes* or *agree* to eight or more of these questions, you are a member of a small but significant minority of Americans who view creativity as a life style. Yankelovich sees the 17 million Americans in this category as experiencing the strong form of the drive for self-fulfillment. They are more concerned with designing their own lives than other Americans are. They are the experimenters.

If you gave an affirmative answer to five or fewer questions, you agree with the majority of Americans that self-fulfillment is important, but that other things are important as well.

Source: Adapted from D. Yankelovich, *New Rules: Searching for Self-Fulfillment in a World Turned Upside Down*, New York: Random House, 1981, pp. 82-84. Copyright 1981 by Random House, Inc.

Chapter Four

SOCIALIZATION

OBJECTIVES

After reading Chapter Four you should be able to give in-depth answers to the following questions:

1. What is socialization?
2. How do heredity and the social environment shape human development?
3. How do Freud's views of socialization differ from those of Cooley and Mead?
4. What are the major agents of socialization?
5. How does socialization extend over the life cycle?

CONCEPTS

You should also understand the following sociological concepts:

socialization/agent of socialization
reference group
positive/negative reference groups
anticipatory socialization
oral, anal, latency, phallic, genital stages
personality
looking-glass self
play and game stages
generalized other/significant other
life cycle
eight stages of man
adolescence
mid-life crisis

CHAPTER REVIEW

I. What is socialization?

Socialization is the lifelong process of social interaction that trans-

forms an infant into, perhaps, a child thirsting for knowledge, maybe a re-
bellious teenager, a worker, a spouse and parent, and eventually into an
elder member of our society. Your text uses a brief biography of the famous
anthropologist Margaret Mead to illustrate the many changes people undergo as
they grow up and grow older. The remainder of the chapter considers how and
why these changes occur, beginning with some very basic questions and answers
about human behavior.

II.   How do heredity and the environment shape human development?

The debate over nature and nurture dates back to the turn of the century.
Social Darwinists (and others) argued that a person's character and position
in society are genetically determined. Behaviorists countered that *exper-
ience is everything.* Contemporary sociologists have developed a synthesis.
They reject both extremes of genetic and social environmental determinism.
Instead, they see development as a result of the interaction of genetic po-
tential and socially derived factors. Genes establish potential and limits.
How much potential is realized depends upon socialization.

Your text describes two main lines of evidence that support the importance of socialization: studies of children raised in near total isolation
(the real-life equivalent of myths of feral children purported to have been
raised by wild animals), and cross-cultural comparisons (such as Margaret
Mead's study of sex and temperament in different societies). If human behavior were genetically determined, children would develop characteristically
human behavior patterns with or without social interaction, and males and females in one culture would behave in much the same way as their counterparts
in another. As the text shows, they do not! *This is a debate that will not
go away, however. If you pay attention to the news and read popular magazines
you will see articles related to this subject on many occasions. Watch for
them!*

III.   What are the major perspectives on socialization?

Your text examines and contrasts two different perspectives on socialization, each of which focuses on a different aspect of human development that
you will need to learn thoroughly.

A. Freud was primarily interested in personality, that is, how the
individual develops characteristic ways of thinking and behaving. He viewed
socialization as a confrontation between a child's innate sexual and aggressive urges and the demands of parents and others to *act civilized.* To
simplify the point, the child says *I will*; society (through the child's
parents says *you won't*; and the resolution of these types of conflicts
determines how the individual will handle future situations. The social control of sexual impulses plays a central role in Freud's theories. He des-

cribed the five critical stages in personality development as the oral, anal, latency, phallic, and genital stages. In mature individuals, the ego mediates between the asocial, pleasure-seeking id, and the punative, guilt-ridden superego.

Freud's theory sees the libido as the driving force, but grants family interactions a major role in personality development. Few social scientists dispute Freud's brilliance or his profound influence on contemporary thinking, but many question the scientific validity of his analysis.

B. Charles Horton Cooley and George Herbert Mead (sociologists, in contrast to Margaret Mead, the anthropologist) were primarily interested in social development, that is, how social interaction shapes the individual's identity or sense of self. Cooley showed that our self-images are largely a reflection of what we see in other people's responses to us (the looking-glass self). Mead identified two stages in the development of the self: the play stage, in which children learn to take the role of the other; and the game stage, in which children learn to participate in reciprocal relationships through games. He distinguished between the impulsive, creative *I* and the *me,* which constantly seeks social approval.

Mead and Cooley saw socialization as a cooperative effort, in which the individual develops a sense of self in relation to others and society is re-created as a generalized other in the individual's mind.

IV. Who/what are the major agents of socialization?

Your text considers five primary agents of socialization that operate independently, and also *interdependently*: the family, school, peer groups, mass media, and reference groups.

A. The family is a primary agent of socialization in the sense that it is the first, and perhaps most important, influence on the individual. Different styles of parenting (authoritarian, permissive, and authoritative) have been linked to social class differences. Parents socialize their children into the world they know, the one into which they, the parents, have been socialized, and with which they are most comfortable.

B. The school gives youngsters experience in dealing with a large, bureaucratic organization in which the same rules are supposed to apply to everyone and individuals are valued in terms of their performance.

C. The importance of peers (or age-mates) increases with age. Peers provide young people with their first experience of egalitarian relationships, opportunities to test what they are taught by adults, and group support for developing alternative norms and values. Look for examples in your own life to illustrate this point, whether in your sorority or fraternity, or back home in your friendship groups. Remember this principle when you become a parent!

D. The mass media (especially television) is a fourth, and controversial, agent of socialization. There is evidence that violence on prime-time programs encourages aggressive behavior and that commercials promote sex stereotyping. But there is evidence also that TV can encourage pro-social behavior and provide positive models for behavior.

E. The term *reference groups* refers to the wide range of groups and social categories individuals use through the life span, both as models and as measures of self-worth. These groups may be positive or negative.

V. How does socialization extend over the life cycle?

Erikson was one of the first social scientists to systematically examine the changes people undergo after adolescence. He sees each stage in life as presenting new crises that require new adjustments. Your text uses his description of the *eight stages of man* as a framework for considering socialization over the life cycle.

A. Erikson sees the central crises of childhood as establishing basic trust (vs. mistrust), autonomy (vs. shame and doubt), initiative (vs. guilt), and industry (vs. inferiority). Like the theorists considered earlier in the chapter, Erikson is concerned with *everychild.* Sociologists point out that not every child's experiences are alike, however.

B. Erikson sees the central task of adolescence as establishing identity (vs. role confusion). Sociological analysis shows that adolescence as we know it is largely a social invention. In other cultures, where individuals do not have to create their own identities and adults are not so ambivalent about teenage sexuality, the transition from childhood to adulthood can be smooth. The identity crisis many young people in our society experience can be traced, first, to the fact that the role of adolescence is ambiguous (teenagers are neither children nor adults) and, second, to the necessity of choosing from among a wide array of life styles and occupations.

C. Erikson sees the central task of adulthood as establishing intimacy (vs. isolation), generativity (vs. stagnation), and integrity (vs. despair). This orderly progression was based on the assumption that most people would finish school and settle down into a career and family, their children would leave home at a certain time, and so on. Things have changed in American society since Erikson first developed his theory. The ages at which individuals attain the traditional markers of adulthood have changed. Norms governing sexual activity have changed, as have work habits. Young adults are postponing the assumption of full-scale adult roles, and the roles of men and women have been altered dramatically. Levinson examines adult roles and finds that the roles of men and women have been altered dramatically. He sees adulthood as a series of crises, of which the most notable outlined in the text is the *midlife* crisis, the last chance to *make it.*

As the country experiences an increase in the number of elderly, the social meaning of reaching sixty-five has changed. Later adulthood is no longer a period of despair and isolation for many. There are more older Americans in better health than ever before, and they are more active. The result is a restructuring of retirement so that it may be enjoyed in the company of others in a similar situation for an increasing number of the elderly.

CONCEPT REVIEW

Match each of the following terms with the correct definition.

a. self
b. play stage
c. reference group
d. looking-glass self
e. personality
f. anticipatory socialization
g. agent of socialization
h. significant others
i. game stage
j. genital stage

k. the "I"
l. positive reference group
m. latency stage
n. negative reference group
o. socialization
p. generalized other
q. phallic stage
r. reaction range
s. anal stage
t. oral stage

1. _s_   Freud's term for the stage of psychosexual development in which babies take pleasure in controlling their bowels.

2. ___   The individual's sense of identity or *who I am.*

3. ___   The individual's patterns of behavior and thought.

4. ___   G. H. Mead's term for the stage in social development when children begin to participate in reciprocal relationships with others.

5. ___   The range of possible responses to different environmental conditions established by a person's genes.

6. ___   Cooley's term for the images of ourselves we form by observing how other people react to us.

7. ___   Freud's term for the stage is psychosexual development in which children discover their genitals and become aware of the differences between the sexes.

8. ___   Freud's term for the stage in psychosexual development in children in which sexual urges are dormant and the child focuses on the mastering of skills for coping with the environment.

9. _D_   The process through which experience shapes personal identity and orientations to social action.

10. ___   A group that a person rejects and does not want to join in the future.

11.___   People whose evaluations a person holds in high esteem.
12.___   Freud's term for the stage in psychosexual development in which infants derive pleasure from nursing and sucking.
13.___   G.H. Mead's term for the internalized image of the structure and norms of society as a whole.
14.___   According to Mead, the impulsive, creative, selfish part of the self.
15.___   Freud's term for the stage in psychosexual development when sexual desires reemerge and the young person begins to seek mature love.
16.___   Learning about and practicing a new role before one is in a position to play that role.
17.___   A group that a person would like to join in the future.
18.___   An individual, group, or organization that influences a person's behavior and sense of self.
19.___   A group or social category that an individual uses as a guide in developing his or her values, attitudes, behavior, and self-image.
20.___   G. H. Mead's term for the stage in social development when children engage in imitative play and begin to take the role of the other.

Answers

1. s   8. m   15. j
2. a   9. o   16. f
3. e   10. n   17. l
4. i   11. h   18. g
5. r   12. t   19. c
6. d   13. p   20. b
7. q   14. k

REVIEW QUESTIONS

1. Most social scientists today would agree with the statement:
   a. Human behavior is largely determined by genes, acting independently of the environment.
   b. Human behavior is largely determined by experience and learning, acting independently of genes.
   c. Genes and environment interact in the process of human development.
   d. Genes and environment have little effect on human development, which is the result of socialization.
   e. None of the above.

2. The agent of socialization that functions to wean young people from the idea that whatever they do is special is:
   a. the family
   b. the peer group
   c. school
   d. the mass media

3. By *taking the role of the other,* G. H. Mead meant:
   a. practicing a new role before actually taking on that role
   b. seeing an image of yourself reflected in other people's eyes
   c. learning to play a game, such as baseball, by the rules
   d. learning to see things from another person's point of view
   e. developing an image of the structure and working of society as a whole

4. Erikson saw one of the major psychosocial tasks of childhood as achieving:
   a. identity
   b. industry
   c. intimacy
   d. integrity
   e. generativity

5. One of the primary differences between peers and parents as agents of socialization is:
   a. Peers engage in open conflict.
   b. Peer relationships are egalitarian.
   c. Peer relationships are not regulated by norms.
   d. Peers and parents have different, conflicting values.
   e. Peers are more fun.

6. Ms. McHugh is thirty-four years old and vice president of a bank. Her friends think of her as one of the most successful career women they know. Suddenly she finds herself looking at babies and wondering if the man she is dating will propose. Ms. McHugh is:
   a. thinking about settling down
   b. experiencing role confusion
   c. going through an identity crisis
   d. experiencing a mid-life crisis
   e. torn between intimacy and isolation

7. Socialization involves:
   a. unconscious modeling
   b. explicit instruction

    c.   acquiring a sense of identity
    d.   learning the values, norms, and skills of one's culture
    e.   all of the above

8. Freud's term for the part of the personality that operates on the pleasure principle, seeking immediate gratification, is:
    a.   the id
    b.   the ego
    c.   the superego
    d.   the libido

9. Your mother has asked you to visit an uncle who is in the hospital. You discover that a movie you have been waiting to see is on TV that night. You're torn, but you decide to visit your uncle. According to G. H. Mead, which part of the self governed your behavior?
    a.   the significant other
    b.   the me
    c.   the generalized other
    d.   the I
    e.   the superego

10. Which of the following theorists saw socialization as a confrontation between the individual and society?
    a.   Sigmund Freud
    b.   Erik Erikson
    c.   George Herbert Mead
    d.   Charles Horton Cooley
    e.   Margaret Mead

11. In his study of class differences in socialization, Kohn found that:
    a.   Middle-class parents are more concerned about their child's performance in school than working-class parents are.
    b.   Middle-class parents are less concerned about neatness and obedience than working-class parents are.
    c.   Middle-class parents are more concerned about teaching their children how to get ahead than working-class parents are.
    d.   Middle-class parents do a better job of socialization than working-class parents do.
    e.   Working-class parents do a better job of socialization than middle-class parents do.

12. According to Cooley, the looking-glass self consists of:
    a.   how we imagine others see us

b.   how we imagine others judge us
c.   how we feel about the reactions of others
d.   how significant others see us
e.   all of the above

13. Although men and women go through the same stages of adult development, they do not have identical experiences. One difference between young men and women is:
    a.   Women are concerned with intimacy; men are not.
    b.   Men in their twenties formulate a dream of their future; women only dream of helping a man to achieve his.
    c.   For men, the *honeymoon stage* of married life ends in the early thirties; for women it is just beginning.
    d.   Women experience a time-crunch in their mid-thirties or early forties; men do not.
    e.   None of the above.

14. Jim's father is a senior partner in a large Washington law firm; his mother is head of a Virginia school district. Most of their friends are as successful and career-oriented as they are. Jim has no interest in what he sees as the *rat race*; he wants to be a cabinetmaker. His parents' circle of friends serve as a:
    a.   primary group
    b.   looking-glass self
    c.   positive reference group
    d.   negative reference group

15. Studies of unfortunate children who have been reared in near-total isolation show they:
    a.   behave like animals
    b.   never recover from the experience
    c.   develop normally without interaction
    d.   catch up with others their age if given proper nutrition and tender loving care

16. According to G. H. Mead, the primary change in the game stage of social development is that:
    a.   Children learn to take the role of the other.
    b.   Children acquire a generalized other.
    c.   Children learn to play by the rules.
    d.   The *me* and the *I* become differentiated.

17. In many ways, the role of adolescents in modern Western societies is unique. Which of the following statements about American teen-agers would

not apply to teen-agers in traditional societies (such as Samoa at the time of M. Mead's study)?

a. Teenagers are expected to unlearn much of the behavior that was expected of them in childhood.
b. Teenagers must cope with puberty.
c. Teenagers must prepare for adult roles.
d. Teenagers must begin to develop an adult identity.
e. Teenagers must choose a life style and occupation.

18. According to your text, since 1965, the number of Americans aged 65 and older has reached:

a. 28 million
b. the same size as the population of Canada
c. 12% of the entire country's population
d. all of the above

19. According to one estimate, an average hour of TV includes how many violent acts, as reported in your text?

a. two
b. four
c. six
d. eight
e. ten

20. Which of the following is not one of the problems associated with prime time TV?

a. the great majority of programs reinforce widely held values
b. advertising tends to reinforce stereotypes
c. TV alters the traditional influences of the family, friends, and school
d. TV alters traditional socialization patterns
e. TV often gives inaccurate portrayals of important events

21. All societies divide the life course into stages, which are institutionalized informal rules which define the ages at which people are allowed to participate in certain activities. Which of the following is an example of that principle in American society?

a. the requirement to attend school
b. a person cannot get married without a permit
c. a person cannot work without a permit
d. we are not entitled to Medicare benefits until we reach 65
e. all of the above

22. As an example of changes occurring in our traditional adulthood roles, the text gave several examples of trends affecting roles. Many of these

trends have to do with the activities of women in American society. Which of the following is not such a trend?

a.   More than half of today's college students are women.

b.   Most college educated women are expected to work for a few years after graduation, and then settle down to raising a family.

c.   The average age at first marriage has risen.

d.   Today, nine out of ten women expect to work after they marry.

e.   Only a small number of men and women enter into a marriage where the wife is a full-time homemaker and the husband the sole breadwinner.

Answers

1.   c: Most social scientists reject both genetic determinism and environmental determinism as oversimplifications of a complex process. (See section entitled The Nature of Human Behavior.)

2.   c: Elementary school is the child's first experience of an organization in which people are evaluated in terms of what they do (not who they are); the same standards are applied to everyone; and activities are governed by formal rules and regulations. (Agents of Socialization)

3.   d: Mead saw the first evidence of this in the play stage, when children pretend to be other people. He maintained that children begin to develop a sense of self only when they discover how it feels to be another person. Only then do they see themselves as social objects. (The Emergence of Self)

4.   b: Erikson believes that achieving a sense of mastery, or industry--a confidence in one's ability to learn, produce, and achieve--in middle childhood is as important as developing a sense of trust in infancy. (The other answers refer to adult stages of development.) (Socialization and the Life Cycle)

5.   b: Parents and children often run into conflicts (answer a). Children often devise and enforce strict rules for their games (c). Youngsters' values may be a more accurate reflection of adult values than adults care to admit (d). And peers can be as demanding, hurtful, or dull as parents (e). That leaves answer b. (Agents of Socialization)

6.   d: The term *mid-life crisis* refers to the feeling many women have in their mid-thirties that this is their last chance to pursue other dreams. Although there is some overlap, the other answers use terms that apply to adolescence (role confusion and identity crisis) and to the twenties (settling down and intimacy vs. isolation). (Socialization and the Life Cycle)

7.   e: The term *socialization* covers the whole range of social activities and experiences that contribute to transforming an infant into a participating member of society. (The Nature of Human Behavior)

8. a: Freud saw the id as a reservoir of primitive, infantile urges, caged in the process of socialization but never entirely tamed. (The Process of Socialization: Psychosexual Development)

9. b: According to Mead, the *me* is the social self, the part of you that seeks social approval. If the *I*--the spontaneous, self-centered part of the self--had been in control, you would have watched the movie. (The Emergence of Self)

10. a: Freud viewed socialization as a taming of the human animal, but he also believed that civilization was a continuing source of discontent. (Psychosexual Development: Freud)

11. b: All parents want their children to do well in school and to get ahead in life, but their own experiences have taught them different routes to success (initiative in the middle-class world; obedience in the working-class world). (Agents of Socialization)

12. e: Cooley believed that our self-image depends not only on the image of ourselves we see reflected in others' eyes, but also on our reaction to those judgments. If someone you do not consider very intelligent tells you that you are stupid, for example, it won't damage your self-esteem. If a significant other makes the same comment, it will have an effect. (The Emergence of Self)

13. e: Answer b is partially correct, but only partially: Some women's dreams center around helping a man, but other women have ambitions of their own. (Transitions to Adulthood)

14. d: Reference groups can be positive or negative. Jim's self-image is based in part on those people he does not want to resemble. (Agents of Socialization)

15. d: In most cases, children who have been kept in isolation have been mistreated in other ways as well. Anna, for example, was severely malnourished. If discovered before too much physical damage has occurred, however, they respond to socialization and make up most of the time they have lost. (The Nature of Human Behavior)

16. b: Mead uses the image of a game to describe this stage because to play an organized game like baseball, a child must understand the relationship between the position he or she is playing and other positions. In other words, the child must have a general image of the game in his or her head. (The Emergence of Self)

17. e: In traditional societies, there are few if any choices in life style and occupation; children literally follow in their parents' footsteps. One reason for role confusion in modern Western societies is that the individual's future is not predetermined. It is a matter of personal choice, and a person's identity depends on what choices he or she makes. (Socialization and the Life Cycle)

18. d: These data also mean that the social meaning of reaching age 65 has changed. Older Americans are in better health than ever before and

represent a new leisure class. Old age, however, does affect men and women differently, especially in regard to economic security. (Socialization and the Life Cycle)

19. d: Albert Bandura has argued that aggressive behavior is promoted by TV violence. Keep in mind that other research (e.g., Josephson) has qualifed Bandura's findings. But, to the extent that his research is accurate, a few hours of TV watched can expose children to a high number of violent acts. Further, violence is seen not only in crime shows and Westerns, but in cartoons like Bugs Bunny. (Growing up with T.V.)

20. a: The great majority of shows teach such widely held values as good over evil, hard work pays off, and honesty is the best policy. (Growing up with T.V.)

21. e: Each of the answers is correct. We must attend public school up to a certain age. If children are not sent to school, both the parents and the children are liable to be the recipients of legal action; marriage permits are required in all states although it is easier to get the license in some states (Nevada) than in others with very little in the way of a waiting period; work permits assure that a Social Security number has been obtained for taxing and entitlement benefit purposes, the legal age has been reached, etc.; and Medicare benefits are associated with formal retirement, the usual age being sixty-five. (Socialization and the Life Cycle)

22. b: Today, nine out of ten college women expect to work after they are married, and the trend is to remain in the work force, leaving only to bear children, and then returning.

MYTH OR FACT?

1. In adolescence, peers become the main agent of socialization; parents have little impact on teenagers. t/f
2. Television encourages children to be aggressive. t/f
3. Middle-class parents do a better job of socializing children than working-class parents do. t/f

Answers

1. *False.* Teenagers may say, and even believe, that what their peers think matters more to them than what their parents think. But research indicates that parents continue to be powerful agents of socialization in this period. Parental indifference is a leading cause of low self-esteem among adolescents.
2. *False.* Studies do show that children who watch violent TV shows are more willing to hurt another child or an inanimate object and more likely

to select violent toys than are children who watch a neutral show. But research also indicates that pro-social shows, like Mr. Rogers, encourage children to help and share things with their playmates. So the reviews on the effects of TV are mixed.

3. *False.* Kohn did find that middle- and working-class parents apply different goals and standards to child-rearing. But he shows that parents of both classes are socializing children for the world as they know it and for the kinds of occupations their children are likely to enter.

CRITICAL THINKING

1. One social scientist has called the phrase *nature vs. nurture* a case of a mistaken conjunctive (or connecting word). The correct phrase is *nature and nurture.* Explain.

2. Most discussions of socialization emphasize the role parents play in socializing their children. But it could also be said that children socialize their parents. Think how the arrival of a child changes a husband's and wife's self-images, social identities, life style, and relationship to one another. Think how their youngest child's departure for college or marriage changes them. What does this tell you about socialization?

3. Men and women in their late thirties and early forties might be described as *ships passing in the night.* Just at the point when men are settling into their chosen careers, many women are wondering if they made the right choices. At the point when many men experience a mid-life crisis, their wives or lovers may be hard at work on fulfilling their own dreams. Why do you think this is so? Are the reasons why the male and female cycles are not synchronized biological? social? both?

Chapter Five

INTERACTION AND SOCIAL STRUCTURE

OBJECTIVES

After reading Chapter Five you should be able to give in-depth answers to the following questions:

1. What are the basic elements of interaction? Of social structure?
2. What does the microperspective reveal about the structure of everyday interaction?
3. What does the macroperspective reveal about the changing shape of human societies?
4. How are the micro- and macroperspectives related?

CONCEPTS

You should also understand the following sociological concepts:

social interaction
social structure
achieved status
ascribed status
master status
role
role set
role strain
role conflict
negotiations
exchange and reciprocity
group
network
social institution
mechanical/organic solidarity
world system
definition of the situation
microperspective
macroperspective

CHAPTER REVIEW

I.   What are the basic elements of social structure?

Social structure is the framework for behavior created by repeated, pat-terned social interaction. Your text uses a football team analogy to illus-trate this concept. The assignment of individuals to specialized, interde-pendent positions, the rules of the game, the boundaries of the field, and so on, transform a collection of people on offense, defense, and special teams into a working unit having specific goals. In much the same way, social structure transforms an assortment of people into groups, a population into a society. The basic elements of social structure are: statuses, roles, inter-personal relationships, and social institutions. Study these thoroughly. They are concepts you will need throughout the course.

A. Social interaction is the basis of social organization and struc-ture. Interactions range from the informal to the formal. But all inter-actions fall into patterns. How we interact depends on the situation. When expectations are unclear, people go through a reconciliation process called *definition of the situation.*

B. A status is a position in society that is either assigned to the individual on the basis of sex, age, race, or other immutable characteristics or achieved through individual action. In everyday conversation we use the word *status* to refer to prestige (as in status symbol). Sociologists use the term to refer to any position in society, high or low. A master status is that which overrides everything else a person is or does. It is the status with which an individual is most identified.

C. A role consists of socially defined rights and responsibilities that accompany a status. If you occupy the status of student, you are expect-ed to play the part of a student. As on the stage, a role establishes guide-lines; how different individuals interpret a role varies. This is an impor-tant aspect of individuality. It is this aspect that leads to a lot of con-fusion in regard to individual decision-making and group influences.

A single status establishes a number of different relationships, known as a role set. Thus a professor is expected to play the role of teacher with students, colleagues, with other faculty members, employees, with the uni-versity administration, and so on. Moreover, an individual occupies a number of different statuses at the same time (professor, spouse, neighbor, black American). Roles simplify social interaction but may also lead to strain, when an individual is unable to fill a role; or conflict, when different roles make incompatible demands. Be sure to understand the difference between role *strain and conflict.*

D. Virtually all human activities involve other people. Interpersonal relationships are characterized by these processes: competition, cooperation, conflict, and exchange. Some sociologists see exchange and reciprocity as the

social glue that binds individuals to one another. Interpersonal relations create networks (loose webs of social connection) and groups (tight
knots of social interaction). This distinction is important when it comes to
understanding communication patterns among people. Imagine networks as
strands which link people together. They become durable, and can survive for
long periods of time. They do not, however, link people on every issue. The
types of issues, however, will be very similar.

E. Social institutions are widely accepted, time-honored blueprints
for social activities that people consider vital to their well-being. The
five major social institutions--the family, education, religion, the political system, and the economic system--deal with basic human needs. They
provide ready-made solutions to life's recurring problems (such as how to
rear children and how to distribute goods and services).

Institutions maintain continuity from generation to generation and group
to group. But institutions also play a role in social change. A change in one
institution--for example, a shift from a peasant to an industrial economy--
inevitably causes changes in other institutions.

II. What does the microperspective reveal about the structure of everyday interaction?

The microperspective is the detailed analysis of everyday behavior. The
emphasis is on how individuals determine their own and other people's statuses and interpret their own roles. Your text looks at two aspects of micro-
structure: defining the situation and presenting the self.

A. In some cases (for example, a football game or a funeral), everyone knows know what is expected, but in others, they do not. Is an invitation
to have dinner with a co-worker of the opposite sex a date or a business
meeting? In such cases, participants must arrive at a collective definition
of the situation. How they act toward one another depends on this definition.
Marriage is an example of two people using an institutionalized ceremony to
define their relationship.

B. Whereas some sociologists view everyday behavior as an unconscious
enactment of the roles society creates, Goffman (among others) argued that
people consciously try to manage the impression they make on others and to
present themselves in the most favorable light. Using a dramaturgical model
(that is, the use of a drama metaphor), Goffman and Fishman pointed out how a
married couple may act one way on stage (in public), and quite another
backstage (in private). Also, they analyzed how individuals use various props
(identity documents and support systems) to establish the role they want to
play with their spouse and others.

One of the most interesting insights was that, in most cases, people support one another's performances, even when they know the other person is
trying to create a false impression. When someone steps out of character, the

audience is often embarrassed and pretends not to notice.

III. What does the macroperspective reveal about the changing shape of human society?

The macroperspective is the analysis of whole societies and long-term social change. The emphasis is on social institutions rather than individual actions. The discussion in your text of the changing structure of human societies illustrates the macro-approach. A society is an autonomous group of people who occupy a common territory and participate in a common culture. The text identifies five types of societies: hunter-gatherer bands, horticultural villages, agrarian states, industrial nations, and the world system.

A. For 99 percent of human history, our ancestors lived as hunters and gatherers. They neither produced nor preserved their food, and lived in nomadic bands of ten to fifty people; members were free to come and go. There were no formal political or economic institutions in these types of societies. Individuals earned respect for their skills. Every adult male was a hunter, and the adult females, gatherers. There was a high degree of freedom; no one worked for anyone else. Warfare was unknown because the human population was small and natural resources abundant (as opposed to today, where much international tension emanates from disputes over the allocation of scarce resources). When bands did not get along with each other, they simply moved apart.

B. About 10,000 years ago, human beings became food producers for the first time. The domestication of plants and animals is associated with the first settled villages, more complex social structure, and war. The Yanomamo, who still practice simple horticulture, live in walled villages of seventy to eighty residents. Membership in a village and rights to surrounding gardens are determined by kinship and marriage. The Yanomamo are tied to their land and to their fellow villagers in a way that hunter-gathers are not. Raids between villages are common. Although each couple provides for itself, defense requires collective effort. Moreover, feasts and gifts are used for political ends. Most villages have a headman, who has demonstrated skill in leading raids and/or settling disputes. Many also have a shaman (a magico-religious specialist). But the major social roles in Yanomamo society are warrior (all adult men) and gardener (all adult women).

C. The agricultural revolution, which began about 6,000 years ago, paved the way for a new and more intricate type of society, the agrarian state. The plow and other inventions made it possible to keep land in continuous cultivation, to establish permanent settlements, and to produce a food surplus. This in turn made it possible for some members of the population to devote themselves full-time to activities other than farming.

The rise of agrarian states is associated with the first cities; the emergence of state religions, divine rulers who had the power of life and death over a population, and a class of religious specialists (a priesthood); the first money economies, the first taxes, and the first clerks; the state-sponsored development of crafts and arts; empire building, militarism, and the creation of standing armies; the division of society into separate and unequal classes (from kings to slaves); the invention of writing, calendars, sailing ships, and much more.

Agrarian states were far more complex than any society known before. The size of society increased; territory expanded; new institutions arose (religion, politics, and economics); and the number of statuses and roles multiplied. The vast majority of the peoples in these societies were peasants.

D. The industrial nation is a comparatively recent invention. The Industrial Revolution, which began in England about 250 years ago, reshaped social structure in a number of ways. First, populations grew and moved to urban centers. Second, the number of occupational specializations increased dramatically. As a result, people are more interdependent than ever before. Only a small percentage of the populations of industrial nations is engaged in food production; very few people produce a complete product by themselves; and hardly any families are self-sufficient. Third, the balance among institutions changed, with the family becoming less powerful and the political system more influential. New institutions, such as science and health care, developed. Fourth, mass participation in government increased and social inequalities were reduced somewhat. Finally, the nature of groups and communities changed, with voluntary and secondary associations replacing traditional ties.

E. The spread of industrialism has led to the emergence of a world system, a network of economic and political ties dominated by core capitalist nations.

IV. How are the micro- and macroperspectives related?

In real life, micro- and macro-events are intertwined. For example, the declining birthrate (a macro-event) is the result of many personal, individual decisions (micro-events). These decisions were themselves influenced by such macro-events as the women's movement and the increasing demand for higher education (which makes it more expensive to raise a child).

CONCEPT REVIEW

Match each of the following terms with the correct definition.

a. role strain
b. microperspective
c. network
d. status

e. society
f. group
g. role
h. social institution

i.   achieved status
j.   ascribed status
k.   role set
l.   definition of the situation
m.   role conflict

n.   macroperspective
o.   master status
p.   norm of reciprocity
q.   social structure
r.   world system

1.___   The focus of analysis on society and culture, along with large-scale social organizations, and social processes.

2.___   What occurs when the different roles an individual is expected to play make incompatible demands. This is different from the process of *within role* imcompatibility.

3.___   An autonomous group of people who are linked to one another through social structure, occupy a common territory, and have a common culture and a sense of shared identity.

4.___   A position in the social structure as opposed to functioning within the structure.

5.___   The cluster of different social relationships in which a person becomes involved because he or she occupies a particular social status.

6.___   The rules that demand that people respond in kind to certain behaviors.

7.___   A social status that is attained through personal effort.

8.___   What occurs when an individual is unable to fullfill social role obligations.

9.___   The framework of social relationships created and maintained through recurrent social interaction.

10.___   The analysis of everyday interaction and behavior; and real-life situations.

11.___   An overall idea of the meaning of a situation, developed through social interaction.

12.___   A social status that is assigned to an individual at birth or at different stages of the life cycle on the basis of characteristics the individual cannot control; normally this status is assigned by others.

13.___   A social status that tends to override everything else the person is or does.

14.___   A web of social relationships that connects people or organizations to each other, directly and indirectly.

15.___   A number of people who engage in frequent face-to-face activities, feel a common identity, and recognize a boundary between *us* and *them.*

16.___   A relatively stable set of norms, values, statuses, roles, groups, and organizations that provides a structure for behavior in a particular area of social life.

17.___ The collection of culturally defined rights, obligations, and expectations that accompany a social status.

18.___ The international structure which results from a division of labor among mutually interdependent nations.

Answers

1. n	7. i	13. o
2. m	8. a	14. c
3. e	9. q	15. f
4. d	10. b	16. h
5. k	11. l	17. g
6. p	12. j	18. r

REVIEW QUESTIONS

1. Which of the following statements about social structure is false?
   a. Social structure provides continuity.
   b. Social structure determines the outcome of social interaction.
   c. Social structure shapes everyday behavior.
   d. Social structure transforms a collection of people into a group, community, or society.

2. Multistranded relationships are characteristic of:
   a. hunter-gatherer societies
   b. horticultural societies
   c. agrarian states
   d. a and b
   e. a, b, and c

3. Which of the following is an example of an achieved status?
   a. judge
   b. convict
   c. wife
   d. homosexual
   e. all of the above

4. One of the defining characteristics of industrial nations is:
   a. the emergence of cities
   b. the development of separate political and religious institutions
   c. mobility (people are not tied to the land)
   d. the increasing importance of achieved statuses

5. A physician's relationships with other physicians, nurses, patients, and

patients' families are part of his or her:
a. status
b. role
c. role set
d. identity documents

6. When people see a couple fighting on a public bus they are likely to:
a. stare
b. rush over and ask if they can help
c. lecture the couple on proper behavior in public places
d. pretend that they don't notice

7. What is the basic unit of social structure in hunter-gatherer societies?
a. the family
b. the band
c. the clan
d. the territory

8. Which of the following is likely to serve as a master status for adults in industrial nations?
a. income
b. age
c. religion
d. occupation

9. The key difference between purely economic exchange and the norms of reciprocity is that the latter:
a. are based on perceptions of equal value
b. do not involve the exchange of goods
c. are subtle and diffuse
d. may be ignored without penalty

10. Which of the following illustrates the microperspective?
a. an analysis of the family system in a South American society
b. a study of racial prejudice in the United States
c. a survey of attitudes toward marriage among American college students
d. a study of ritualized behavior at a football game

11. The political system in the United States is an example of:
a. a set of norms and values
b. a formal organization
c. a social institution
d. a set of statuses and roles
e. a macroperspective

12. Which of the following perspectives holds that the history of society moves from simple to complex forms?
    a.   population perspective
    b.   microperspective
    c.   macroperspective
    d.   network perspective

13. Which of the following applies to some (not all) human societies?
    a.   Members of a society occupy a common territory.
    b.   Members of a society have a common culture and sense of identity.
    c.   Members of a society are linked through a common political system.
    d.   All of the above.
    e.   None of the above.

14. *Homosexual* is an example of:
    a.   an ascribed status
    b.   a master status
    c.   a role set
    d.   role conflict

15. The majority of the population in agrarian states:
    a.   lives in urban centers
    b.   specializes in crafts such as metalwork or pottery
    c.   engages in military action
    d.   lives as peasants

16. A sick person's obligation to stay in bed and follow doctor's orders is an example of his or her:
    a.   status
    b.   role
    c.   presentation of self
    d.   institution

17. Which of the following incidents is an example of *offstage* behavior?
    a.   a wife covering up for an inconsiderate remark by her husband (*He's only joking*)
    b.   a doctor telling his nurse that Patient X, with whom he just consulted for half an hour, is an annoying hypochondriac
    c.   a student carrying his athletic equipment everywhere he goes
    d.   a woman telling a man she just met that she never goes to singles bars; a friend insisted she come

18. The so-called superwoman syndrome, which holds that a woman ought to be able to keep house and raise a family while pursuing a full-time career

is an example of:
a. role strain
b. role conflict
c. institutionalized sexism
d. identity confusion

19. Social inequality is most pronounced in:
a. hunter-gatherer bands
b. horticultural societies
c. agrarian states
d. industrial nations

20. An analysis of the social functions of the family in horticultural villages would be an example of:
a. the changing shape of society
b. macrosociology
c. everyday interaction
d. microsociology

21. The oft-quoted statement by W. I. Thomas, *If men define situations as real, they are real in their consequences,* means:
a. People often deceive themselves.
b. Reality is a social construct.
c. Seeing is believing.
d. People are prisoners of society.

22. The basic unit of social organization in horticultural societies is:
a. the family
b. the band
c. the clan
d. the tribe

23. *Senior citizen* is an example of
a. a status
b. a role
c. a group
d. a social institution

24. Which institution is concerned with giving meaning and purpose to life?
a. the family
b. education
c. religion
d. the political system
e. the economic system

Answers

1. b: Social structure establishes *the rules of the game* and assigns *players* to positions (or statuses), but how individuals play the game depends on their skills, efforts, and imagination. (See section entitled Defining the Situation.)

2. e: Even in agrarian states, most relationships are personal and multi-faceted. Appointment to public positions is based on kinship and/or friendship; marriage is seen as an economic contract between families; and so on. The shift from many multistranded relationships to numerous single-purpose relationships occurred with the rise of industrial nations. (Relations Among Societies)

3. e: An achieved status is a social position that results from the individual's own behavior. It may or may not be considered an *achievement* (a praiseworthy accomplishment) in the eyes of society. (Status and Role)

4. d: Although the ascribed statuses of sex, age, and racial or ethnic identity are still important in industrial nations, achieved statuses--such as education, occupation, and income--are also socially significant. (Status and Role)

5. c: The status *physician* generates an array of different relationships to people in other statuses (sometimes resulting in role strain or conflict). (Status and Role)

6. d: According to Goffman, everyone is embarrassed when someone loses face. The most common reaction to scenes like this is studied non-observance. (Status and Role)

7. a: Although the hunter-gatherers live in bands, membership in a band is flexible. Members are free to come and go as they like. Thus the nuclear family is the basic building block of hunter-gatherer societies. (Relations Among Societies)

8. d: In industrial nations, *you are what you do.* This is not the case in other types of societies, in which most adults do the same kinds of work (hunting and gathering or farming). (Relations Among Societies)

9. c: Whereas economic exchange is concrete/limited, reciprocity is vague and more demanding. Gifts and favors cannot be safely ignored. (Relations Among Societies)

10. d: Microsociology is detailed analysis of routine behavior that people take for granted. (Emphasis is on behavior in the here and now; a survey doesn't qualify.) (Defining the Situation)

11. c: As an institution, the political system includes norms and values, statuses and roles, groups and formal organizations. The term that describes this entire set of social arrangements is *institution.* (The Structure of Societies; Institutional Structure)

12. c: Technology is seen as the driving force in sociocultural evolution. New technologies enable a society to support a larger population; and the population, in turn, requires more complex forms of organization. (Relations Among Societies)

13. c: Hunter-gatherer bands and horticultural villages do not have formal political institutions or political leaders. Rather, they rely on informal mechanisms of social control. Government as we know it first appeared in agrarian states. (Relations Among Societies)

14. b: When people learn that an individual is gay, they are likely to see this as a defining characteristic and to reinterpret his or her past behavior in light of this identity. (Status and Role)

15. d: Although cities, craft specialties, and standing armies all emerged with the agrarian state, most citizens of these states are engaged in food production. (Relations Among Societies)

16. b: As Parsons pointed out, someone who does not play the role described here will be evicted from the status of *patient* and considered a malingerer. (Status and Role)

17. b: The doctor has dropped the mask of *concerned physician.* All of the other answers describe onstage behavior--the self-conscious attempt to manage impressions. (The Presentation of Self)

18. b: Role strain (answer a) occurs when a person cannot live up to the expectations of one role. Role conflict occurs when different roles make competing demands. (The Structure of Social Relationships)

19. c: There is very little difference in standard of living from one family to the next in hunter-gatherer bands, and horticultural villages. And while inequality persists in industrial nations, it is not as extreme in agrarian states, where kings were often treated as gods and peasants and slaves as beasts of burden. (Relations Among Societies)

20. b: Macrosociology is concerned with overall patterns, not everyday interaction. The discussion of different types of societies in your text uses this approach. (Defining the Situation)

21. b: Thomas held that reality is not something *out there,* waiting to be discovered, but the product of collective definitions of situations. (Defining the Situation)

22. c: In most horticultural societies, the right to live in a village and plant gardens around it is determined by membership in, or marriage into, a clan, what is essentially an extended kin group. (Relations Among Societies)

23. a: *Senior citizen* is a position in society, or social status. The role a senior citizen plays depends on the expectations of the people around him or her (whether they feel an older person would be active or take it easy, advise younger relations or acknowledge that they are strangers in the modern world, and so on). (Status and Role)

24. c: All institutions depend on shared values and agreement on the meaning

and purpose of life. Religion is the institution that is directly responsible for reinforcing values, especially when people are dis-
heartened (for example, when a family member dies). (The Structure of
Societies; Institutional Structure)

MYTH OR FACT?

1. Although the American family is changing, the social
    institution of the family is *alive and well* in the
    United States today.   t/f
2. Advanced technology, with its numerous labor-saving
    devices, has created a *leisure society.* People
    today do not have to work nearly as hard as their
    ancestors did to earn a living.   t/f
3. The violent atmosphere in prisons today reflects the
    personal characteristics of inmates and the fact
    that they are not free to *check out* whenever they
    they like.   t/f

Answers

1. *True.* The American family is changing: People are living together
    before they get married, marrying later, having fewer children, and get-
    ting divorced more than in the past. Even so, the fact is that the vast
    majority of Americans do get married at least once, and most couples have
    at least one child.
2. *False.* Life in small, technologically simple societies is far more
    leisurely than it is in modern, technologically advanced societies. Hun-
    ter-gatherers, who collect and produce everything they need by working
    about fifteen hours a week, are a better example of a leisure society
    than we are.
3. *False.* Zimbardo's experiment suggests that the social structure of
    prisons promotes the kinds of behavior we attribute to prisoners (and
    guards). The subjects in this study were normal, law-abiding college
    students. Moreover, they were free to quit at any time. Assigning them
    prison roles produced an authoritarian, sadistic streak in guards and a
    subservient posture in prisoners--results that no one (least of all
    Zimbardo) would have predicted.

CRITICAL THINKING

1. In the early 1960s, Elliot Liebow conducted a yearlong field study of the
    men who congregated on a particular street corner in a poor, black neigh-
    borhood in Washington, D.C. Most of the chapters in his report, publish-

ed as *Tally's Corner*, describe the men's daily, face-to-face relationships (microperspective). Then, in the last chapter, he explains their inner world and behavior as a direct response to the larger society and the position they occupy in that society (macroperspective.)

One of the major points of articulation between the inside world and the larger society surrounding it is in the area of employment. The way in which a man earns a living and the kind of living he makes have important consequences for how the man sees himself and is seen by others. . . .

Making a living takes on an overriding importance at marriage. The young, lower-class Negro gets married in his early twenties, at approximately the same time and in part for the same reasons as his white or Negro middle- or working-class counterpart. . . . He wants to be publicly, legally married, to support a family and be the head of it, because this is what it is to be a man in our society, whether one lives in a room [in a black ghetto] or in an elegant house in the suburbs.

Although he wants to get married, he hedges on his commitment from the beginning because he is afraid, not of marriage itself, but of his ability to carry out his responsibilities as husband and father. His father failed and had to *cut out,* and the men he knows who have been or are married have also failed or are in the process of doing so. . . . However far he has gone in school he is illiterate or almost so; however many jobs he has had or however hard he has worked, he is essentially unskilled . . . .

In general, the menial job lies outside the job hierarchy and promises to offer no more tomorrow than it did today. The Negro menial worker remains a menial worker so that, after one or two years of marriage and as many children, the man who could not support his family from the beginning is even less able to do so as time goes on. . . . He has little vested interest in such a job and learns to treat it with the same contempt held for it by his employer and society at large. From his point of view, the job is expendable; from the employer's point of view, he is. For reasons real or imagined,. . . he frequently quits or is fired.

He carries this failure home where his family life is undergoing a parallel deterioration. . . .[1]

Liebow suggests that these men have "three strikes against them": their jobs do not allow them to fill the role of breadwinner; the expectation of failure functions as a self-fulfilling prophecy (see Chapter One); and they are black. Which of these obstacles is located in the men's inner worlds? Which are created by society?

2. In *Anger: The Misunderstood Emotion*, the social psychologist Carol Tavris examines something we usually think of as a psychological pheno-menon from the sociological point of view. Tavris writes,

> Most angry episodes are social events: they assume meaning only in terms of the social contract between participants. The beliefs we have about anger, and the interpretations we give to the experience, are as impor-tant [as] the emotion itself. . . . This is why people don't always know why they are angry; sometimes it takes a friend or a therapist or a whole movement to persuade them. It is why people can feel very angry and not know why, or at what. There is no one-to-one correspondence be-tween feeling angry and knowing why, because "knowing why" is a social convention that follows cultural rules.[2]

Would you agree with this view? Can you recall a time when you didn't realize that you were angry, or why you were angry, until you discussed some-thing with a friend? Tavris says that talking over anger doesn't reduce the feeling, but rather rehearses it. What does she mean?

3. A few years ago, the social psychologist Stanley Milgram asked a group of New York male graduate students to participate in a simple experiment. All the student had to do was to get on a subway, pick out one passenger in the crowd, and ask that person to give him his seat. Milgram's stu-dents thought he was crazy. "A person could get killed that way." One brave student agreed to try. To his great surprise, half of the people he approached gave him their seat without asking for an explanation. When Milgram tried it himself, he found the most difficult part was making the request. The words stuck in his throat.[3] The sociologist Harold Garfin-kel has asked students to commit similar violations of folkways--for ex-ample, attempting to bargain for items in a department store (something Americans do not ordinarily do) or breaking the rules in a game of tic-tac-toe by erasing their opponent's first move.[4] How would you feel about participating in one of these experiments? What does your reaction tell you about the unconscious, habitual level of social structure? About the presentation of the self?

Notes

[1] Elliot Liebow, *Tally's Corner: A Study of Negro Streetcorner Men,* Boston: Little, Brown, reprinted by permission of the publisher: 210-212, 1967.

[2] Carol Tavris, *Anger: The Misunderstood Emotion*, New York: Simon and Schuster, reprinted by permission of Simon and Schuster, Inc.: 18, 1982.

[3]Carol Tavris, The Frozen World of the Familiar Stranger: A Conversation with Stanley Milgram, by Carol Tavris, *Psychology Today* 8: 70-80, 1974.

[4]H. Garfinkel, *Studies in Ethnomethodology*, Englewood Cliffs, NJ: Prentice-Hall, 1967.

EXERCISE: Society and Identity--The Presentation of Yourself

This test has two parts (and no right or wrong answers). First, complete the following sentence: I am...

1.

2.

3.

4.

5.

6.

7.

8.

9.

10.

11.

12.

13.

14.

15.

If you are like most people, you began by listing your social statuses (twenty-six years old, male, student, captain of the track team) and then personality characteristics (friendly or shy, driven or easygoing, intelligent or average, and so on). Underline the personality characteristics you listed. Would someone expect a person who occupies your statuses to exhibit these traits? Do you fit the role?

Having examined your *social address,* now consider the ways in which you attempt to manage the impression you make on others. Look at what you are wearing and, if you are at home, look around your room. (If you are not at home, picture it in your mind.) Would someone know *who you are* simply by looking at you? What identity props do you use? What would a stranger learn about you by visiting your home? Do the pictures on your wall and the things on your shelves express your dominant identity? Would a stranger see clues to your reserve and relic identities (a flute you no longer play, books on religion or travel that you'd forgotten, a gift from an ex-lover)? In other words, how do you set the stage?

EXERCISE: Identifying Your Networks

Diagram your twenty closest friends, including relationships they have among each other. Then (a) identify which are most likely to form a social group getting together on some occasion, and which are unlikely to be gathered together; (b) suppose you had to decide where to spend a vacation--e.g., at home, at school (e.g., for a summer job or summer session), or traveling with friends. Will your choice bring you closer to one cluster than another? Or is there such a high overlap between your friends at home and at school that you would be with the same people regardless?

Chapter Six

DEVIANCE AND SOCIAL CONTROL

OBJECTIVES

After reading Chapter Six you should be able to give in-depth answers to the following questions:

1. What are deviance and social control?
2. What is labeling theory?
3. What is crime?
4. How does the criminal justice system work?

CONCEPTS

You should also understand the following sociological concepts:

deviance
social control
informal/formal social controls
sanctions
anomie
conformists
innovators
rebels
retreatists
ritualists
differential association
labeling theory
deviant career
deviant subculture
moral entrepreneurs
crime
absolute number of crimes
crime rate
crimes without victims
organized crime
white-collar criminals

CHAPTER REVIEW

I. What are deviance and social control?

Your text examines the social phenomena of deviance and social control, and considers the relationship between the two. This chapter contains a lot of information that will seem strange to you. Stay with it. Examine how you will see reports of deviance and crime in newspapers differently from now on. You *should* see them differently. If not, you missed the major points.

A. Psychologists are concerned with the question of why certain individuals engage in particular forms of deviance. Learning theory psychologists emphasize that the causes of deviance lie within the individual learning process; and that reinforcement, punishment, and imitation shape individual behavior.

B. Sociologists are concerned with the question of why rates of deviance vary from group to group, place to place, and time to time. The underlying assumption is that the social environment influences behavior. Durkheim traced deviance to anomie, to a breakdown in the social order that leaves people without social guidelines. (Updating Durkheim, Hirschi details a loss of attachments, commitment, involvement, and belief in the value of social rules.) In contrast, Merton sees deviance as a product of contradictions in the social order. Cultural norms and values set the same goals for everyone, but the social structure denies some people legitimate opportunities to achieve those goals. Individuals respond to the gap between socially prescribed goals and socially approved means in one of five ways: conformity, innovation, ritualism, retreatism, or rebellion. Those most likely to be considered deviant are innovators (who resort to disapproved means of achieving recognized goals) and rebels (who substitute new goals, and new means for achieving them). The text points out that which strategy people adopt depends on the illegitimate opportunity structure of their society.

A second group of theorists traces deviance to socialization by a subculture that flouts conventional rules for behavior. Like Merton's innovators and rebels, these subcultures can be seen as a response to limited opportunities and social inequality. What would some of these limited opportunities be? And, what would some of the important aspects of social inequality be?

II. What is labeling theory?

Labeling theory emphasizes the social definition of deviance and the unintended consequences of branding certain activities and actors as deviant. A deviant label invokes a cluster of stereotypes that usually cause conventional people to shun a person in this category. As a result, individuals may be pushed into deviant careers and subcultures. In other words, the label functions as a self-fulfilling prophecy. (People assume that *once a criminal, always a criminal,* and refuse to hire an ex-convict; unable to find a legitimate job, the ex-convict again turns to crime--thus fulfilling the prophecy.) Labeling theorists hold that the creation of deviant categories is the result of moral enterprise, implying that social control is arbitrary. (In theory, left-handed people or people who like ice cream could be treated as deviant.) This may be true in some cases, such as labeling marijuana but not alcohol as a dangerous drug. In others (child molestation, terrorist attacks), deviance is a clear violation of widely held norms which seem to be accepted universally.

III.   What is crime?

A crime, quite simply, is a violation of the law. Not all deviant behavior is criminal, and not all crimes are considered deviant. Coming to grips with such statements may be difficult at first, but stay with the ideas, and trust that the research evidence is accurate on these points. Your text examines four types of crime in detail, and then looks at crime rates in the United States. Study these carefully. This knowledge will serve you well in your everyday life as well as in the course.

A. *Common crime* refers to violent and property crimes (murder, assault, robbery, burglary, etc.). In terms of absolute numbers, most common crimes are committed by whites. But both the crime rate and the victimization rate are higher for minorities. *White-collar crimes* are illegal acts committed by individuals or corporations engaged in legitimate businesses, either to benefit the business or for personal gain. Although long regarded as a minor problem by the courts and public, such acts are now seen as being widespread, costly, and criminal. *Organized crime* refers to organizations specializing in providing illegal goods and services. Like legitimate businesses, organized crime has evolved from family enterprises into sophisticated operations. *Crimes without victims* are acts that injure no one except (perhaps) the person who commits them. They are controversial because the public is divided between those who feel the police and courts should enforce morality and those who believe the government has no right to regulate private behavior. This difference of opinion seems to persist and has been heightened in recent years.

B. Calculations of crime rates are complicated by the existence of different measures of crime. The Uniform Crime Report is based on police data --the National Crime Survey is based on victimization surveys. The best data indicate that crime rates increased steadily in the United States during the 1960s and 1970s, then leveled off in the 1980s.

IV. How does the criminal justice system work?

The criminal justice system is best described as a funnel. Only about 50 percent of all crimes are reported to the police, and only about half of these crimes are *cleared by arrest.* Less than half of those suspects who are arrested are tried and convicted, and only a small percentage of these people are sent to prison and complete their sentences. The main reason is that the police, the courts, and the prisons are given considerable discretion in applying sanctions. Decisions may be based on practical or personal considerations, not *the letter of the law.* Whether the threat of punishment acts as a deterrent to crime is the subject of much debate, much of which sorts out on political grounds (e.g., liberal/conservative).

Concept Review

Match each of the following terms with the correct definition.

a. innovators
b. formal social controls
c. deviant subculture
d. crime
e. anomie
f. crime rate
g. ritualists
h. white-collar criminals
i. social control
j. moral entrepreneurs
k. crimes without victims

l. conformists
m. deviance
n. differential association
o. informal social controls
p. labeling theory
q. deviant career
r. sanctions
s. retreatists
t. rebels
u. organized crime
v. absolute number of crimes

1.___ A violation of a norm that is codified in a law and backed by the power and authority of the state.
2.___ Sutherland's term for the learning of criminal or violent behavior through exposure to predominantly procriminal norms and values or to situations that reward criminal behavior.
3.___ Subtle pressures to conform to society's norms and values.
4.___ A condition of normlessness in a society.
5.___ Merton's term for the people who accept both the goals their culture holds out as desirable and the approved means.
6._p_ The view that deviance is an interactive process whereby a society, or a group within a society, defines certain behavior as deviant, labels people who engage in that behavior as deviants, and then treats them as outcasts.
7.___ Crimes that harm no one, but offend widely shared/accepted public morals.
8._i_ Efforts to prevent and/or correct deviance.
9.___ Merton's term for people who reject both the socially approved goals and socially approved rules, and substitute new goals

and new means of achieving them.

10.___ Merton's term for people who have given up both on goals and on the means for attaining them.

11.___ Social rewards for conforming behavior and punishments for deviant behavior.

12.___ The number of crimes per 100,000 population in a given time period.

13.___ Becker's term for people who make it their business to see that offenses are recognized and offenders treated as such.

14.___ Behavior that violates widely held norms.

15.___ Institutionalized, codified, public, highly visible mechanisms for preventing or correcting deviant behavior.

16.___ Merton's term for people who are determined to achieve conventional goals but are willing to use unconventional means.

17.___ Organizations that exist primarily to provide, and profit from, illegal goods and services.

18.___ A life style, according to your text, that includes habitual or permanent deviance.

19.___ Individuals (and corporations), engaged in an otherwise legitimate business, who either conduct business by illegal means or take illegal personal profits at the expense of their employers, customers, or the government.

20.___ Merton's term for people who are so compulsive about following social rules that they lose sight of the goals.

21.___ A group that is distinguished from other members of society by deviant norms, values, and life style.

22.___ The number of crimes committed during a given time period, often measured in terms of the number of crimes *known*.

Answers

1. d	8. i	15. b	22. v
2. n	9. t	16. a	
3. o	10. s	17. u	
4. e	11. r	18. q	
5. l	12. f	19. h	
6. p	13. j	20. g	
7. k	14. m	21. c	

REVIEW QUESTIONS

1. Which of the following theories holds that to understand deviance one must study the rule makers as well as the rule breakers?
   a. control theory

    b. labeling theory
    c. the theory of anomie
    d. learning theory

2. According to Erikson, one of the functions of deviance is:
    a. to provide employment for police, court workers, and prison guards
    b. to discourage innovation and ritualism
    c. to establish group boundaries and promote internal stability
    d. public entertainment

3. A major difference between small, traditional societies and modern societies is:
    a. Deviance does not exist in small, traditional societies.
    b. In modern societies, formal controls replace informal social controls.
    c. Social controls are not necessary in small, traditional societies.
    d. Informal controls are often sufficient in traditional societies.

4. Edwin Sutherland coined the term *white-collar crime* in 1939. Since then:
    a. White-collar crime has decreased.
    b. White-collar crime has increased.
    c. White-collar criminals are more often prosecuted and sent to prison.
    d. The public feels one is more likely to become a victim of white-collar crime than of any other type of crime.

5. Two students are working late in their college computer center. By chance, they unlock a program containing the questions and answers for the final exam in Psychology 301. They spend two nights memorizing the answers and both get A's on the exam. This is an example of:
    a. conformity
    b. innovation
    c. ritualism
    d. retreatism
    e. rebellion

6. Which of the following statements about police work is false?
    a. Half of all crimes committed are not reported to the police.
    b. Most crimes are solved through detective work.
    c. In practice, police are selective about which crimes they investigate.
    d. Most crimes reported to police do not result in arrest.
    e. All of the above are false.

7. Merton uses the term *rebel* to describe people who:
    a. pursue culturally approved goals by illegitimate means

b. abide by society's rules but lose sight of the goals
c. abandon culturally approved goals and legitimate means to achieve them
d. reject cultural values and norms, but substitute new goals and rules for action

8. Which of the following people are not moral entrepreneurs?
    a. members of the right-to-life movement
    b. members of the Baptist church
    c. participants in the ban-the-bomb demonstrations
    d. founders of the National Organization for the Repeal of Marijuana Laws

9. Which of the following is an example of behavior that has only recently been recognized as deviant and treated as criminal?
    a. sexual harassment in the workplace
    b. smoking marijuana
    c. homosexuality
    d. political corruption
    e. all of the above

10. One of the criticisms of labeling theory is that:
    a. It overlooks white-collar crime.
    b. In focusing on crimes without victims, it implies that the social definition of deviance is entirely arbitrary.
    c. It assumes that people who are labeled as deviant are defenseless.
    d. All of the above.

11. Which of the following sociologists emphasized the role of *differential association* in generating deviance?
    a. Robert Merton
    b. Richard Cloward and Lloyd Ohlin
    c. Edwin Sutherland
    d. Travis Hirschi

12. Studies of crime deterrents indicate that:
    a. Increasing police patrols reduces crime rates.
    b. Increasing police patrols has no effect on crimes rates.
    c. Public executions reduce the murder rate.
    d. Public executions increase the murder rate.
    e. All of the above.

13. Which of the following is not an example of white-collar crime?
    a. suppressing a study that shows workers in a paint factory are being exposed to high levels of toxic substances

b. using intimidation (threats of sabbotage, violence, etc.) to obtain a contract for garbage collection
c. using bribery to obtain a contract for garbage collection
d. embezzling money from a bank

14. The top management of a corporation may encourage white-collar crime by setting impossibly high goals for middle management and blocking efforts to discuss methods of achieving those goals. Top management is encouraging:
a. conformity
b. ritualism
c. innovation
d. retreatism
e. rebellion

15. Which theory holds that deviance is the result of socialization?
a. psychoanalytic theory
b. Durkheim's theory of anomie
c. labeling theory
d. cultural transmission

16. John lost his job six months ago. His wife left him shortly thereafter, taking their young daughter with her. When he tries to get together with friends from the company where he used to work, they make excuses. The bank is threatening to repossess his car. He is drinking heavily, spends most of his time alone watching TV, and jokes that the bottle is his best friend. Which of the following theorists best describes his behavior?
a. Erikson
b. Durkheim
c. Hirschi
d. Cloward and Ohlin

17. Which of the following is not a crime without victims?
a. using cocaine
b. selling cocaine
c. acting in a pornographic movie
d. concealing that a candidate for public office has a homosexual lover
e. All (a-d) are crimes without victims

18. In a classic study of streetwalkers,[1] Nanette Davis found that most had drifted from casual sex into prostitution. Although they had accepted gifts or money in exchange for sexual favors, they had not thought of

themselves as prostitutes. The turning point came when they were arrested, or when the man with whom they lived started to demand that they work the streets. From this point on, they began to avoid straight friends and to associate with other *working girls* who did not condemn their activities. This study supports:

a. social learning theory
b. labeling theory
c. cultural transmission theory
d. the social bond
e. none of the above

19. Which of the following statements about crime and deviance is accurate?
a. Not all crimes are considered deviant.
b. Not all deviant acts are considered crimes.
c. Criminal deviance elicits formal, official sanctions.
d. All of the above.

20. Since the 1970s when the women's movement redefined rape as a crime of violence:
a. Rape trials have become even more difficult to prosecute.
b. The victim of a rape is less often blamed.
c. Rape trials have become easier to prosecute.
d. b and c.

21. About ____ people are sentenced to death in the U.S. each year.
a. 6,000
b. 10
c. 250
d. none of the above

Answers

1. b: Labeling theorists view deviance as the result of social interaction. This approach draws on both symbolic interactionism and conflict theory (which stresses power differentials). (See section entitled Labeling Theory.)
2. c: Erikson reasons that all groups in a society must establish boundaries to ascertain where a group starts and where it ends, who belongs and who does not. (Functions of Deviance)
3. d: Deviance and social control exist in all societies. In small, traditional societies, where people know one another personally and share a common heritage and way of life, informal social controls may be sufficient. In complex, modern societies, where people must deal with strangers and with members of subcultures that endorse different

norms and values, formal social controls are essential. (Deviance and Social Structure)

4. d: Most white-collar crimes that come to public attention are only *the tip of the iceberg.* Often such crimes are treated as *internal matters,* and not brought to police attention. Hence it is impossible to say whether white-collar crime has increased or decreased. But polls do show that the public is more concerned about white-collar crime than was true in Sutherland's day. When convicted, white-collar criminals are still more likely to be fined than to be given prison terms. (Types of Crime)

5. b: The students are pursuing a widely held goal (that is, attempting to obtain good grades in college) by socially disapproved means. (Types of Crime)

6. b: Many crimes go unsolved. When crimes are solved, it is often because the victim can identify the offender or because witnesses come forward. (The Criminal Justice System)

7. d: Anarchists are one example. Members of unconventional religious sects that require members radically to alter their life style are another. (Theories of Deviance)

8. b: All of the other answers refer to people who are making an active effort to alert the public to what they consider to be a moral outrage. (Labeling Theory)

9. a: Smoking marijuana and homosexuality are examples of behavior that is in the process of being decriminalized and socially tolerated, if not approved. In contrast, sexual harassment in the workplace was often tolerated in the past but is now being treated as a violation of decency. (What Is Deviance?)

10. d: For the most part, labeling theorists have not dealt with all of these issues. (Labeling Theory)

11. c: Sutherland held that learning deviant values is as significant as learning deviant skills and that we learn values from our close associations. (Types of Crime)

12. e: Studies of attempts to reduce crime by stepping up social control yield mixed results (*all of the above* sections). This does not necessarily mean that more police and stiffer penalties have no effect on crime. Rather, the relationship between crime and social control is complex. Increased police action may deter some crimes but promote others. (An Evaluation of the Justice System)

13. b: The use of physical intimidation is associated with organized crime. Note that the line between organized and white-collar crime is a fine one. Using bribery to obtain a contract is also illegal, and exposing workers to toxic substances causes physical harm. (Types of Crime)

14. c: In effect, the corporate heads are asking middle management to achieve accepted goals by illegal means. Note that they create a *corporate*

climate that encourages innovation, while, at the same time, avoiding any personal responsibility for illegal activities. (Types of Crime)

15. d: The theory of cultural transmission is based on the idea that people learn deviant life styles in the same way, and for the same reasons that other people learn conforming or *straight* life styles-- namely, through socialization. This view contrasts psychoanalytic theory, which attributes deviance to a breakdown in socialization; Durkheim's theory of anomie, which attributes deviance to a breakdown in the social order; and labeling theory, which views deviant life styles as a response to being treated as an outsider. (Theories of Deviance)

16. c: Hirschi emphasizes the importance of the social bond in maintaining conformity. John's commitment to his job did not *pay off*, he isn't involved in conventional activities, and his attachments to his wife and child and to friends have been cut off. The social bond has snapped. (Theories of Deviance)

17. b: Whereas the use of cocaine is a victimless crime, pushing cocaine (an addictive drug that may cause harm) is not. The distinction here is between private and public behavior. (Deviance and Social Structure)

18. b: According to labeling theory, being labeled as deviant may lead a person to adopt a deviant identity and life style. Other theories treat labeling as a consequence of deviant behavior. (Labeling Theory)

19. d: Although not identical, crime and deviance overlap. (What Is Deviance?)

20. d: During the 1970s the women's movement succeeded in having rape redefined as a crime of violence Since that time, not only have rape trials become easier to prosecute, but public attitudes have changed. The definition of rape has shifted so that now date rape is included. (What Is Deviance?)

21. c: Currently, about 250 people are sentenced to death in the U.S. each year. Of these, however, less than one in ten are actually executed. (An Evaluation of the Justice System)

Notes

[1] N. Davis, Prostitution: Identity, Career, and Legal-Economic Enterprise. In J. M. Henslin and E. Sagarin (eds.). *The Sociology of Sex: An Introductory Reader, New York: Shocken: 195-222: 1978.*

MYTH OR FACT?

1. *Once a junkie, always a junkie.*   t/f
2. Crime rates in the United States have risen steadily.   t/f

3. In the United States today, about half of the people
    confined to jail or prison have not been convicted
    of a crime.   t/f
4. A majority of Americans support a woman's right to
    abortion.   t/f

Answers

1. *False.* This is an example of deviant stereotyping. Studies of
    veterans who used heroin in Vietnam indicate that almost 90 percent
    stopped when they returned to the United States, where heroin is less
    readily available, more expensive, and socially disapproved. Note that
    the social context is operating here.
2. *True.* According to the *Uniform Crime Reports*, crime rates in this
    country climbed in the 1960s and 1970s, leveled off between 1980-85, and
    since 1985 have been increasing again.
3. *True.* About half the inmates in the U.S. detention facilities are
    awaiting trial in jail because they cannot raise bail.
4. *False.* In a recent poll, 21 percent of respondents said abortions
    should be legal under all circumstances; 55 percent, under certain
    circumstances. Further questioning revealed that 55 percent thought
    abortions should be legal only in cases of rape or incest, or when the
    mother's life is in danger.

CRITICAL THINKING

1. According to psychoanalytic theory, "We are all. . . born criminals. We
    do not learn to become criminals; rather some of us learn to control the
    criminality with which we are afflicted, while some do not."[1] Explain
    this quotation. Do you agree?

2. For the next week, read all the articles on crime (robberies, muggings,
    rapes, arrests for drugs and prostitution, political scandals) in your
    local newspaper. Underline the paragraphs and quotations that attempt to
    explain the crime. What theories of deviance is the reporter, expert, or
    eyewitness using?

3. Some years ago, eight sane people voluntarily committed themselves to
    mental hospitals. On admission, they reported one "symptom": they had
    heard voices repeating the words "empty" and "hollow." Otherwise, they
    answered questions truthfully. After being admitted, they behaved
    normally and, when asked, said the voices had stopped. A number of pa-
    tients realized that they were imposters. But not one staff member recog-
    nized that they were sane. Why? D. L. Rosenhan, who organized this ex-

periment, explains that once people have been labeled mentally ill, their behavior is interpreted in terms of their diagnosis. Normal activities are treated as symptoms. (For example the pseudopatients kept notes; one staff member reported this in the records as *patient engages in writing behavior*.) The staff segregated themselves from patients, as if they thought mental illness was contagious. When they walked through the wards, they treated the patients almost as if they were invisible. When one pseudopatient approached a doctor to ask about ground privileges, the doctor acted as if he had not spoken. *Good morning, Dave. How are you?* he said, moving on without waiting for a reply. When released after an average stay of nineteen days, their records were labeled *schizophrenia in remission.*[2]

Would you consider conducting a modified version of this experiment yourself? Suppose you told a few classmates, that you had been confined to a mental hospital for six months, or had recently graduated from a drug rehabilitation program? How do you think they would react to such a revelation?

4. Most people think of deviance as an either-or condition: you are either a criminal or a law-abiding citizen; either a social drinker or an alcoholic; either a heterosexual or a homosexual. As one team of researchers found, this either-or mentality functions as a self-fulfilling prophecy. Philip Blumstein and Pepper Schwartz interviewed eight women who had relationships with both men and women.[3] These women reported that they were under just as much pressure from homosexuals to commit themselves one way or the other as they were from heterosexuals. Their lesbian friends ridiculed them as *fence sitters*, dismissed their homosexual relationships as sexual experimentation. This suggests that a woman who has a homosexual relationship but also wants to date men believes that one relationship reveals her *true nature.* How would you feel if a woman friend told you she had had an affair with another woman? Would you feel that her current interest in men was an attempt to flee or deny her true identity? Why do you think both heterosexuals and homosexuals are uncomfortable with the idea of bisexuality?

Notes

[1] Albert K. Cohen and James F. Short, Jr., Crime and Juvenile Delinquency. In R. K. Merton and R. Nisbet (eds.), *Contemporary Social Problems*, 4th ed., New York: Harcourt Brace Jovanovich, 70, 1976.

[2] D. L. Rosenhan, On Being Sane in Insane Places, *Science* 179: 250-259, 1973.

[3] Philip W. Blumstein and Pepper Schwartz, Bisexual Women. In J. P. Wiseman (ed.), *The Social Psychology of Sex*, New York: Harper & Row, 154-162, 1976.

EXERCISE: The Hidden Criminal in You

The labeling theorist Howard Becker holds that for every individual who is caught breaking the law and sent to jail, there is one who never gets caught, one who is caught but manages to *get off the hook,* and another who is falsely accused but cannot convince his accusers of his innocence. Do you think Becker is right? exaggerating? Before you answer, complete the following checklist.

Indicate below those activities in which you have participated after turning thirteen years of age. Please check only if they have not (to your knowledge) come to the attention of the police. The numbers in parentheses indicate the maximum number of years you could spend in prison if you were caught and convicted in Georgia.

1. Tried to hit another person, but did not succeed. (1)
2. Gave someone a broken nose or black eye (or other disfiguring of the body) during a fight. (20)
3. Set fire to an unoccupied building, car, boat, or airplane. (20)
4. Intentionally damaged the property of another without his consent. (5)
5. Entered a *No Trespass* area without the owner's permission. (1)
6. Entered and remained in another person's home, car, or place of business without that person's permission. (20)
7. Wrote a check for an amount which you knew was more than that in your account (even though you were going to deposit enough to cover it the next day). (1)
8. Sold an item as a certain quantity (ounce, pint, etc.) without actually weighing it. (1)
9. Shoplifted minor articles (e.g., cigarettes, magazines). (1)
10. Shoplifted major articles (over $100 values). (10)
11. Kept money or property (e.g., billfold, purse, etc.) which you believed and later learned had been misplaced or lost. (10)

✓ 12. Received, disposed of, or retained property (e.g., home entertainment equipment) which you knew or believed was stolen. (10)

✓ 13. Entered a movie theater, carnival, or other type of show or entertainment place without paying. (10)

___ 14. Participated in sexual activity involving the sex organs of one person and the mouth of another. (20)

___ 15. Participated in sexual activity with an animal. (5)

___ 16. Persuaded, by false promise of marriage or other fraudulent means, a virtuous unmarried female to engage in sexual intercourse. (5)

___ 17. While married, had voluntary sexual intercourse with a person other than your spouse. (1)

✓ 18. While unmarried, had voluntary sexual intercourse with another person. (1)

___ 19. Performed, offered, or consented to perform an act of sexual intercourse for money. (1)

✓ 20. Offered or agreed to procure a prostitute for another; or directed another to a place of prostitution. (1)

___ 21. Engaged in sexual intercourse with any female under the age of fourteen. (20)

___ 22. Showed still or moving pictures to friends while strongly suspecting such pictures would be considered *obscene* by many, if not most, members of your community. (5)

✓ 23. Were in a fight involving two or more persons in a public place. (1)

✓ 24. Used obscene, vulgar, or profane language in the presence of a female or male under the age of fourteen. (1)

✓ 25. Littered. (1)

✓ 26. Placed a bet on the outcome of any type of sporting event or played cards (bridge, poker, etc.) for money. (1)

___ 27. Hid a firearm or knife on your person while outside your home. (1)

___ 28. Pointed a gun or pistol, either loaded or unloaded, at another person. (1)

___ 29. Discharged a gun or pistol within fifty yards of a public highway. (1)

✓ 30. Worked at your ordinary job on Sunday. (1)

Source: Adapted from Philip J. Reichel, Classroom Use of a Criminal Activities Checklist, *Teaching Sociology* 3:1, by permission of the publisher, Sage Publications, Inc.: 85-86, October 1975.

If you ever engaged in any of the activities on this list, you have violated the law in Georgia (and possibly your home state as well). Philip Reichel (1975) has given this questionnaire to more than 1,000 students. Not one could say he or she had never broken the law. At the very least, Reichel's students owe the state one year in jail. The average student could be imprisoned for twenty-five years! These lawbreakers do not think of themselves as *criminals.* Their friends and family do not think of them as *deviants.* They were sitting in a classroom when they filled out this questionnaire. Yet all of them could have been in jail. What does this tell you about labeling theory? about the criminal justice funnel?

Chapter Seven

COLLECTIVE BEHAVIOR AND SOCIAL MOVEMENTS

OBJECTIVES

After reading Chapter Seven you should be able to give in-depth answers to the following questions:

1. How do sociologists view collective behavior and social movements?
2. What are the preconditions for collective behavior?
3. Why do crowds become violent?
4. How do social movements take shape?
5. When and why do social movements become revolutions?

CONCEPTS

You should also understand the following concepts:

collective behavior ✓
collective action theory ✓
mass hysteria ✓
craze
structural conduciveness
structural strain
generalized belief
precipitating incident
breakdown of social control
mobilization
crowd
mob
emergent norms
social movement
social revolution
rising expectations
relative deprivation
functionalism

CHAPTER REVIEW

I.   How do sociologists view collective behavior and social movements?

Collective behavior refers to episodes of unconventional behavior involving such large numbers of people that it requires special explanation. Mass hysteria, riots, social movements, and revolutions all fall into this category. The basic question among sociologists is whether such behavior is rational or irrational.

Functionalists emphasize the spontaneous, irrational, emotional aspects of collective behavior. They trace mass departures from convention to a breakdown in social order. In other words, collective behavior is symptomatic of a flaw in a social system. When people are faced with an ambiguous situation, when their normal routines seem threatened, they act without thinking. In contrast, collective action theorists emphasize the roles of rational calculation, planning, and organization in collective behavior. Mass departures from the norms are not a symptom of social breakdown, but seen as a sign of social reorganization.

Your text takes the position that both views have something to contribute. Whereas functionalist theories tend to underestimate the roles of rational choice and planning in collective behavior, collective action theory tends to ignore the emotional aspects of these phenomena. Functionalist theories may explain mass hysteria and some aspects of crowd violence, but collective action theories are needed to explain social movements and revolutions.

II.   What are the preconditions for collective behavior?

Smelser's functional theory of collective behavior holds that for discontent to be translated into collective action, six conditions must be met. (1) Structural Conduciveness: the social structure must create uncertainty and channels for communication of discontent. (2) Structural Strain: people must feel that things are getting out of control. (3) Generalized Belief: people must develop shared ideas about what is threatening them and how to respond. (4) Precipitating Incident: something must happen to confirm their suspicions. (5) Mobilization: someone (or some group) must take charge, provide direction. (6) Breakdown of Social Control: even if the first five conditions have been met, collective behavior will not occur if conventional sources of social control (from the family to the police) intervene.

Your text uses the mass suicide in Jonestown, Guyana, to illustrate this theory. The press explained this horrifying event in terms of Jim Jones' personality and brainwashing; using Smelser's theory, your text identifies the social and structural factors. In its early days, the People's Temple provided a haven for people who were not coping well in the outside world. When Jones came under attack, the temple moved to a remote location in Guyana, where they were completely cut off from the usual social controls. Jones passionately argued, and convinced his followers, that they were under constant threat of attack and torture from the CIA, FBI, and Ku Klux Klan. A visit from a Congressman accompanied by reporters confirmed their fears. The community was already mobilized: Jones had held suicide drills in the past. When he ordered them to drink poisoned Kool-Aid, most complied without question. *As difficult as it is to believe, it happened,* and it can happen again under similar conditions. This incident shocked the nation, but little in the way of social policy initiatives has been undertaken.

III. Why do crowds become violent?

Crowd violence (riots and revolutions) are the most frightening form of collective behavior. In the summer of 1965, for example, Watts--a black ghetto in Los Angeles--exploded. For four days, mobs roamed the streets, burning, looting, and sniping at police and firefighters. At one point, rioters controlled fifty square miles of the city. The National Guard was called in. Before order was restored, thirty-four people had been killed, 1,000 injured, and 4,000 arrested. Property damage was estimated at $40 million. The question of why crowds become violent can be answered on both the micro- and macrolevels.

A. Some theories of mass violence focus on *crowd psychology.* Contagion theory holds that large numbers of people milling about tend to pick up, repeat, and reinforce one another's behavior. Violence is contagious; reason is abandoned. Convergence theory holds that riots attract violent people --in popular terminology, *riffraff* and *rabble rousers* (militant agitators). Studies of Watts and other riots in the 1960s do not support either theory. In Watts and elsewhere, rioters were selective: they attacked the symbols of white power (police and white-owned stores). Black-owned stores and homes were spared. Thus the rioters' behavior was guided by emergent norms. Studies showed that the Watts riot was not instigated by social dropouts or by outside agitators. Although most residents of Watts did not participate, a majority approved. They saw the riot as a form of protest, not an outbreak of crime. Moreover, the *typical* rioter was a resident of Watts and somewhat better educated and better off than the average resident. The Watts riot is best described as a spontaneous, desperate, but not ineffective way of calling the nation's attention to the problems of the black ghetto in Los Angeles.

B. Macrolevel theories of crowd violence focus on social conditions. Common sense suggests that social movements arise when conditions become unbearable. In this case, sociological analysis shows common sense is wrong. The theory of rising expectations traces social movements to a long period of economic and political gain followed by a short reversal. According to this view, people will tolerate poverty and oppression for generations if they see no alternative. Only when the situation has begun to improve do they believe that a better life may be possible. Only then does a loss of freedom or economic gains make them feel they are deprived of things to which they are entitled. The theory of relative deprivation holds that whether or not people feel deprived depends on their social environment. If everyone else in society is *in the same boat,* they may not feel deprived. If theirs is the only boat in the fleet that is sinking, they will see their situation as unjust.

IV. How do social movements take shape?

When large numbers of people organize to bring about social change, we think of a social movement. Social movements differ from collective behavior in four ways: they last longer, they are goal oriented, they are more structured, and they involve a larger segment of the population.

A. Tilly holds that collective action is part of the normal fabric of everyday life. Small-scale or not, localized collective action which becomes a full-scale social movement depends on interests (people developing a sense of common purpose), organization (informal, preexisting groups and networks may lay the groundwork and formal organizations develop later on), mobilization of resources (workers, a *conscience constituency,* money, votes, perhaps weapons), and opportunity (a key factor in Tilly's view). Mobilization of the handicapped illustrates how this combination of factors enables people to overcome physical difficulties as well as social stigmatization.

B. The relationship between social movements and social change is complex. A social movement may be diffused by token concessions or coopted by more powerful groups, or may mobilize the opposition. Or it may bring about changes in consciousness that lead to concrete social change. Your text discusses the emergence of a student social movement in China (expressed in the unrest seen in June of 1989), the long-term results of which are yet to be seen.

V. When and why do social movements become revolutions?

Skocpol defines social revolution as a rapid transformation of a nation's political system, social-class structure, and ideology.

Skocpol challenges the popular view that revolutions are started by small bands of radicals, driven by an ideology, and intent on political upheaval. The structure of international relations (especially the threat of invasion), conflicts among powerful groups within the society, and preexisting organizations that facilitate mass uprisings are key. More often than not, leadership emerges after a revolution has taken place and creates a more centralized, bureaucratic government than existed under the old regime. The ideology or rationalization also develops after a revolution is under way.

The revolution in Iran conformed to social revolutions in some ways: Iran was under international pressure, powerful groups were alienated from the

Shah, and the popular uprising was spontaneous (not instigated) and had grass-roots organization and support. However, the Iranian revolution departed from the usual pattern in one important aspect--it was guided by the traditions and ideology of Shiite Islam from the start.

CONCEPT REVIEW

Match each of the following terms with the correct definition.

a. collective behavior
b. mob
c. structural strain
d. precipitating incident
e. structural conduciveness
f. social movement
g. breakdown of social control
h. emergent norms
i. mobilization

j. generalized belief
k. crowd
l. craze
m. collective action theory
n. mass hysteria
o. social revolution
p. rising expectations
q. relative deprivation
r. functionalism

1. _e_ Smelser's first condition for collective behavior; an element within the structure that invites or drives people to depart from convention. (Study Smelser's model carefully. It will help you understand styles of collective behavior.)

2. _b_ A pejorative term for crowds that are viewed as disorderly, riotous, or lawless.

3. _j_ Smelser's third condition for collective behavior; the shared perception among individuals about who or what is threatening them, what the enemy is like, and how they should respond.

4. _f_ The more or less organized effort of a large number of people to produce some social change.

5. _c_ Smelser's second condition for collective behavior; the tension that develops when people sense an immediate, ambiguous threat and they feel helpless.

6. _m_ The view of collective behavior that emphasizes rational decisions on the part of individuals and planning and organization on the part of collectivities.

7. _d_ Smelser's fifth condition for collective behavior; the actions of a leader who provides a model for behavior.

8. _l_ A type of collective behavior that takes the form of wild enthusiasm about some person, object, or event.

9. _g_ Smelser's sixth condition for collective behavior; the absence of leadership capable of correct misinformation, convincing people that the threat is imaginary, or intervening to redirect behavior.

10. _A_   Large numbers of people engaging in nonroutine activities that violate social expectations.

11. _d_   Smelser's fourth condition for collective behavior; the dramatic event that confirms people's fears and suspicions and focuses their attention.

12. _h_   Definitions of the situation during a riot or rebellion.

13. _o_   A rapid, fundamental transformation of a country's political system, social-class structure, and dominant ideology.

14. _k_   A collection of people who come together on a temporary basis.

15. _n_   Collective behavior that results from the *contagious* spread of fear or anxiety.

16. _p_   A condition where the gap between what people expect and what they have becomes intolerable.

17. _r_   In regard to collective behavior, this theory holds that such behavior is symptomatic of a breakdown in the social order.

18. _q_   Feelings of deprivation are contingent on the groups to which people compare themselves (reference groups).

Answers

1. e	7. i	13. o
2. b	8. l	14. k
3. j	9. g	15. n
4. f	10. a	16. p
5. c	11. d	17. r
6. m	12. h	18. q

REVIEW QUESTIONS

1. Functionalists and collective action theorists would agree on one of the following points. Which one?
   a. Collective behavior expresses hidden social conflict.
   b. Collective behavior occurs when ordinary channels break down.
   c. All collective behavior, from fads to revolutions, can be explained in the same basic terms.
   d. Explanations of collective behavior must distinguish between brief, small-scale outbreaks and sustained, goal-oriented action over a longer period of time.

2. Which of the following conditions did not characterize the student uprising in the People's Republic of China (Tiananmen Square), from mid-April to early June 1989?
   a. turmoil
   b. cultural crisis

   c. spontaneity
   d. corrupt leadership in the Communist Party

3. Which of the following is the best illustration of Smelser's fifth condition for collective behavior, mobilization?
   a. Several books describing the aftermath of a nuclear war make the
      best-seller lists.
   b. A committee is formed to contact church congregations, heads of stu-
      dent governments, women's groups, environmental groups, and others who
      might be concerned about the arms race.
   c. Local officials refuse to grant a permit for a demonstration.
   d. News media give coverage to antinuclear demonstrations in Europe.

4. Gustave LeBon, *the grandfather of collective behavior theory,* is associated with which of the following theories of crowd violence?
   a. collective action theory
   b. crowd psychology
   c. the theory of rising expectations
   d. resource mobilization

5. Riots broke out in Watts and other black ghettos in the late 1960s
   because the civil rights movement and civil rights legislation had
   promised but failed to deliver concrete change. This view reflects:
   a. the theory of relative deprivation
   b. the theory of rising expectations
   c. convergence theory
   d. contagion theory

6. Which of the following is not an example of collective behavior?
   a. a wildcat strike
   b. a protest at a nuclear power plant
   c. the St. Patrick's Day parade in New York City
   d. the revolution in Iran

7. The *precipitating incident* at Jonestown was:
   a. Jim Jones' madness
   b. the suicide drills
   c. the arrival of an investigative committee
   d. rumors that the community was in danger

8. Riots may be explained at the micro- and macrolevels. Which of the
   following is a microlevel explanation?
   a. emergent norms
   b. relative deprivation

    c. the *riffraff* theory
    d. the *rabble rouser* theory

9. According to the functionalist view, fads, crazes, and hysterias may be explained in:
    a. terms of real grievances
    b. terms of rational calculation
    (c.) psychosocial terms
    d. they can't be explained

10. The revolution in Iran differed from social revolutions in other nations in several ways, including:
    (a.) It did not involve prolonged armed conflict between rebels and government troops.
    b. Many segments of the elite were alienated from the Shah.
    (c.) It led not to modernization and secularization, but to a return to religious fundamentalism.
    d. It led to the creation of a more centralized, bureaucratic government than existed before the revolution.
    e. a and b.
    (f.) a and c.

11. Which of the following characteristics applies to both collective behavior and social movements?
    a. Collective action is unplanned.
    b. Collective action is short-lived.
    c. Collective action involves large numbers of people.
    (d.) Collective action is goal oriented.

12. In the Florida land boom of the 1920s, thousands of Americans poured their savings into Florida real estate, convinced this was a sure way to get rich quick. This was an example of:
    a. social movement
    b. mass hysteria
    (c.) a craze
    d. crowd psychology

13. Skocpol emphasizes the role of international forces in social revolutions. She found that revolutions are most likely to take place when:
    a. Foreign agitators introduce a new ideology into a country.
    b. A developed nation's economy begins to falter.
    (c.) An undeveloped nation is threatened or attacked by a technologically more advanced nation.
    d. International alliances fall apart.

14. In the winter of 1986, French students took to the streets to protest a planned increase in tuition and decrease in university admissions. Confrontations between police and students resulted. This was an example of:
    a. mass hysteria
    b. social revolution
    c. collective action
    d. a social movement

15. The term *conscience constituency* refers to:
    a. people who are directly affected by a social movement
    b. people who are not directly affected by a social movement, but sympathize with and support the cause
    c. professional organizers and fund raisers
    d. hangers-on

16. One of the criticisms of Smelser's functionalist theory of collective behavior is:
    a. It is irrational.
    b. It puts too much emphasis on planning and organization.
    c. It overstates the differences between collective and everyday behavior.
    d. It underplays emotional factors.

17. One of the criticisms of collective action theory is:
    a. It is irrational.
    b. It puts too much emphasis on generalized beliefs.
    c. It overstates the differences between collective action and everyday behavior.
    d. It underplays emotional factors.

18. A precipitating incident in the popular uprisings in Iran was:
    a. disgust with the Shah's militarism and ties to the United States
    b. the announcement of plans to close the Teheran bazaar
    c. the taking of U.S. hostages
    d. the Shiite tradition of martyrdom

Answers

1. a: Functionalists hold that people usually do not know why they are engaging in collective behavior, whereas collective action theorists hold that people engage in collective behavior for rational reasons. Further, functionalists see social conflict as unusual, as a break in social routines; collective action theorists view conflict as part of normal, everyday social interaction. (See section entitled Rational

or Irrational.)

2. c: Your text argues that the student movement was not spontaneous in terms of being chaotic or even unprecedented. The movement was the latest in a series of protests dating back to 1919. The 1989 movement was very carefully organized, and used preexisting organizations for a different purpose. (Box: Communist Societies in Transition)

3. b: According to Smelser, discontent will not be translated into collective behavior unless people are organized. (Smelser's Functionalist Theory)

4. b: LeBon noted that, to some degree, people lose their reason in crowds. Social scientists today reject his strong statement of this position, but some believe there is an element of contagion in crowd behavior. (Microperspectives: Crowd Psychology or Collective Action?)

5. b: Although the civil rights movement brought significant changes for blacks living in the South, it had little impact on those living in northern cities. The unrealized hope of improvements made the realities of the ghetto more unbearable. (Macroperspectives: Rising Expectations and Relative Deprivation)

6. c: The St. Patrick's Day parade is a scheduled event, structured by traditional norms and values. (The rowdy enthusiasm and occasional destructive behavior of crowds after the parade does fit the definition of collective behavior, however.) (Collective Behavior as a Breakdown in Social Order)

7. c: All of these factors played a role in the Jonestown tragedy (including Jim Jones' delusions). But the event that triggered mass suicide was the arrival of Congressman Ryan. (Smelser's Functionalist Theory; An Evaluation)

8. a: Microlevel theories focus on interpersonal relations--in this case, how people decide how to behave in an ambiguous situation. The concept of emergent norms highlights the observation that, even in riots, behavior is not random. (Microperspectives: Crowd Psychology or Collective Action?)

9. c: The functionalist view differentiates between responses to varying degrees of stress and strain which result from breakdowns in the social order. Thus fads, crazes, and mass hysterias may be explained in psychosocial terms. (Microperspectives: Crowd Psychology or Collective Action?)

10. f: Most social revolutions have involved prolonged, bloody conflict; most have led to modernization and centralization. The Iranian revolution did not. (Answers b and d apply not only to Iran, but to most social revolutions.) (The Iranian Revolution; An Evaluation)

11. d: Analyses of the mass suicide at Jonestown and the riot in Watts show that even though collective action may have been based on misinformation, it was goal oriented. (Functionalists might not accept this answer, however.) (Social Movements as Collective Action)

12. c: A craze is a burst of wild enthusiasm. When the bubble bursts, as it did regarding Florida real estate, crazes may turn into mass hysteria. (Collective Behavior as a Breakdown in Social Order)

13. c: Skocpol's primary example is the Russian revolution, which began when Russia was threatened by the German military machine. (Skocpol's Theory of Social Revolution)

14. c: The student protest in France was best described as collective action. The aim was to resist government policies, not to transform French society (as in a revolution). Moreover, the demonstrations were short-lived (not prolonged, as in a social movement). (Social Movements as Collective Action)

15. b: An example would be men who are members of NOW, and make contributions to feminist causes. (Social Movements and Social Change)

16. c: Collective action theorists, in particular, argue that the line between everyday conflict and collective behavior is never definite. In their view, a major problem for social scientists is distinguishing what is and what is not collective behavior. (Social Movements as Collective Action)

17. d: Collective action was developed as a critique of functionalist theories of collective behavior. In the effort to correct what they saw as flaws in functionalist theory, collective action theorists may have gone too far in the direction of depicting collective behavior as cool and rational. (Tilly's Collective Action Theory)

18. b: The plan to bulldoze the Teheran bazaar was the *final straw*. It had the unintended consequence of galvanizing support for Islamic rebels among shopkeepers. (Macroperspectives: Rising Expectations and Relative Deprivation)

MYTH OR FACT?

1. People are most likely to join a revolution when they are deprived of the necessities of life and basic human dignity. t/f
2. The wave of riots that erupted in black ghettos in the late 1960s was inspired by militant agitators. t/f
3. Most of the people who took part in the mass suicide in Jonestown were mentally unbalanced.   t/f
4. The 1989 student movement in China was spontaneous.   t/f

Answers

1. *False.* People are most likely to take up arms when conditions have improved, they expect more, and their raised expectations are thwarted.

2. *False.* Many whites wanted to believe that the riots were led by small groups of malcontents and radicals, but the President's Commission on Civil Disorders found no evidence of this.

3. *False.* Some of the people who joined the People's Temple were social outcasts; Jones himself may have been psychologically disturbed. But Smelser's analysis shows that structural strain, mobilization (including suicide drills), and a breakdown of social control created this tragedy.

4. *False.* The 1989 student movement was the latest in a series of student protests dating back to May of 1919. The 1989 episode was carefully organized, using existing organizations for new purposes. For example, students marched by school, and within schools, by class.

CRITICAL THINKING

1. When people go to a championship football game or a rock concert, they expect to get excited and they usually do. A naive observer might conclude that "anything goes" in these settings. Having studied collective behavior, you know better. The next time you attend such an event, take notes. What patterns of behavior do you see? What emergent norms is the crowd following? How does behavior spread from one section of the audience to another? Where do people draw the limits?

2. In *The Feminine Mystique* (1963), Betty Friedan, one of the founders of the National Organization for Women (NOW) described the housewife syndrome as "the problem that has no name." Women are discontented, she said, but they don't know why; they don't know how to put their problems into words. Friedan attacked the glorification of "the little housewife" and "the sexual sell" that confined women to the home and the beauty shop. Published three years before the creation of NOW, the book became a national best-seller. Many people feel it played an important role in the women's movement. Where would this book fit in Smelser's list of preconditions? What other conditions had to be met for discontent to be translated into collective behavior? collective behavior into a social movement? (You might want to look ahead, to the description of the women's movement in Chapter Ten of your text.)

3. Your text points out that social movements may inadvertently undermine their own goals by mobilizing the opposition. What are some recent examples of countermovements? How successful have they been in blocking change? Or have they given new life to the movements they opposed?

PART THREE: SOCIAL INEQUALITY

Chapter Eight
SOCIAL STRATIFICATION

OBJECTIVES

After reading Chapter Eight you should be able to give in-depth answers to the following questions:

1. What is social stratification?
2. What is the degree of social stratification in the United States?
3. Who gets ahead in America?
4. Identify the major changes in the profile of poverty in America.
5. What are some of the major impacts of poverty?
6. Why are human societies stratified?
7. How and why did the global system of stratification come into being?

CONCEPTS

You should also understand the following sociological concepts:

social stratification
social class
wealth
power
prestige
closed system
open system
social mobility
structural mobility
poverty line
black underclass
working poor

CHAPTER REVIEW

I.   What is social stratification?

Social stratification is the division of society into layers (or strata), such that people in the upper classes enjoy opportunities that are denied people in the lower classes. In a stratified society, inequality is built into the social structure.

II. What is the degree of social stratification in the United States?

Most sociologists, and most Americans, would agree that there are five social classes in the United States: the upper, upper-middle, lower-middle, working, and lower classes. These classes are distinguished by occupation and life style, as well as by income and wealth.

Your text focuses on the top and bottom strata of American society.

A. The distribution of wealth in the United States today is highly uneven. The wealthiest fifth of the population owns more than three-quarters of the nation's stocks, bonds, real estate, and other assets, and earns more than the poorest three-fifths of the population. Half of all Americans own no assets whatsoever.

B. At the opposite extreme are some 34 million Americans (15 percent of the population) who live in poverty. This group can be divided into the *working poor* (who do not earn enough to support their families), the *new poor* (out of work as a result of recent structural changes in the economy), and the *underclass* (the chronically unemployed). The majority of the poor in the United States today are urbanites, members of minority groups, and women and dependent children (note that these are the same variables used to describe the homeless).

The impact of poverty on life chances is clear, and has been the subject of much policy debate for many years. The poor are far more likely to lose their children in infancy, endure chronic and occupational diseases, suffer from severe mental disorders, and die prematurely than are other Americans. They pay a higher price for shifts in the economy. And they are less likely to have a stable family life, to participate in politics, and to profit from education.

According to the *culture of poverty* thesis, poverty promotes the development of a self-defeating life style that is passed from generation to generation. This view has been questioned, however. The structural theory of poverty interprets the life styles of the poor as an adaptation to blocked opportunity. *This is the view that often gets labeled in popular culture as the liberal bias.*

III. Who gets ahead in America?

Sociologists distinguish between two types of social stratification. In a closed system, social status is ascribed at birth and there are few, if any, opportunities for social mobility. The caste system in India is an example. In an open system, social status is awarded on the basis of merit and personal achievement, and there are few obstacles to social mobility. The United States falls between these two extremes.

Generations of Americans have been raised to believe that ours is the land of opportunity and that anyone who works hard can get ahead. There is some truth to this belief--but only some. Most Americans are slightly better off than their parents were. But these improvements in the standard of living are due more to structural mobility (not individual success stories). There is little evidence that the United States offers more opportunities for social mobility than do other Western societies.

IV. Identify the major changes in the profile of poverty in America.

Changes in the profile of America's poor are the result of two decades of economic stagnation in the U.S. The working poor, who are employed yet still unable to sufficiently provide for themselves and their dependents, the black underclass, which consists of an increasing number of blacks trapped in decaying inner city neighborhoods who are unable to earn a decent wage or maintain a stable family life, and the homeless, those Americans who are incapable of affording shelter, are America's new poor. Their numbers are growing at an alarming rate.

V. What are some of the major impacts of poverty?

The major impacts of poverty are best exemplified by health care issues. Poor women experience many more prenatal problems than middle-class or upper-class pregnant mothers. Poor children have a significantly larger number of health care problems than their middle- and upper-class counterparts. And, poor adults are more likely to suffer from chronic, serious infections of all types, a variety of occupational diseases (when they can find work) than the rest of the work force, and emotional disorders. They are also more likely to be institutionalized or incarcerated.

VI. Why are human societies stratified?

Your text considers four theories of social stratification, beginning with Karl Marx's analysis of class conflict.
    A. An economic determinist, Marx traced social stratification to the *means of production.* Throughout recorded history, he argued, societies have been divided into a ruling class, which controls the means of production, and an oppressed class, which has lost control of the products of its labor.[1] The ruling class is in a position not only to exploit the laboring class, but also to dominate the political, social, and intellectual life of that society. As the mode of production changes, the composition of these classes also changes. In feudal societies, the ruling class was composed of landowners and the oppressed class of serfs; in an industrial, capitalist society, the ruling class is the bourgeoisie (the owners of industry) and the

oppressed class is the proletariat (propertyless workers). Marx held that industrial capitalism would inevitably lead to revolution and the creation of a workers' socialist state. For the first time in history, the majority of the population would control the means of production. Class distinctions would eventually disappear.

B. Weber saw social stratification as multidimensional. An individual or group's position in society depends not only on wealth, but also on power and prestige. By wealth, Weber meant rights over economic resources and decisions as well as ownership of property. Power is the ability to achieve one's goals, despite opposition. Prestige is a social honor and esteem. The three do not necessarily go together. An artist may enjoy high esteem but have little wealth and no formal political power, for example. Weber did not deny the role of economics in social stratification, but argued that prestige and power are also important.

C. Functionalists view stratification as an inevitable part of social life. If a society is to motivate talented people to fill roles that require long and difficult training and entail unpleasant work, it must offer these people special rewards. Underlying the functionalist view is the ideal of meritocracy, in which positions in society are distributed solely on the basis of merit.

D. Lenski's evolutionary view of stratification is based on an analysis of the history of human societies. Through most of human history, advances in technology have widened the gap between the rich and poor. Within industrial societies this trend has reversed somewhat. However, industrialization has widened the gap between rich and poor nations.

VII. How and why did the global system of stratification come into being?

The global system of stratification can be traced to the period of European colonization. Global stratification persists because of uneven development (economic diversification in rich nations, specialization in poor nations), control of technology by rich nations, and demography (ever-increasing dependent populations in poor nations).

CONCEPT REVIEW

Match each of the following terms with the correct definition.

a. prestige
b. structural mobility
c. wealth
d. poverty line
e. open system
f. meritocracy

g. social stratification
h. social class
i. social mobility
j. closed system
k. power

1. *c*   Ownership of objects and rights over desirable objects.
2. *j*   A society in which opportunities to better one's social position are severely limited, if they exist at all (sometimes called a caste system).
3. *h*   People who occupy the same layer of the socioeconomic hierarchy in a society.
4. *a*   The degree of respect and/or esteem a person receives.
5. *i*   Movement up or down the socioeconomic ladder in society.
6. *k*   The ability of an individual or group of people *to realize their own will in a communal action even against the resistance of others who are participating in that action* (Weber).
7. *b*   Changes in social position that occur because technological innovations, urbanization, economic booms or busts, wars, or other events have altered the number and kinds of occupations available in a society.
8. *d*   The federal government's estimate of a minimum budget for a family of four.
9. *g*   The division of society into layers whose occupants have unequal access to social opportunities and rewards; and which affects virtually every aspect of life.
10. *f*   A system in which social rewards are distributed on the basis of achievement.
11. *e*   A society that attempts to minimize the obstacles to social mobility by providing equal opportunity to all (sometimes called a class system).

Answers

1.	c	7.	b
2.	j	8.	d
3.	h	9.	g
4.	a	10.	f
5.	i	11.	e
6.	k		

REVIEW QUESTIONS

1. The wealthiest fifth of the American population controls about what percentage of the nation's stocks, bonds, and other assets?
   a. 20 percent
   b. 50 percent
   c. 75 percent
   d. 100 percent

2. Weber used the term *prestige* to refer to:
   a. conspicuous consumption
   b. social status
   c. social influence
   d. social honor and esteem
   e. rights over property

3. Which of the following thinkers recognized a global system of stratification?
   a. Marx
   b. Weber
   c. Wallerstein
   d. Lenski
   e. none of the above

4. Which of the following problems is associated with being a member of the lower class and/or being at or below what is termed the *poverty line* in the United States?
   a. a high risk of infant mortality
   b. chronic diseases
   c. a high incidence of severe mental disorders
   d. a high rate of separation and divorce
   e. all of the above

5. Studies of the economy indicate that the *pay escalator* has slowed down; people now in their twenties and thirties cannot expect their income to grow at the rate that their parents' generation experienced. Buying houses and supporting families are becoming increasingly more difficult. This is an example of:
   a. upward mobility
   b. downward mobility
   c. structural mobility
   d. personal mobility
   e. lateral mobility

6. Which of the following best exemplifies the difference between *relative* and *absolute* poverty?
   a. Absolute poverty is permanent; relative poverty is temporary.
   b. Relative poverty is subjective; absolute poverty is objective.
   c. Absolute poverty exists only in poorer nations; relative poverty exists only in wealthy nations.
   d. Absolute poverty can be explained in terms of cultural adaptations; relative poverty must be explained in terms of structural obstacles.

7. Sociologists use the term *wealth* to refer to:
   a. income
   b. property
   c. privilege
   d. ownership of scarce resources
   e. rights to economic resources

8. Which following statement about social mobility in the U.S. is accurate?
   a. The U.S. is a land of unlimited opportunity.
   b. Social mobility in the U.S. usually takes the form of small steps up (or down) the social ladder.
   c. There is more mobility in the U.S. than in any other Western nation.
   d. Structural mobility has not much affected the standard of living in the U.S. over the years.

9. One of the major changes in the profile of poverty in the United States in the past decade is:
   a. the increasing number of elderly people living in poverty
   b. the percentage of minority group members living in poverty
   c. the percentage of women who are poor
   d. the percentage of men who are unemployed

10. Which of the following statements is *false*?
    a. Most societies can be characterized as having either closed or open social systems.
    b. In a closed social system, status is ascribed on the basis of characteristics over which the individual has little or no control.
    c. In an open social system, social status is achieved through personal talent and effort.
    d. In a closed social system, opportunities for social mobility are severely limited.
    e. In an open social system, obstacles to social mobility are minimal.

11. Critics of the culture of poverty thesis attribute the persistence of poverty generation after generation to:
    a. the structure of society
    b. contempt for work in the lower classes
    c. personal and social disorganization
    d. feelings of powerlessness and fatalism
    e. an impulsive, present-time orientation

12. Which of the following statements applies to advanced industrial nations?
    a. Social stratification has been institutionalized for the first time.
    b. Social stratification has disappeared.

 What D think will be on the test

    c. Social inequalities have been reduced, but have not disappeared.
    d. Social class has virtually no impact on life chances.

13. Poverty in the United States is:
    a. a temporary problem for the country
    b. a temporary condition for most people
    c. a persistent problem for the country
    d. a lifelong problem for most people
    e. b and c

14. Which of the following statements is *not* correct?
    a. Marx saw social stratification as the result of competition for scarce resources.
    b. Marx held that the religion and political ideologies of a society reflect economic relationships.
    c. Weber held that economics does not play a part in social stratification.

15. As of the mid-1980s, approximately how many Americans were living below the poverty line?
    a. 5 million
    b. 20 million
    c. 35 million
    d. 50 million

16. Which of the following statements reflects the functionalist view of social stratification?
    a. Supreme Court justices obtain their positions because of their upper-class backgrounds.
    b. Schoolteachers have low salaries because they often come from a lower-middle-class background.
    c. Physicians have high incomes because medical schools limit the number of admissions so that doctors are scarce.
    d. Physicians have high incomes because their work requires long training and is important, difficult, and often unpleasant.

17. The expression *You are what you do* captures one of the features of:
    a. hunter-gatherer bands
    b. horticultural villages
    c. agrarian states
    d. industrial nations

18. One of the major reasons for the global system of stratification that exists among nations today is that:

a. Industrial nations still control most of the natural resources in Third World nations.
b. Third World nations lack the natural resources for industrialization.
c. Industrial nations control much of the technology of production and distribution.
d. Third World nations have become too economically diversified.

19. The term *working poor* refers to:
    a. people who are collecting welfare and working at the same time
    b. people who work but do not earn enough to support themselves and their dependents
    c. people who earn their livings through illegal jobs
    d. people who have lost their jobs and are temporarily poor

20. The number of homeless persons in the U.S. is best estimated by which of the following parameters:
    a. 1 to 2 thousand
    b. 250,000 to 3 million
    c. not known
    d. 20 million

Answers

1. c: In contrast, the poorest fifth of the population owns less than 0.5 percent of the nation's wealth. (See section entitled Distribution of Wealth in U.S.)
2. d: Weber emphasized that individuals who are neither wealthy nor powerful may nonetheless enjoy high regard in their society. Saints and artists are examples. (Marx on Class Struggle)
3. c: Marx, Weber, and Lenski looked to history for insights into the causes of social stratifications, but they were concerned with inequalities *within*, rather than *between* nations. (Global Stratification)
4. e: In addition, the poor may be handicapped in education (for reasons we analyze in Chapter Thirteen). (The Impact of Poverty)
5. d: The term *structural mobility* refers to changes in standard of living that result from changes in the economy, not individual fortune. (Getting Ahead or Falling Behind?)
6. b: This does not mean that relative poverty is not painful, humiliating, and difficult to escape. (The Black Underclass)
7. e: As Marx and Weber emphasized, possession of valuables may not be as important as the rights to land, minerals, technology, labor, and other means of creating and maintaining wealth. (Marx on Class Struggle)
8. b: Leaps from rags to riches are extremely rare. Most changes in social position take the form of modest gains (or losses) and most can be at-

tributed to structural mobility. (Getting Ahead or Falling Behind?)

9. c: Female-headed households are five times more likely to be living in poverty than households with male workers. (Who Are the Poor?)

10. a: Closed and open social systems are ideal types. Most societies contain at least some elements of both ideal types. (Open and Closed Social Systems)

11. a: All of the other answers are drawn from the characterization of the culture of poverty. (The Black Underclass)

12. c: Inequalities in wealth, power, and prestige are not as *extreme* in industrial nations as they are in agrarian states, but persist nonetheless. (Global Stratification)

13. e: In the 1950s, many people believed poverty in America had all but disappeared, in part because it was largely a rural problem and hidden from public view. Today poverty is more an urban problem, and most Americans are aware of it. Contrary to popular belief, however, most people are not locked into poverty, but slip in and out. (The Distribution of Wealth in the U.S.)

14. c: Weber did not deny the role of economics in social stratification. Rather, he disagreed with Marx's economic determinism. (Marx on Class Struggle)

15. c: This figure is controversial, however. Some analysts argue that if the government counted such *kin kind* aid as food stamps, the number of poor in the United States would drop to 4 million. Others argue that the 40 million Americans who earn less than the median income should be counted as poor. (Who Are the Poor?)

16. d: All of the other answers reflect the conflict view of social stratification, which holds that those in power preserve their positions by limiting access to important and lucrative positions. (Functionalists and Meritocracy)

17. d: In simpler societies, most people do the same kinds of work. With the rise of industrialization, the number and diversity of jobs increase dramatically and occupation becomes a major source of prestige. (Global Stratification)

18. c: Some Third World nations are rich in natural resources (such as oil); in general, Third World nations tend to be economically specialized, not diversified. A major obstacle for these nations is dependence on imported technology (including the technology of management in some cases). (Global Stratification)

19. b: This term refers to people who want to work and do work, but whose skills and opportunities confine them to marginal jobs. (The American Class System)

20. b: The exact number of homeless persons is difficult to determine. Current estimates indicate that the number is between 250,000 and 3 million or more. (Box A-1.)

MYTH OR FACT?

1. Heart disease, ulcers, high blood pressure, and other illnesses that have been associated with stress and diet are *diseases of the rich.*　　　　　　　　　　　t/f

2. America is the land of opportunity--that is, one of the most open social systems in the world.　　　　　t/f

3. Most of the Americans who are living below the poverty line are white.　　　　　　　　　　　　　　t/f

Answers

1. *False.* The incidence of these and other chronic and infectious diseases is much higher in the lower than in the upper class.

2. *False.* The rate of social mobility in the United States is no higher than in other industrial nations. Indeed, an individual probably has a better chance of *getting ahead* in Norway, Australia, or West Germany than in this country.

3. *True.* Minority groups are overrepresented in the statistics on poverty (that is, a higher percentage of minority groups members are poor), but in terms of numbers the majority of the poor are white.

use for paper?

CRITICAL THINKING

1. Your text asserts that "social stratification can be a matter of life and death." Explain this statement.

2. In a recent issue of the *Annual Review of Sociology,* James Kluegel and Eliot Smith summarized the literature on beliefs about social stratification in the United States. The studies they reviewed focused on three questions: Is America the land of opportunity? Why is there poverty in one of the richest nations on earth? Is the distribution of wealth in the United States today just?

    Americans endorse the statement that theirs is the land of opportunity where anyone who works hard can get ahead. . . .

    Studies of beliefs about the poor consistently show a prevailing negative view--i.e., the poor are blamed, partially or totally, for their poverty. They are seen as lacking work motivation, ability, or proper morals. Partial blame involves the theme that while there are obstacles to self-betterment by the poor, such obstacles would be surmountable if it were not for the debilitating personal characteristics of the poor. . . .

The common evaluation of fairness in the distribution of income is based on a balancing of need and equity. . . . First, there is popular agreement that all workers, regardless of job, should earn a certain minimum income. . . . Second, there is little general support for equality of income, principally because it violates norms of equity. An unequal distribution of income based on education, occupation, marital status, and number of children is generally believed in. . . . [M]any hold with the functionalist principle that inequality serves to select and motivate people for the larger benefit of society. . . . Third, many people believe that an equitable earnings distribution would have a narrower range than does the present distribution.

[Kluegel and Smith point out one exception to these patterns.] Blacks are somewhat less likely than whites to emphasize individualist factors and are much more likely to see structural factors as the cause of poverty.[2]

Do your beliefs about social stratification in America coincide with those summarized here? On what points do you agree with the majority of Americans? On what points do you disagree?

3. A journalist returning from West Africa reports on the heart of the problem on that continent.

For much of Africa, the village is where the heart is. It defines where one stands, and what is proper and what should be. . . .

Urban areas in Africa, like urban areas anywhere, demand a great deal from the hinterland. In Africa, however, the luxuries and power of urban life are rarely shared with the countryside, where basic government services--such as health care, roads, water projects, education and electricity--are available in only the most rudimentary form, if at all. . . .

With the discovery of mineral resources on the continent, many African countries focused their entire economic activity on the oil or the copper that was to catapult them into the modern world. In the dash to meet world demand for these critical minerals, most African countries neglected, almost to the point of abandonment, their traditional economic strengths, particularly agriculture. Zambia, for example, became a mining economy almost overnight after vast reserves of copper were discovered. There was a mass migration from the countryside to the newly affluent cities--resulting in a near collapse of the farming sector.

The chasm between village life and urban centers of political and economic power is much of what Africa is about today. Whether the village and its strengths survive will say a great deal about the survival of the nations of this continent.[3]

Does this news piece support the points made in your text about global stratification? What does it add?

Notes

[1] Note that Marx did not have access to the anthropological and archaeological data on prehistoric societies Lenski used in his evolutionary analysis of stratification.

[2] James R. Kluegel and Eliot R. Smith, Beliefs about Stratification, *Annual Review of Sociology* 7, 1981, pp. 30-32, 41. Reproduced with permission, from the *Annual Review of Sociology* 7, 1981, by Annual Reviews Inc.

[3] Edward A. Gargan, In the Heart of Africa, *The New York Times Magazine*, December 7, 1986. Copyright 1986 by the New York Times Company. Reprinted by permission.

Chapter Nine

RACIAL AND ETHNIC INEQUALITY

OBJECTIVES

After reading Chapter Nine you should be able to give in-depth answers to the following questions:

1. What are the sociological definitions of race, ethnic group, and minority group?
2. What historical patterns have shaped racial and ethnic relations in the U.S.?
3. Where do racial minorities stand in the U.S. today?
4. What are the leading theories of racial inequality?
5. How is the racial/ethnic composition of the U.S. continuing to change?
6. How has the composition of the native-born U.S. population changed?
7. What is the recent history of race relations in this country?

CONCEPTS

You should also understand the following sociological concepts:

race
ethnic group
minority group
assimilation
cultural assimilation
primary assimilation
structural assimilation
prejudice
discrimination
racism
institutionalized racism
nativism
white flight
pluralism
ethnic struggle

amalgamation
glasnost
perestroika
arpartheid
de facto segregation
de jure segregation
genocide
affirmative action

CHAPTER REVIEW

I. **What are the sociological definitions of race, ethnic group, and minority group?**

The definitions of race, ethnic group, and minority group are not as straightforward as one might expect, but reflect changing social perceptions.

Sociologists define a race as a category of people who are considered *different* because of inherited physical traits. To outsiders, the classification of individuals into distinct social groups because of height or skin color may seem arbitrary. But such classifications have definite social consequences.

An ethnic group is a category of people who are considered *different* because of their cultural heritage. The same people may be viewed as a race at one time and place, an ethnic group at another. Pay very special attention to this point.

According to Lewis Wirth, the defining characteristics of a minority group are that members are disadvantaged; they are held in low esteem; their membership in the group is involuntary; and they are conscious of being *a people apart.* Note that members of a minority group may constitute a numerical majority in a society. Blacks in South Africa and women in the United States are examples.

II. **What historical patterns have shaped racial and ethnic relations in the United States?**

Relations among races and ethnic groups may take many different forms, ranging from peaceful coexistence (as in Switzerland) to genocide (as in Nazi Germany). The patterns of relations in the United States, which has drawn peoples from around the world, are especially complex. Following Steinberg, your text identifies four episodes in our racial and ethnic history: settlement, expansion, agricultural development, and industrial development. Each episode is associated with a different pattern.

A. The settlement phase established an Anglo-Saxon, Protestant blueprint for the nation. Non-British settlers were admitted reluctantly, out of economic necessity.

B. The expansion phase began after the Revolution, when the colonial population began to grow and to compete with Native Americans for land. One by one, Native American tribes were forced to leave their ancestral lands or die. By 1890, Native Americans had been reduced to colonial status. The expansion phase also included the conquest of the Southwest and its Mexican-American inhabitants in 1846.

C. The agricultural development of the South laid the foundation for a third phase in the nation's racial and ethnic history: black slavery. Your text suggests that slavery was institutionalized because it was profitable; because racist beliefs rationalized the denial of freedom to blacks; and because Africans were visible and far from home (making escape difficult). Although slavery was outlawed in 1863, the *Jim Crow* laws of the post-Reconstruction years reestablished black servitude.

D. The industrial expansion in the North during the post-Civil War years led to the fourth phase of our ethnic history, the waves of immigrants from northern and later eastern and southern Europe. Immigrants supplied much of the labor for the industrialization of America. (Blacks were hired only for menial jobs or as a last resort in northern factories in the early part of the century.) The history of the newest immigrants, many of whom are Hispanic or Asian, has yet to be written. Research on this topic is under way, however.

E. How have the many racial and ethnic groups that make up the American population been assimilated (or incorporated) into one society? Your text suggests that cultural assimilation is a prerequisite for structural assimilation (acceptance into businesses and professions), which is in turn a prerequisite for primary assimilation (acceptance in private life). While many white ethnic groups have made the first two steps, intermarriage between religions is still unusual. The groups we commonly refer to as minorities--especially the blacks, Hispanics, and Native Americans--have not gone that far.

III. Where do the different racial minorities stand in the United States at the present time?

In recent years, blacks, Hispanics, and Native Americans have been admitted to schools, occupations, and neighborhoods that were closed to them in the recent past. But these individuals and families are exceptions to the rule of continuing racial inequality. The percentage of Hispanics living below the poverty line is twice, and the percentage of blacks three times, that of whites.

IV. What are the leading theories of racial inequality?

Several theories of racial inequality have been advanced. One emphasizes biological differences; another, prejudice and discrimination; and a third, institutionalized racism.

A. Echoing Social Darwinists, a small number of scientists have argued that racial inequality is the result of hereditary differences. One area of controversy is IQ test scores. The average score for blacks is lower than that for whites. But is this the result of hereditary differences or bias in the tests? A study that found that black children adopted into white families scored above the national average indicates it is the latter.

B. Others attribute racial inequality to continuing prejudice and discrimination. Prejudice is an unfavorable attitude toward members of a group, based on stereotypes of that group. Discrimination is the denial of rights and respect to individuals because they are members of a group. It may take the form of laws designed to isolate members of a group, informal agreements to exclude them, or avoidance of intimate relationships. Whether or not discrimination continues depends in large part on whether it is profitable or costly. Prejudice can function as a self-fulfilling prophecy. If people are seen as inferior, they may be denied education and employment, and the fact that they therefore lack skills and jobs may then be cited as evidence of their alleged inferiority.

C. A third theory holds that once inequality has become part of the social structure, it develops a life of its own and persists even though prejudice and deliberate discrimination decline. This is the theory of institutionalized racism. Racial inequality in the United States today is an unintended consequence of accepted practices that seem to have no relationship to discrimination. The banking practice of *red lining* neighborhoods that are high risks for housing loans, for example, has the unintended consequence of denying mortgages to minorities.

V. How is the racial and ethnic composition of the native-born U.S. continuing to change?

The majority of today's immigrants come from the Third World. Formerly, they came from the Old World. In 1987, 600,000 legal immigrants arrived in the United States. The largest proportions were Mexicans, Filipinos, and Koreans.

VI. How has the composition of the native-born U.S. population changed?

Birthrates for Americans of European descent have been declining. Birthrates for Americans of non-European ancestry have held steady. By the year 2010, more than a third of American babies will be black, Hispanic, or Asian.

VII.   What is the recent history of race relations in this country?

Your text traces the history of race relations back to the Supreme Court decision in *Brown* v. *Board of Education* (1954). This decision overturned the *separate but equal* doctrine which had supported segregation by law.

A. The civil rights movement, which began with the bus boycott in Montgomery, Alabama in 1956 and culminated in the March on Washington in 1963, prompted Congress to pass the Civil Rights and Voting Rights acts. The strategy of nonviolent protest (which provoked beatings, jailings, and a number of deaths) provided a model for other protest movements of the 1960s and 1970s. In may ways, however, combating de facto segregation (or unofficial discrimination) in the North proved as difficult as fighting de jure segregation in the South. Busing children to integrate schools and affirmative action (programs designed to seek out qualified members of minority groups) were and are controversial. But there is little evidence of the white backlash many observers anticipated. In recent years, however, programs to assist minorities have been cut back and enforcement of civil rights has been relaxed somewhat.

B. Table 10-4 summarizes movement toward, and obstacles to, racial inequality; e.g., on the positive side, nearly as many blacks as whites complete high school. The negative is that education requirements for jobs have risen, so that a high school degree is worth less today.

The debate over the current state of race relations carries over into sociology. Wilson and others argue that the significance of race per se is declining and that the problems blacks encounter today result from social class, not the color of their skin. Others feel Wilson is deceiving himself.

CONCEPT REVIEW

Match each of the following terms with the correct definition.

a. ethnic group
b. de jure segregation
c. affirmative action
d. genocide
e. majority group
f. nativism
g. primary assimilation
h. race
i. structural assimilation
j. prejudice
k. cultural assimilation
l. minority group

m. institutionalized racism
n. assimilation
o. de facto segregation
p. racism
q. discrimination
r. white flight
s. pluralism
t. amalgamation
u. ethnic struggle
v. perestroika
w. glasnost

1. _d_ The systematic attempt to murder members of a racial or ethnic group.

2. _B_ The separation of racial and ethnic groups by law.

3. _h_ A category of people who see themselves and are seen by others as different because of characteristics that are assumed to be inherited.

4. _i_ The admission of members of minority groups into major businesses and professions.

5. _k_ An immigrant's adoption of the host country's cultural patterns.

6. _a_ A category of people who see themselves and are seen by others as different because of their cultural heritage.

7. _e_ A category of people who have gained a dominant position in society and guard their power and position, excluding others from their ranks.

8. _q_ The denial of opportunities and social esteem to individuals because they are members of a devalued group or category.

9. _m_ Established social patterns that have the unintended consequence of limiting the opportunities of certain social groups.

10. _l_ A category of people whose members are disadvantaged, held in low esteem, involuntarily excluded from valued social positions, and conscious of being *a people apart.*

11. _f_ The view that American institutions must be protected from immigrant influences in order to preserve what is considered to be the *right* way to do things (America for Americans).

12. _g_ Acceptance of members of minority groups into the majority's private clubs and friendship cliques.

13. _o_ Separation of racial and ethnic groups resulting from informal social patterns, not public policy.

14. _c_ Programs designed to seek out members of a minority group for positions from which they were excluded in the past.

15. _j_ A negative prejudgment of members of a social group or category that is based on stereotypes and cannot be influenced by new information.

16. _n_ The incorporation of different ethnic and racial groups into the mainstream of society.

17. _p_ The belief that a group considered a racial group is innately inferior and that this justifies discrimination against and exploitation of members of that race.

18. _ll_ A society in which two or more groups vie for power.

19. _s_ A society in which racial and ethnic groups maintain their distinctiveness, but treat one another with respect and get along with one another.

20. _Ω_ The alleged departure of white, middle-class families for the cities or the suburbs.

21. _t_ The melting pot. A society in which different ethnic and racial groups intermingle, producing an entirely new and distinctive genetic and cultural blend. *amalgamation*

22. _w_ A new strategy of *openness* in Soviet society. *glasnost*

23. _v_ A program aimed at restructuring or revitalizing the economy of the Soviet Union. *Parastroika*

Answers

1. d	9. m	17. p
2. b	10. l	18. u
3. h	11. f	19. s
4. i	12. g	20. r
5. k	13. o	21. t
6. a	14. c	22. w
7. e	15. j	23. v
8. q	16. n	

REVIEW QUESTIONS

1. Which of the following groups does not qualify as a minority group in the United States?
   a. black Americans
   b. the poor
   c. women
   d. homosexuals

2. Which of the following strategies were employed by the civil rights movement in the 1950s and 1960s?
   a. civil disobedience (deliberate violation of laws that were considered unjust)
   b. nonviolence (passive resistance to verbal and physical abuse)
   c. economic boycotts
   d. a and b
   e. all of the above

3. The *newest immigrants* differ from earlier generations of immigrants in that a higher proportion are:
   a. women
   b. political or Third World refugees
   c. highly educated professionals
   d. all of the above

4. One of the major problems facing colonists during the settlement phase of U.S. ethnic history was:
   a. discouraging immigration
   b. attracting settlers
   c. assimilating Native Americans
   d. acquiring new territory

5. Many city schools are predominantly black because the neighborhoods in which they are located are predominantly black. This is an example of:
   a. prejudice
   b. discrimination
   c. de facto segregation
   d. de jure segregation

6. Which of the following created the waves of immigration to the United States in the late nineteenth and early twentieth centuries?
   a. racism
   b. population growth in Europe
   c. famines and job shortages in Europe
   d. industrialization in America
   e. all of the above

7. The average score of black Americans on IQ tests is lower than that of white Americans. What this *means*, however, is debatable. Which of the following statements is false?
   a. IQ tests measure cultural knowledge as well as cognitive ability.
   b. The average IQs of Jews, Poles, Chinese, and other groups have changed significantly over time.
   c. Black children adopted by white, middle-class families score above the national average on IQ tests.
   d. Average IQs of a group enable educators to predict how an individual member of that group will perform on the test.

8. The incorporation of the Southwest and its Hispanic population into the United States was part of which phase of U.S. ethnic history?
   a. settlement
   b. expansion
   c. agricultural development
   d. industrial development

9. The main difference between a race and an ethnic group is that members of an ethnic group are socially defined as *different* because of their:
   a. physical traits
   b. cultural traits

    c. consciousness of kind
    d. ancestry

10. So-called Jim Crow laws were:
    a. slavery statutes
    b. rules governing sharecropping
    c. laws that forbade discrimination against blacks
    (d.) laws enacted after Reconstruction that formalized segregation

11. Colonial Brazil provided an example of:
    (a.) a melting pot/amalgamation
    b. cultural pluralism
    c. Anglo-conformity
    d. genocide

12. Which of the following is an example of affirmative action?
    a. the federal prohibition on granting government contracts to firms that discriminate against minorities
    b. the 1963 March on Washington
    (c.) a plan to recruit minority members for a police force
    d. laws against discrimination in education, employment, and housing

13. Mr. James brags to his small-town relatives about the ethnic diversity of his neighborhood in the city. He is impressed by how quickly the Asian children in his daughter's class learn English. He has hired Jamaicans and Hondurans in his business. Yet he is deeply distressed when his son announces that he is engaged to a Puerto Rican woman. What level of assimilation has Mr. James *not* accepted?
    a. cultural assimilation
    b. structural assimilation
    (c.) primary assimilation
    d. none of the above

14. The division of the human species into different races:
    a. is a biological fact
    b. is a pseudoscientific myth
    c. has no social significance
    (d.) has social consequences

15. Which of the following is an example of discrimination?
    a. the statement that *Jose is bright--for a Chicano*
    b. the belief that blacks have *natural rhythm*
    c. worrying that property values will fall and the character of the neighborhood will change if a black family moves onto the block

   d. voting against admitting a family to a private club because the family is Jewish

16. Most major cities in the United States have a Chinatown, a Little Italy, a Spanish quarter. These ethnic enclaves are evidence of resistance to:
   a. cultural assimilation
   b. structural assimilation
   c. primary assimilation
   d. cultural pluralism

17. The sociologist William J. Wilson has argued that:
   a. Blacks and whites have equal opportunities in America today.
   b. Opportunities for black Americans have not changed in the last quarter-century.
   c. Racial inequality persists because of continuing prejudice and discrimination.
   d. Racial inequality persists because of lingering social-class differences.

18. During the expansion phase of U.S. ethnic history, the Native American population was reduced from an estimated 1.5 million to:
   a. 1 million
   b. 500,000
   c. 250,000
   d. 100,000

19. Of the following groups, which is growing the fastest in America today?
   a. blacks
   b. Hispanics
   c. Asians
   d. Eastern Europeans

20. Which of the following developments contributed to the institutionalization of black slavery in the American South?
   a. the land and climate of the South
   b. European ethnocentrism
   c. the invention of the cotton gin
   d. industrialization in Britain
   e. all of the above

21. Which of the following is an example of institutionalized racism?
   a. the bombing of a black church in Birmingham, Alabama
   b. opposition to school busing
   c. the exclusion of blacks and other minorities from private clubs

    d. the poor have only themselves to blame for their economic situation
   (e.) the high unemployment rate among black teenagers

22. In recent years, the education gap between blacks and whites has:
    a. remained about the same
   (b.) almost closed
    c. widened

23. In Switzerland there are four ethnic groups: the Schwzer tush, the French, the Romansh, and the Italians. Their ability to coexist as equals, maintaining their own distinctive cultural heritages and group identities, is an example of:
    a. amalgamation
    b. assimilation
    c. ethnic struggle
   (d.) pluralism

24. Gorbachev's reform programs aimed at revitalizing the Soviet economy include:
    a. glasnost
    b. nationalities policy
    c. perestroika
    d. all of the above
   (e.) both a and c

25. South Africa's government is controlled by White Afrikaners who constitute _____ % of the country's population.
    a. 9%
    b. 73%
    c. 50%
   (d.) 15%

Answers

1. b: The poor are disadvantaged, held in low esteem, and involuntarily confined to their status, but they do not have the group consciousness or feeling of solidarity that Wirth saw as a defining characteristic of minority groups. (See section entitled Minority Groups.)
2. e: Following Mahatma Ghandi, Martin Luther King added nonviolent resistance to such traditional forms of civil disobedience as marches, rallies, and boycotts. (The Civil Rights Movement)
3. d: In the past, a majority of immigrants were male, from rural backgrounds, and more often economic than political refugees. They were also far more likely to be Old World immigrants as opposed to Third

World. (Other American Minorities)

4. b: This problem was solved through indentured servitude; paying someone's passage to the New World in exchange for seven years' labor. (The Peopling of the U.S.)

✓5. c: *De facto segregation* is another term for institutionalized racism: practices and policies that seem to have nothing to do with racial issues but have the unintended consequence of perpetuating racial inequality. This is a very difficult issue for most Americans to deal with unemotionally. (Institutionalized Racism)

6. e: The inclusion of racism on this list may have surprised you. But the fact that northerners did not want to attract large numbers of freed slaves to their towns and cities led factory owners to look elsewhere for labor. (The Peopling of the U.S.)

7. d: Averages do not provide information about individuals. Many blacks score well above, and many whites well below, the national average on intelligence tests. (The IQ Controversy)

8. b: The Southwest was won by force of arms. In theory Hispanics were guaranteed full rights as citizens under the Treaty of Guadalupe Hidalgo (1848); in practice most were overwhelmed by Anglo settlers and Anglo courts of justice. (The Peopling of the U.S.)

9. b: Both races and ethnic groups are defined as different, and feel themselves different, because of ancestry. But whereas with races the emphasis is on physical traits, with ethnic groups it is on cultural traits. (The Social Definition of Race and Ethnicity)

10. d: Steinberg describes the period of Jim Crow laws as the re-creation of black servitude. (Fighting Racial Inequality)

11. a: Although people of Portuguese origins dominated the government, there was a good deal of cultural exchange and intermarriage in colonial Brazil. As a result, the racial composition and culture of Brazil is unique. (The treatment of tribal peoples in Brazil today is characterized as genocide, however.) (Patterns of Intergroup Relations)

12. c: Affirmative action programs are controversial because they are not color blind, but require some degree of *reverse discrimination* to ensure that minorities are not excluded. (Affirmative Action)

13. c: People may accept and even enjoy ethnic and racial diversity in their public lives, yet resist close connections. (Blacks and Whites Today)

14. d: Whether biologically significant or not, the social fact that the human species is perceived as being divided into different races has social consequences. (Theories of Racial Inequality)

15. d: The term *prejudice* refers to attitudes; the term *discrimination* refers to actions that deny opportunities to members of minorities. (Prejudice and Discrimination)

16. d: Although many members of these ethnic groups have joined the mainstream of American society, others have resisted enculturation.

The fact that many non-Chinese and non-Italians flock to these neighborhoods for meals and festivals is evidence of some degree of cultural pluralism in the U.S. (Patterns of Intergroup Relations)

17. d: But, Wilson's is not a majority view. (Theories of Racial Inequality)

18. c: Many Native Americans died in battle, but many more died from exposure to diseases for which they had no immunity, forcing migration to regions unsupportive of their way of life. (The Peopling of the U.S.)

19. c: The number of Asians and Pacific Islanders in the U.S. more than doubled in the 1970s, reaching an estimated 3.5 million. (Other American Immigrants)

20. e. The inclusion of the industrialization of Britain may have surprised you. But the mechanization of the textile industry in Britain contributed to the institutionalization of slavery indirectly, by creating an expanding market for cotton. (The Peopling of the U.S.)

21. e: Undoubtedly some employers turn down teenaged applicants simply because they are black. These are acts of individual racism. But the high unemployment *rate* among black teenagers is an unintended consequence of automation, the movement of factories from inner cities to suburbs, and other factors that have reduced the demand for unintended skilled labor. Because a high percentage of black teenagers live in cities and have only a high school diploma or less, they are hardest hit by these changes. (Institutionalized Racism)

22. b: As of the late 1970s, the median number of school years completed was 12.5 for whites, 11.9 for blacks--a difference of less than one year. But that year can make a significant difference: fewer blacks than whites complete high school (12 years). (Blacks and Whites Today)

23. d: A pluralist society is a *nation of nations*. Races maintain their distinctiveness. (Patterns of Intergroup Relations)

24. e: Glasnost, literally meaning openness, refers to Gorbachev's attempt to introduce some degree of freedom into Soviet society. Perestroika, meaning reorganization, was designed to reform both the economy and government. (Box: Ethnicity in the USSR)

25. d: Whites, who make up only 15% of South Africa's population, enjoy the political freedoms and economic opportunities of Western democracies. (Box: Apartheid)

MYTH OR FACT?

1. Blacks are natural athletes.   t/f
2. Ethnicity is as important to Americans today as it was twenty-five or fifty years ago.   t/f
3. Affirmative action programs, e.g., busing, created a white backlash, antagonizing whites who might otherwise have approved of black Americans' efforts to achieve equality   t/f

4. The last minority group to win the right to vote in the
United States was that of the Native Americans.   t/f
5. Some 600,000 new immigrants arrived in the U.S. in 1987.
Of these the largest groups were Africans, West Germans,
and Canadians.   t/f

Answers

1. *False.* If blacks are prominent in professional sports today, it is
because sports was one of the first highly paid, highly visible careers
to be integrated in the United States. Success has provided an incentive
for them to devote more time and energy to sports than other youngsters.
2. *True.* Some sociologists argue that the importance of ethnicity is declining in the United States today; others argue that it is increasing.
The authors of your text take a middle position: the role of ethnicity in
American society may be changing, but it is not disappearing.
3. *False.* There is no evidence of white backlash. Although loud, sometimes violent, protests against school busing received widespread coverage in the press, these were exceptions to the rule.
4. *True.* Black men won the right to vote after the Civil War, women were
granted suffrage in 1920, and Native Americans in 1924. If you count
young people as a minority group, however, eighteen-year-olds were the
last to be allowed into the polling booth (1972).
5. *False.* The majority of today's immigrants are from Third World nations. The largest group of *legal* immigrants to arrive in 1987 were
Mexicans, followed by Filipinos and Koreans.

CRITICAL THINKING

1. Many Americans would like to think that racism is a thing of the past.
Unfortunately, this is wishful thinking. On December 15, 1986, *The New
York Times* reported:

Officials Voice Growing Concern Over Racial Incidents on U.S. Campuses[1]

By LENA WILLIAMS

WASHINGTON, Dec. 14--Educators and civil rights leaders are becoming increasingly worried over what they fear is a proliferation of racial incidents on college campuses around the country. Though no one keeps compre-
hensive figures on such incidents and there appears to be no direct
connections among those that have received attention recently, officials
at the colleges and experts in race relations say that they seem to be
part of an alarming and growing pattern of bigotry and animosity toward

minority students at predominantly white schools.

The episodes include fights between black and white students at the University of Massachusetts, the arrest and subsequent release of a black male student at the University of Chicago, threats by a University of Texas group called Aryan Collegiates to rid the campus of "outspoken minorities," and the burning of a cross in front of a new black sorority house at the University of Alabama in Tuscaloosa. . . .

College officials and civil rights groups cite various factors underlying the recent activity, including perceived differences in the standards applied by college admissions officers to minority students, cutbacks in Federal student aid, and political divisions over anti-apartheid protests, with many white students voicing irritation at the idea that opposition to the divestment of stocks related to South Africa can be equated with support for South Africa's racial policies.

"We have seen resentment on the part of white students who perceive that black students have been given a free ride, so to speak," said Dennis Wynn of the Community Relations Service, a Justice Department agency that acts to resolve discrimination complaints and community disputes. "White students often feel that blacks have attained admission through affirmative action; that they don't have the ability to compete academically, or to be evaluated objectively on their own merit," he said.

Although some college administrators maintain that incidents of racial violence and harassment are rare and are sometimes blown out of proportion by the press, officials at many of the institutions where there has been violence against minority students acknowledge that the incidents appear to be racially motivated. . . .

Joseph D. Duffey, Chancellor at the University of Massachusetts, has asked the Massachusetts Commission Against Discrimination to investigate the fight that erupted between black and white students on the campus after the seventh game of the World Series.

The police said a heated exchange ensued between black fans of the New York Mets and white fans of the Boston Red Sox and the activity soon intensified into a stampede of 500 to 1,000 white students chasing 6 to 10 black students. At least 12 students were injured.

Mr. Duffey called for the outside inquiry after hearing reports from students of certain "names" and "uses of language" the night it happened. "People seem less embarrassed with racial slurs or jokes," he said.

2. In addition to those racial problems occurring on America's college cam-
    puses, increases in racial incidents have been experienced by many of
    America's communities. The violent deaths of two young black men, in
    Howard Beach, New York, and in Bensonhurst, New York, demonstrate this
    increase. The youth killed in Howard Beach had entered that predominately
    white community to seek assistance after his car broke down on a nearby
    freeway. He was chased into the path of a speeding car by a gang of white
    teenagers. The second black was harassed by a group of young Italian-
    Americans, one of whom shot him in the chest. He had gone into Italian
    Bensonhurst to look at a used car he had seen advertised in the local
    newspaper. (See *Time* and *Newsweek*, 1/4/88, pages 38 and 25,
    respectively; *Nation* 9/25/89, page 30; *Newsweek*, 9/4/89, page 25
    for accounts of the incident).

    Residents of Bensonhurst, responding to the violence in their community,
    felt that the young black did not have any business in their neighbor-
    hood, and shifted the blame to the victim! This is a common pattern in
    communities where ethnic and racial tensions exist. A sense of turf and
    proprietorship prevail--almost as though, "this neighborhood belongs to
    us. You enter at your own risk."

    Residents of Queens, New York, were reported as being very supportive of
    the youths who were convicted of manslaughter and assault in the Howard
    Beach Case. Can you think of cases like this in your own community, or
    where families and friends came to the side of the perpetrators of a
    racially motivated incident?

    The significance of these incidents and the angry reactions of some
    community members toward them seems to indicate a reemergence of both
    racial intolerance and polarization in American society. America's racial
    history, almost three decades after the birth of the civil rights
    movement, remains unresolved.

    Have there been incidents like these on your campus? Have you ever
    considered the possibility that racial conflict might erupt at your
    school? Do you agree with the explanations given in this news reports? Is
    Mr. Duffey correct when he says that racial slurs have become more
    acceptable among students? How would you characterize the degree of
    "assimilation" of minority group members on your campus?

3. Other articles published in newspapers recently have alluded to the de-
    bate at the end of Chapter Nine in your text about the declining sig-
    nificance of race. The evidence cited in this article is the assimilation
    of "the newest immigrants."

Suburbs Absorb More Immigrants, Mostly the Affluent and Educated[2]

By John Herbers

UNIVERSAL CITY, Tex.--Many new immigrants are bypassing congested central cities and settling in affluent suburban neighborhoods, skipping what historically has been the first and most difficult step of becoming assimilated into American life, recent studies show.

Many of these legal immigrants are members of ethnic or racial minorities--Asian, black and Hispanic--who are well-educated and have above-average incomes.

Great numbers of recent immigrants arrive speaking fluent English and holding advanced degrees in the professions and business.

Indeed, Leon F. Bouvier and Robert W. Gardner, in a new study for the Population Reference Bureau in Washington, wrote that because of current laws and regulations "generally only the better educated and better trained can hope to pay for and negotiate the hurdles that lie in the path of someone wishing to immigrate legally to the United States."

According to population surveys conducted by the Census Bureau from 1975 to 1985, almost half the 4.7 million Asian, Hispanic and non-Hispanic black people who moved to the United States from abroad in that 10 year period settled in suburban and non-metropolitan areas rather than in the central cities. . . .

For the most part, the legal immigrants settling in affluent areas report little opposition from native whites. . . . At the same time, according to recent census surveys, it is mostly American-born members of minorities--poor black and Hispanic people--who remain unassimilated in growing urban concentrations of unemployment, crime and inferior housing as the legal immigrants settle immediately in areas where employment opportunities are greatest and incomes are highest.

The way foreign immigrants with dark skin have spread out through the population lends support to the contention of some social scientists that the continued isolation of large numbers of the black and Hispanic poor in the central cities is more a result of class than of race. In urban centers virtually all the blacks, and many of the Hispanic people, are native to this country. . . .

"As avenues of opportunity have opened up for upwardly mobile and educated members of racial minority groups to move to suburbs and better-off urban neighborhoods, the people left behind in the ghetto, the hidden city, are more isolated," he said.

Are there new immigrants in your neighborhood? your college? the shops and businesses in your area? the professions (doctors, lawyers, and the like)? How would you characterize the degree of assimilation of these minorities? Do you agree with the point of view in this article? Explain.

3. It has been said that "the function of minority groups [in the United States] has always been to serve as point men in ferreting out the contradictions of American democracy. They begin by noticing the color-coded aspects of privilege, and they end by raising questions about fundamental issues of rights and the distribution of benefits."[3] Did the civil rights movement of the 1950s and 1960s serve this function? Explain your answer.

4. In *Ethnic America: A History*, Stanford University economist Thomas Sowell wrote, "The history of American ethnic groups has implications that reach beyond ethnicity. In an individualistic society, ethnic history reminds us of the enduring consequences of centuries-old patterns into which each individual is born."[4] Explain.

Notes

[1] *The New York Times*. (December 15, 1986), p. A18. Copyright by The New York Times Company. Reprinted by permission.

[2] *The New York Times*. (December 14, 1986), A1, 44. Copyright 1986 by The New York Times Company. Reprinted by permission.

[3] J. Dreyfuss and C. Lawrence, *The Bakke Case: The Politics of Inequality.* New York: Harcourt Brace Jovanovich: 140, 1979.

[4] T. Sowell, *Ethnic America: A History*, New York: Basic Books: 273, 1981

Chapter 10

GENDER AND AGE STRATIFICATION

OBJECTIVES

After reading Chapter Ten you should be able to give in-depth answers to the following questions:

1. How do biology and socialization combine to create sex differences?
2. Why are women (52 percent of the population) a minority group in the United States today?
3. Why did feminism in the United States disappear in the 1920s and then reemerge in the 1960s?
4. What position do the elderly occupy in the American stratification system?

CONCEPTS

You should also understand the following sociological concepts:

sex
sex role
gender
sexism
institutionalized sexism
feminism
role strain
ageism

CHAPTER REVIEW

I. How do biology and socialization combine to create sex differences?

Your text looks at sex differences from both biological and sociological points of view.

A. There is no denying the obvious fact that males and females are biologically different. Taking the broad, evolutionary view, Rossi concludes that differences in size, strength, and other traits evolved during the long period when our ancestors were hunters and gatherers. As a result, men are better adapted to some activities and women better adapted to others. Mothering comes more naturally to women, for example, but this does not mean that men cannot learn to care for babies. They can. For most activities in the modern world, sex differences are irrelevant.

B. Cross-cultural studies show that ideas about what is appropriate masculine and feminine behavior vary widely. But whatever the ideas, parents and others go to great lengths to distinguish girls from boys and to socialize them *appropriately.* Parents perceive male and female babies as different, even when they are not (as in the experiment with the same baby). Girls and boys are given different playthings, taught different hidden curricula in school, and exposed to different models in the mass media. Given such intensive, pervasive sex-role socialization, it's a wonder that sex differences are not greater than they are!

II. Why are women (52 percent of the population) a minority group in the United States today?

Although a numerical majority, women in America fit Wirth's definition of a minority group: they are not treated as equals and are aware of discrimination (the objective and subjective criteria for a minority group). Things are changing rapidly, but much work remains to be done if women are to achieve true equality.

Your text analyzes inequality in the workplace and the home. A majority of women hold jobs today, including many mothers of small children. Some women work in previously all-male, high-paying, high-prestige occupations, but the majority do not. The worlds of *men's work* and *women's work* are still separate and unequal. Most women hold such traditionally female jobs as secretary, *salesgirl, nurse, or schoolteacher, and earn only 64 cents for every dollar men earn. Education does not pay off* for women as it does for men. Few women reach the top levels of management. And women confront role conflicts that men seldom face, most of which are accounted for by the transition out of the household into the work force.

Inequality extends into the family. Married women have more legal rights today than they did in the past, and most couples like to think of themselves as equal partners. But the realities of daily living seldom meet this egalitarian ideal. A majority of women hold two jobs: one outside the home and one inside. Even when men help out, women usually have final responsibility for housekeeping and child care. Even when women take responsibility for everyday decisions, men usually have the final say in major decisions. When families break up, women are far more likely than men are to experience a decline in their standard of living.

Many explanations of sex inequality have been put forward (including human capital theory, overcrowding theory, and dual labor market theory). The best explanation seems to be institutionalized sexism: established practices that have the unintended consequence of discriminating against women. The fact that most offices and factories operate on a nine-to-five schedule and award promotions on the basis of seniority and continuous commitment automatically creates problems for women who are also mothers. (The United States is the only industrial nation that does not have a national program for child care.)

III. Why did feminism in the United States disappear in the 1920s and re-emerge in the 1960s?

Feminism has a longer history in the United States than many people realize. Your text identifies three phases in women's struggle for equality in this country: the early feminist movement, retrenchment, and the contemporary women's movement.

A. Although women may have enjoyed practical equality in colonial America, industrialization reduced their status in two ways. Middle-class women were barred from the workplace and thus forced to become financially dependent; poor women were forced to work long hours for little pay. But deprivation does not necessarily lead to rebellion. The early feminist movement was an offshoot of the abolition, temperance, and other late nineteenth and early twentieth century social movements. Female activists in these movements often found their efforts were ridiculed. Around the turn of the century, radical feminists were replaced by a generation of female reformers who portrayed themselves as *society's housekeepers.* Female suffrage became the rallying point for the modern feminist movement which characterizes the current period.

B. Ironically, the ratification of the Nineteenth Amendment, which gave women the vote, marked the beginning of a period of retrenchment. The Great Depression and two world wars overshadowed women's issues. Then the *baby boom* and attending suburbanization added segregation during the workday to the already existing sex-role differentiation. Although many women worked in a variety of important and visible jobs, a *woman's place* was still considered to be in the home.

C. Your text cites two main reasons for the emergence of the women's movement in the 1960s. First, it was a decade of instability, social change, and social reform. Like the early feminist movement, today's women's movement grew out of other social causes that sensitized women to discrimination. Second, many women were already working outside their homes. In this sense, *women's liberation* was a fact before it became a social movement.

The women's movement has scored victories (the legalization of abortion) and suffered defeats (the failure to ratify the ERA). The fact that it has a broad base of support and has addressed a broad range of issues makes it unlikely that this movement will disappear, as the early feminist movement did.

IV. What position do the elderly occupy in the American stratification system?

All societies use age as a basis for distributing rights and privileges, and America is no exception. Your text focuses on the elderly.

One of the most dramatic changes in the American population is the increase in the percentage of citizens aged sixty-five and older. Although it would be an exaggeration to call the elderly a *minority group,* they are victims of prejudice and discrimination. Stereotypes about aging make it difficult for the elderly to find work. Although most older Americans are not isolated, many have lost a spouse. Social Security does not replace lost income, and most retired people experience a drop in their standard of living. But, the lower position the elderly occupy in America today may change in the near future.

CONCEPT REVIEW

Match each of the following terms with the correct definition.

a. gender
b. role strain
c. institutionalized sexism
d. sex role
e. feminism
f. sex
g. sexism
h. ageism

1.___   Established social patterns that have the unintended consequence of limiting women's opportunities.
2.___   A person's subjective or psychological sense of being masculine or feminine.
3.___   The behavior, attitudes, and motivations a culture defines as appropriate for males or females.
4.___   The belief that innate sex differences justify discrimination against and exploitation of women.
5.___   The belief that women are equal to men.
6.___   A person's biological identity as male or female.
7.___   The feeling that a social role makes incompatible demands.
8.___   Prejudice and discrimination against older people.

Answers

1. c   2. a

3. d   4. g
5. e   6. f
7. b   8. h

REVIEW QUESTIONS

1. One of the differences between women and other minority groups is that:
    a. Women are not covered by the Civil Rights Act.
    b. Women have never been segregated from the majority (i.e., males).
    c. Women have only recently become aware of sex discrimination.
    d. Women are singled out for differential treatment in American society.

2. Cross-cultural studies challenge many common assumptions about sex differences. Which of the following statements is false?
    a. Gender inequality is universal.
    b. All societies attach social significance to sex differences.
    c. Not all societies attach social significance to sex differences.
    d. Definitions of masculinity and femininity vary widely across cultures.

3. When older Americans speak for themselves, they say their greatest fear is:
    a. loneliness
    b. not having enough to do to keep busy
    c. crime
    d. poor housing

4. Recent government reports classify 16 percent of working women as professional/technical workers. Which of the following professions are women most likely to follow?
    a. physician
    b. college professor
    c. elementary schoolteacher
    d. engineer

5. The greatest increase in women's employment has been among:
    a. young single women
    b. married women with no children
    c. married women with small children
    d. married women with teenage and college-age children.

6. In which of the following ways is the contemporary women's movement like the early feminist movement?
    a. Both had grass-roots support.
    b. Both developed in climates of social change and were to some extent

by-products of other social movements.
c. Both practiced single-issue politics.
d. Both were short-lived.
e. All of the above.

7. Over the past decade, the economic position of elderly Americans has:
a. improved substantially
b. improved somewhat
c. remained about the same
d. declined somewhat

8. The term *sex role* refers to:
a. a person's biological identity as male or female
b. the behavior and attitudes people consider masculine or feminine
c. an individual's inner sense of being masculine or feminine
d. all of the above

9. Studies on gender socialization indicate that contemporary parents:
a. perceive male and female babies as similar
b. treat male and female babies the same
c. engage in more talk with male babies
d. feel that male and female babies behave differently

10. In about how many states does a man have the legal right to have sex with his wife, with or without her consent?
a. six
b. fifteen
c. thirty
d. forty-four

11. Most older Americans:
a. depend on their middle-aged children for financial support
b. expect their children to support them
c. want to live with their children and grandchildren
d. assist their children financially as often as the reverse

12. Social Security is best described as a form of:
a. welfare
b. insurance
c. investment
d. health care

13. In its early days, one of the leading issues of the contemporary women's movement was a woman's right to work for pay outside the home.

Analysis suggests that:
a. The women's movement explains (i.e., caused) the increase in working wives and mothers.
b. The fact that many women were already working in the 1960s explains why the women's movement *caught on.*
c. Most women only work for a little extra *pocket money.*
d. Husbands were pressuring their wives to get jobs.

14. The difference between stratification based on age and stratification based on sex, race, or ethnicity is that age grades:
a. are acquired statuses
b. are master statuses
c. periodically change
d. affect everyone

15. For some time, the Jamesons have been discussing whether to send their son to private school. Mr. Jameson decides that the time has come. Mrs. Jameson collects information on different schools in the area, talks to other parents, fills out the applications, and takes young Paul for interviews at two schools. In this short, short story:
a. The husband exercises orchestration; the wife, implementation power.
b. The husband is exercising implementation power; the wife is exercising orchestration power.
c. The husband and wife are playing equal roles in a major decision.
d. The child's rights and desires are being ignored.

16. Women gained the right to vote in the United States in:
a. 1774
b. 1822
c. 1920
d. 1950

17. In 1900, the proportion of Americans who were sixty-five or older was one in thirty. Today it is more than:
a. one in twenty
b. one in ten
c. one in five
d. one in three

18. The contemporary women's movement differs from the early movement by:
a. its grass-roots support
b. its relationship to other social movements
c. its use of single-issue politics
d. its brief life span

19. Today, the percentage of working wives earning more income than their husbands is?
   a. one-fourth (25%)
   b. half (50%)
   c. three quarters (75%)
   d. none of the above

20. Sam Smith is a truck driver who dropped out of school after ninth grade. Sally O'Brian is a nurse with fourteen years of education. Which of the following statements is likely to be accurate?
   a. Sally earns about $4,000 more a year than Sam.
   b. Sally earns about $2,000 more a year than Sam.
   c. Sally earns about the same income as Sam.
   d. Sam earns about $4,000 more than Sally.

21. In what country does the government provide free day care or 90 percent of a parent's salary for those who elect to stay home to care for a new baby for up to a year?
   a. France
   b. Sweden
   c. West Germany
   d. the United States

22. Maccoby and Jacklin's survey of the literature revealed that many alleged sex differences are myths. Which of the following beliefs about the sexes is probably true?
   a. Girls are more impressionable than boys.
   b. Boys are more ambitious than girls.
   c. Girls tend to be more compliant than boys.
   d. Boys tend to be better at solving spatial and mathematical problems.

23. Ages twenty-five to thirty-five are usually the years when a person *gets ahead*--when a manual laborer advances to skilled worker or a lawyer becomes a partner in the firm. These also happen to be the years when women are most likely to take time off from work to have babies. This is an example of:
   a. human capital theory
   b. overcrowding in the labor market
   c. sex discrimination
   d. institutionalized sexism

24. A majority of senior citizens today:
   a. are confined to nursing homes
   b. live in retirement communities

   c. maintain their own households
   d. live with their children or other relatives

Answers

1. b: Whereas members of other minority groups nearly always achieve second-
    ary assimilation (acceptance in work situations) before they achieve
    primary assimilation (acceptance in private, intimate associations),
    the reverse is true for women. (See section entitled Explaining Gen-
    der Inequality.)
2. c: Every known society has explicit ideas about what is appropriate for
    either sex (or sex roles). In nearly all societies, men's roles are
    considered more valuable than women's roles. (Women: The 52 Percent
    Minority)
3. c: Younger Americans believe that not having enough money to live on and
    loneliness are major problems for older Americans. When the elderly
    speak for themselves, however, they mention crime as their greatest
    fear, followed by poor health. (Living Situations)
4. c: By and large, when women do go into professions, it is in the lower
    ranks of those professions--as nurse not physician, elementary school
    teacher not professor, and so on. (Inequality at Work)
5. c: Overall, the percentage of women who hold jobs has increased 20 per-
    cent since 1960; the percentage of mothers holding jobs has increased
    38 percent. (Inequality at Work)
6. b: Many of the early suffragettes were female activists who had been
    turned away by the abolitionist and other movements; many of the foun-
    ders of the contemporary women's movement were activists in the civil
    rights and anti-Vietnam war movements who found that male activists
    considered female concerns trivial. (Equality for Women: A Century of
    Struggle)
7. b: Two major reasons are cost-of-living adjustments in Social Security
    benefits and Medicare. (Nevertheless, 3.5 million older Americans are
    living below the poverty line.) (Living Situations)
8. b: Sociologists distinguish between cultural definitions of masculinity
    and femininity (sex roles), the individual's biological identity (or
    sex), and the individual's psychological identity (or gender). (Gender
    Socialization)
9. d: Parents today say that they have the same socialization goals for
    males and females (they want both to be neat, both to be athletic, and
    so on). But they also say that their male and female children behave
    differently. (Gender Socialization)
10. d: As of this writing, only six states allow a woman to charge her hus-
    band with rape. (Inequality in the Family)
11. d: A majority of older Americans do not accept financial support from

their children, expect their children to support them, or want to move in with them. Indeed, older Americans are as likely to assist their children with money, gifts, and services as they are to receive assistance. (Living Situations)

12. b: All retired Americans (and their spouses) are entitled to Social Security, regardless of their financial situation. (Social Security)

13. b: Conventional wisdom holds that the women's movement gave women the idea, the incentive, and the support they needed to go out to look for jobs. In fact, the reverse seems to be true: The fact that many women were already working gave support to the movement. (The Contemporary Women's Movement)

14. c: All of these are acquired statuses; all may function as master statuses; and gender stratification also affects everyone. Age grade is the only one of these statuses that changes. (Age Inequality)

15. a: Although both partners are participating in this endeavor, it is the husband who made the major decision. The wife's responsibility and power are limited to carrying out his decision. (Inequality in the Family)

16. c: Paradoxically, winning the vote defused the early feminist movement, leading to a period of relative quiet in the battle of the sexes. (Retrenchment)

17. b: The *graying of America* is the result of both increases in longevity and decreases in the birthrate. (The Graying of America)

18. a: Unlike the early feminist movement, whose supporters came from the upper-middle class, the contemporary women's movement has broad-based support. This, plus the fact that it has addressed a broad range of issues, help to explain its longevity. (The Contemporary Women's Movement)

19. b: According to the U.S. Bureau of Census about one-quarter of working wives--some eight million women--earn more than their husbands do, twice the number of just a decade ago. (Box: When the Wife is the Breadwinner)

20. d: This is not an isolated case. As a rule, traditionally male occupations (such as a truck driver) are higher paid than traditionally female occupations (such as nursing), regardless of the amount of training required. (Inequality at Work)

21. b: France and West Germany also have national programs for child care; the United States is the only industrial nation that does not. In the United States, the only parents who receive government support are women without husbands (welfare mothers). (Explaining Gender Inequality)

22. d: Boys tend to have superior mathematical and spatial abilities; girls tend to have superior verbal abilities. Why this pattern exists is a matter of speculation. (The Origins of Sex Differences)

23. d: In this case, the facts of reproductive life and the facts of business

life *conspire* against career women who want to be mothers, but there is no overt intent to discriminate. (Explaining Gender Inequality)

24. c: Eighty-five percent maintain their own households. Indeed, 70 percent own their own homes. Moreover, most do not want to live with their children or other relatives. (Living Situations)

MYTH OR FACT?

1. Males are the weaker sex. t/f
2. Girls are more sociable and more concerned about their playmates' opinions than boys are. t/f
3. Although women still earn less than men do, their incomes have improved over the past two decades. t/f
4. Women working is a contemporary phenomenon. t/f
5. Many women do not want men to take equal responsibility for cooking, cleaning, and other housework. t/f

Answers

1. *True,* at least in terms of health. More males than females are miscarried, stillborn, or die in infancy; males are more likely to suffer from stress-related illnesses, and they have a shorter life span.
2. *False.* Maccoby and Jacobson's research showed this is myth. Boys tend to be more *other* oriented than girls are.
3. *False.* In 1955, women earned an average of 64 cents for every $1 men earned; today the figure is down to 60 cents.
4. *False.* In most societies and times, women have engaged in economically productive work (farming, herding, weaving, trading, and so on). The brief period in American history when women did not hold jobs was exceptional. Even then, women worked, but not for pay.
5. *True.* There is some evidence that women are reluctant to surrender this area of expertise to men. But how many women feel this way is difficult to say.

CRITICAL THINKING

1. In interviews with a cross-section of American wives, Anne Taylor Fleming[1] found many were happy with their lives, but. . . . Fleming attempts to explain the qualifying "but" by looking at women whose lives, on the surface, seem quite different.

. . .Laura Handman Ickes is trying to do it all by the 80's script, which means she is trying to do it all. A lovely young woman with a high-paying, high-prestige New York law career, a husband with a similar career and a new baby, some days she feels pulled apart. For 34 years it was straight ahead, straight up, until she ran into motherhood and it stopped her dead, her heart did, when she beheld and held her newborn. What is corporate life, after all, beside the miracle of life?

That's the question a lot of young wives are asking themselves. . . . "There is always this tension of a man wanting independence, privacy and a woman always tearing at it. I've learned to reduce my smothering instinct; I can thank my career for that. . . but you can't smother a baby." . . .That's what babies are giving women, as they no doubt gave them for centuries, a love with no lines, with an intimacy that is easier and often sweeter than sex.(pp. 32, 34)

. . .If you live in a four-bedroom house with five children and a husband who makes $34,000 a year and you're home all day and you want to be left alone for a minute, you've got no place to go but the bathroom. That's where Linda Branch periodically hides . . . .

Linda misses the days when she had a waist, when she and [her husband] Mike were best friends and when he was different, not so much the head-of-the-household he's become now.

"It's not like it used to be," she says. "As the kids have gotten older, he's gotten harder, with me too. I guess I expected more of a partnership, though I don't know anyone who has a 50-50 relationship. I make $75 a week babysitting and I piddle in Avon, but his attitude is 'Well, if you go out and make as much as I do, then we'll be equal . . . .'

Life at this level is very different from Laura Handman Ickes's. . . . It is a life in which a night out means dinner at Burger King with the kids; where the wife does all the housework whether she also has a job or not; where pregnancy is not the great magic miracle it is to the so-called super-woman but a fate, a curse, an accident that happened in her teens or early 20's, setting her life off on a course she struggles to control. (pp. 34, 36)

What do these women have in common? First, they have a fear of being alone, of losing the status of "wife." Women like Laura Ickes say that they are tired and "hard" at the end of the workday, and wonder if their husbands will be attracted to a woman who isn't quite so career oriented. Women like Linda Branch worry that their husbands will be drawn to a woman who is more career oriented, more modern in outlook. The author points out that their fears are grounded in demography: Both groups intuitively know that men spend most of their lives married (remarrying quickly after a divorce), whereas women are more likely to be single for a significant portion of their lives. Second, both groups lack clear cultural guidelines. "Right now, at a time when there is no discernible women's movement left, so many [American wives] seem caught between parts of themselves they can't reconcile--the part that wants a hero for a husband and the part that wants a partner; the part that wants to be the perfect, ever-present mother and the part that wants to be the perfect career woman." (p. 39)

Do you agree with the author's analysis? What other social and economic factors might cause their discontent?

2. Contrary to popular belief, Social Security is not an investment program but a government-sponsored, tax-based insurance program for retired workers. The rising cost of Social Security is due not only to the growing number of elderly Americans, but also to changes in the law. The original Social Security Act, passed in 1935, established benefits for retired workers. In 1939, Congress added benefits for dependents and survivors; between 1940 and 1950, domestic workers, some federal civilian workers, self-employed workers, and the armed forces became eligible for benefits; in 1956, disabled workers were added; in 1961, Congress permitted workers retiring at age sixty-two to receive partial benefits; Medicare became part of the program in 1965; in 1972 Social Security benefits were indexed to the cost of living to adjust for inflation. In 1975, retirement benefits paid out exceeded revenues from payroll taxes for the first time. In 1977, Congress passed huge increases in Social Security taxes. Even so, Social Security had to borrow from other trust funds to make required payments. The impact on individual taxpayers has been dramatic. In 1945, there were thirty-five wage earners for every Social Security recipient and the maximum payroll tax was $30. In 1981, there were only three workers for every recipient and the maximum payroll tax had risen to almost $2,000.

Proposals for rescuing the system include raising taxes on workers, delaying cost-of-living increases for recipients, taxing payments to recipients with incomes of $20,000 or more a year, including federal workers now covered by a separate pension plan in the program, and using other sources of revenue. If you were a thirty-year-old worker with no dependents, which plan would you favor? What if you were a sixty-four-year-old worker?

Note

[1] Anne Taylor Fleming, The American Wife, *The New York Times Magazine.* (October 26, 1986), pp. 29-39. Copyright 1986 by The New York Times Company. Reprinted by permission.

PART FOUR: THE CHANGING SHAPE OF SOCIETY

Chapter 11

FORMAL ORGANIZATIONS

OBJECTIVES

After reading Chapter Eleven you should be able to give in-depth answers to the following questions:

1. What is a bureaucracy?
2. What are some important dysfunctions of bureaucracy?
3. What are some alternative organizational forms to bureaucracy?
4. How are formal organizations affected by their environments?
5. What new forms of organization have been proposed for the future? What are the advantages of these new forms?

CONCEPTS

You should also understand the following sociological concepts:

formal organization
bureaucracy
collectivist organization
charismatic authority
rational-legal authority
traditional authority
collegial association
organizational inertia
iron law of oligarchy
flexible specialization
post-entrepreneurial organization
informal structure
trained incapacity
ideal type

CHAPTER REVIEW

I.   How do formal organizations differ from other groups?

A formal organization is a large, complex secondary group (such as a corporation or government agency) that was created for some specific purpose. Your text presents Weber's ideal model of bureaucracy, points out some of the flaws in bureaucracies, and considers several alternative forms of organization. Please take note that Weber's *ideal type* does not mean a *preferred* type. It means, instead, a model against which organizations *can be compared.*

A. Weber defined bureaucracy in terms of six characteristics: (1) a clear-cut division of labor; (2) hierarchical organization (decisions are made at the top and carried out at the bottom); (3) formal rules and regulations (so that each situation does not have to be dealt with as an individual case); (4) impersonality (rational judgments take precedence over personal considerations); (5) technical qualifications, not personal or family connections, determine one's position; and (6) a clear distinction between the public and private spheres. In bureaucracies, authority is vested in the office, not the officeholder. Weber maintained that bureaucracies are more rational than organizations based on traditional or charismatic authority.

B. Whereas Weber saw bureaucracies as essentially democratic organizations, Michels argued that any large organization promotes the emergence of an executive clique that acts in its own best interests. The result is oligarchy (rule by a few). Michels' main example was the German labor movement, but the law of oligarchy applies to other types of organizations as well.

C. Research by Lipset, Trow, and Coleman supports Michel's view. Oligarchy thrives on *apathy in the rank and file.* When workers feel that they are limited to low-status jobs, they tend not to identify with the job. The lower the status of the job, the wider the gap between union leaders and the rank and file. Leaders tend to hold onto their positions. The conditions for oligarchy are, therefore, met.

C. Weber's model was based on the formal structure of organizations--the official rules and regulations. But all organizations have an informal structure, made up of *off the record* arrangements and unofficial procedures workers develop to cut corners and deal with unanticipated situations. The informal structure may undermine organizational goals. But Dalton found it can also provide the flexibility and speed that formal procedures lack. In fact, such informal procedures can enhance the capability of an organization to meet its stated goals.

D. Other sociologists argue that the dysfunctions of bureaucracy can equal or exceed its functions. Notable dysfunctions include routinization (inflexibility in dealing with special cases); trained incapacity (the inability to see or respond to change); depersonalization; and *Parkinson's Law* (work expanding to fill the time available).

E. Alternatives to bureaucracy have been tried in both large and small organizations. One that has attracted a great deal of attention in recent years is the Japanese corporation, in which lifelong employment is guaranteed, the emphasis is on collective rather than individual performance, and the company takes some responsibility for almost all aspects of employees' lives.

Another is the *collectivist* form of organization. This type is a non-bureaucratic form in which authority is shared and rules are subject to negotiation. *Collegial* associations are organizations in which members regard one another as equals, based on having achieved the same things, and sharing a body of specialized knowledge.

II. How are organizations affected by their environments?

All organizations are affected by the environments within which they are located. Indeed, sociologists have come to believe that organizations cannot be understood outside of their contexts.

A. AT&T was probably the largest privately owned corporation in the world in the 1950s, with an operating budget of about $3 billion! During the 1960s, the company began to lose its grip in the telecommunications market. Research by Taffler indicated that radical changes were occurring in the marketplace, that is, in the *external* environment of the company. AT&T couldn't keep up with the radically changing conditions. Under pressure from the federal government, AT&T divested itself of a number of major divisions in order to gain better control over the probability of its survival.

B. Organizational ecology is the examination of how organizations and their environments interact. Social, political and economic forces in the environment contribute to the birth and death rates, successes, and failures of organizations.

C. The text presents a series of studies which show how environmental forces operate: (1) research in medicine and metal working shops in Italy are used to illustrate the value of *networks* in organizations; (2) a study of the birth and death rates of San Francisco newspapers indicated that political climate is the most important factor in the foundation of a new newspaper there, thus pointing out the effects of environmental *opportunities*; (3) discussions of the animal rights movement, and the growing numbers of anti-smoking advocates are used to illustrate the impact of *technical constraints* and *institutional limitations*; (4) *organizational inertia* is born out of a reluctance to change and adapt to environmental circumstances. It is important to recognize that organizations can fail because of inertia.

D. To some extent, organizational survival rates depend on the size and age of the organization. Large, old organizations are subject to inertia. Small, new organizations produce a larger share of new products and procedures. But, these too have problems, which are outlined in the text. Review the case studies of Kodak and Apple Computers.

III. How will companies adapt to the future?

The corporate climate is changing. New forms of organizations have been suggested by sociologists.

Piore and Sabel propose *flexible specialization*, whereby *craft production* is much better suited to today's markets. They use the computer industry as an example.

B. Kanter focuses on the internal structure of organizations, suggesting that the *post-entrepreneurial* corporation must create divisions with independence and the hierarchy of authority is broken down. Such a corporation concentrates on what it does best and, in some cases, contracts certain services out to other companies.

CONCEPT REVIEW

Match each of the following terms with the correct definition.

a. collectivist organizations
b. collegial organizations
c. rational-legal authority
d. bureaucracy
e. flexible specialization
f. traditional authority
g. perestroika

h. Japanese corporations
i. authority
j. charismatic authority
k. formal organization
l. technical constraints
m. glasnost
n. technology

1.___ A hierarchical organization governed by formal rules and regulations.
2.___ Organizations in which rules are subject to negotiation.
3.___ What is necessary for craft-type production.
4.___ Soviet version of openness.
5.___ Goal-oriented organizations.
6.___ The legitimate right to command.
7.___ Companies which provide lifetime employment.
8.___ Authority that is based on and limited by a formal system of rules and laws.
9.___ Organizations normally consisting of professionals.
10.___ Authority that is based on and limited by custom.
11.___ Scarce resources, size of markets, number and types of competitors, etc.
12.___ Authority that is based on special personal qualities.
13.___ A restructuring of the Soviet economy and government.
14.___ Whatever means (e.g., raw materials, processes) formal organizations use to pursue their goals.

Answers

1. d	6. i.	11. l
2. a.	7. h	12. j
3. e	8. c	13. g
4. m	9. b	14. n
5. k	10. f	

REVIEW QUESTIONS

1. In early human societies, most organizations were organized:
   a. like modern Japanese corporations
   b. through personal relations
   c. in bureaucratic forms
   d. in collectivist fashion

2. In the late nineteenth century:
   a. most people were self-employed
   b. about a third of the work force were women
   c. large department stores were first developed
   d. bureaucracy first came into being

3. Research on organizations which focuses on the impact of organizations on individual behavior operates on the:
   a. bureaucratic level
   b. structural level
   c. social psychological level
   d. environmental level
   e. all of the above

4. Formal organizations contain:
   a. structure
   b. participants
   c. goals
   d. technology
   e. all of the above

5. Which of the following characteristics of Japanese management is least likely to be accepted by American workers?
   a. lifelong employment
   b. the use of bonuses to reward performance
   c. collective promotion
   d. holistic concern for employees

6. Which of the following is most likely to be a collectivist organization?
   a. a national bank
   b. a hospital
   c. a public school district
   d. a small advertising agency
   e. a chain supermarket

7. A city board of education authorizes the schools in its district to pur-
   chase a specified number of computerized instruction programs. The teachers and the PTA at P.S. 125 want the new systems, but the principal argues that children must learn from reading and writing. The principal's
   response illustrates:
   a. routinization
   b. trained incapacity
   c. vested interests
   d. Parkinson's law

8. Which of the following does *not* fit Weber's model of a bureaucracy?
   a. a clear-cut division of labor
   b. negotiated decisions
   c. formal rules and regulations
   d. reliance on technical qualifications
   e. rationality

9. The chairman of Chrysler Corporation exercises:
   a. traditional authority
   b. charismatic authority
   c. rational-legal authority
   d. personal authority

10. The *iron law of oligarchy* was proposed by:
    a. Weber
    b. Michels
    c. Tonnies
    d. Durkheim

11. If people operate *off the road*, have open secrets in organizations,
    and/or engage in practices not specified in the rules, we refer to:
    a. the organization chart
    b. informal structure
    c. iron law of oligarchy
    d. specialization

12. *In Men and Women of the Corporation*, Kanter discovered that access to

the informal structure affects how things get done. Which of the following is *not* one of the informal sources of power, according to Kanter?
a. luck
b. sponsorship
c. alliances with peers
d. subordinates

13. Bureaucracy in the Soviet society:
a. is relatively new, born out of the 1917 revolution
b. is flexible and innovative
c. stretches back to the time of the czars, before the revolution
d. none of the above

14. Which of the following is *least* problematic in a bureaucracy, according to the text?
a. routinization
b. trained incapacity
c. informal structure
d. depersonalization

15. Problems experienced by AT&T evolved from:
a. changing technology
b. changing life styles of Americans
c. changing work force
d. all of the above

16. The formation of women's medical societies illustrated that successful development of such associations was heavily dependent upon:
a. money
b. increasing members of female physicians
c. where women were networked
d. being located in rural areas

17. The most important factor in the foundation of newspapers, according to one study was:
a. a good economy
b. good leadership
c. large cities
d. political turmoil

18. Organizational survival rates often depend on the size of an organization. The reason is:
a. larger organizations have the resources to maintain market strength
b. smaller organizations are more innovative

   c. neither of the above
   d. both of the above

19. Flexible specialization:
   a. emphasizes mass production
   b. is the type of production system most characteristic of the U.S.
   c. emphasizes craft production
   d. none of the above

20. The post-entrepreneurial corporation, according to Kanter:
   a. focuses on a less hierarchical structure than organizations have re-
      lied upon in the past
   b. is limited to high-tech production
   c. emphasizes craft production
   d. none of the above

Answers

1. b: Families worked together in small farms, producing most of what they needed themselves. Formal organizations are not exclusively modern, but their number and influence over our lives do distinguish modern societies. (See first page of Chapter 11.)

2. a: Today more than 90% of the labor force works for someone else. More than 50% work for 2% of the nation's employers. (First page)

3. c: Organizations are seen as the context within which interaction occurs; and an influence on interaction. (Second page)

4. e: Organizations contain all of these elements, *plus* they operate within a larger social system. (The Elements of Organizations)

5. c: American workers would not refuse bonuses; many would appreciate a guarantee of lifelong employment; and some are pressing for a more *holistic* approach (company exercise classes, day-care centers). But most would feel cheated if they were promoted with the group of workers hired the same year they were, rather than evaluated on the basis of individual performance. (Alternative Organizational Forms)

6. d: Collectivist organizations may be most useful with small-scale operations that depend on individual talent and collaboration. (Alternative Organizational Forms)

7. a: Rules that make sense in one context may make no sense at all in others, and impede efficiency. (The Dysfunctions of Bureaucracy)

8. b: In a classic bureaucracy, decisions are made at the top of the hierarchy and passed down to the rank and file. (Bureaucracy)

9. c: His authority derives from his position in the company and is limited by company rules and regulations--unlike traditional leaders, whose authority derives from custom, or charismatic leaders, whose authority

is based on exceptional personal qualities. (Bureaucracy)

10. b: Michels' theory was based on his studies of the German labor movement, which began as a democratic, grass-roots movement but produced its own elite. (Michels' Iron Law of Oligarchy)

11. b: Informal structures can operate to either help or hinder an organization in its operations. *Every* formal organization has an informal structure within it. Donald H. Roy was one of the first sociologists to study informal organizations. (Weber's Model)

12. a: Luck has little to do with success. Having a mentor, connecting with peers, and having dependable subordinates can make the difference. (Box: Women of the Corporation)

13. c: Peter the Great established ranks and titles among government officials. This system was replaced by a very complicated bureaucracy after the revolution. (Box: Bureaucracy in the U.S.S.R.)

14. c: Some types of informal structure can be problematical, but they can also be helpful. Indeed, informal structures often overcome problems associated with a, b, and d above. (Dysfunctions of Bureaucracy)

15. d: The U.S. political scene changed as well. New regulations forced changes in operating practice in companies like AT&T, including divesting itself of some of its divisions. (Organizational Survival)

16. c: Preexisting networks provided women with contacts and skills needed to form and maintain societies of their own. (Importance of Networks)

17. d: Political unrest creates interest in news. Also, newspapers can *contribute* to such turmoil. (Environmental Opportunities)

18. d: Large organizations do have the resources, but also can suffer from organizational inertia. Smaller organizations are more innovative, but also have problems getting and maintaining financing. (Organizational Survival)

19. c: Piore and Sabel offer their model as a means to adapt to the future, become more competitive, and take advantage of technological change. (Flexible Specialization)

20. a: Kanter argues that creating divisions, and subcontracting some functions to other companies will allow corporations to concentrate on their strengths. (Post-entrepreneurial Organization)

MYTH OR FACT?

1. Bureaucracies are depersonalizing.   t/f
2. Environmental constraints consist of *both* technical and institutional limitations.   t/f
3. Organizations breed inertia.   t/f
4. All women and minorities need to succeed in corporations is the job; the rest will take care of itself.   t/f

Answers

1. *True.* The ideal bureaucrat, according to Weber, is impartial, setting rational decisions above personal considerations and treating clients as cases. The functions of depersonalization in a bureaucracy are to eliminate favoritism and promote efficiency.
2. *True.* These include the availability of resources, size of markets, number of competitors, and government regulations (technical); and cultural ideas about what type of goals and activities are legitimate (institutional).
3. *True.* The investment of time and money, and cultivating an organizational culture create a resistance to change.
4. *False.* Women and minorities need mentoring, networks, and dependable subordinates in order to be competitive, according to the researcher, Rosabeth Kanter.

CRITICAL THINKING

1. Recall the text discussion on organizations and environments. Could a collectivist organization compete with a company like General Motors in building and selling cars? Why or why not? What would you see as limits for such organizations in modern markets? As you think through the issues, consider the following: size of the organization, type(s) of labor needed, facilities, location, product development, employee benefits, accounting system, support staff, legal staff. Are some bureaucratic principles simply not expendable in view of these issues?

2. To say that the political changes in Eastern Europe which began in 1989 are spectacular is an understatement. A unified Germany? A free Poland and Czechoslovakia? We have even witnessed the beginnings of the breakup of the U.S.S.R. (remember that the R is plural, as in Republics) in 1990. Who could have imagined such a dismantling of the Soviet-controlled Eastern Bloc?
   In any case, let's look back a bit and try to understand what has happened here. Take another look at the sections on Organizational Inertia, Bureaucracy in the U.S.S.R. (Box), and Adapting to the Future. What parallels can you see between the text discussion of organizations (e.g., using AT&T and Kodak as case studies) and the present political events in Eastern Europe?

Chapter 12

THE FAMILY

OBJECTIVES

After reading Chapter Twelve you should be able to give in-depth answers to the following questions:

1. How do the structure and functions of the family vary across cultures?
2. How have American families changed?
3. How are courtship, marriage, and parenthood socially patterned?
4. What causes family violence?
5. Who gets divorced?
6. What is the future of the family in the United States?

CONCEPTS

You should also understand the following sociological concepts:

nuclear family
extended family
modified extended family
stepfamilies
monogamy
polygamy
polygyny
polyandry
serial monogamy
homogamy
divorce rate

CHAPTER REVIEW

I. How do the structure and functions of the family vary across cultures?

All societies have families, but the structure and function of this social institution vary.

Polygyny (one man with several wives) is the preferred form of marriage in 75 percent of human societies. In practice, however, few men achieve this ideal. Monogamy (one man and one wife) is the accepted form of marriage in 25 percent of societies. In practice, serial monogamy (one exclusive marriage followed by another or others) is common in American society.

In most traditional societies, the family is the basic unit of social structure and performs four key functions: the regulation of sex; the replacement of members (reproduction); the socialization of children; and the distribution of goods and services (or economics). In modern societies, other institutions have taken over all or part of these functions. But the family has taken on a new function: emotional gratification.

II. How have American families changed?

Families not only vary from culture to culture, but they change over time. In the 1950s, the ideal of the multigenerational extended family gave way to the ideal of independent nuclear families. (Your text points out that realities do not always match ideals: Extended families were not as common, and nuclear families not as isolated, as many people imagine.) Family ties remain strong, however. A majority of Americans keep in touch with their extended families, looking to them for financial aid and help with daily problems.

The major change in the American family in recent decades is variety. Today most Americans live in a variety of family types over the course of their lifetime: Singlehood, single parenthood, and childless marriages have all increased dramatically in the past two decades. For most individuals, however, these are temporary arrangements before, between, and/or after conventional marriage.

III. How are courtship, marriage, and parenthood socially patterned?

Your text examines the social rules that govern courtship, marriage, and parenthood, and how these have changed.

A. Unmarried couples living together have become both more common and more socially acceptable in recent years. Most couples see living together as a stage in courtship, not as a substitute for marriage.

B. Americans like to think that people marry for love. But, love is not random. Most people marry someone who is like themselves in religion, education, and other attributes society considers important (homogamy). Most women marry a man who is a few years older than they are. Exchange theories hold that how serious a relationship becomes depends on conscious and unconscious calculations of relative value. Only those individuals who are high in self-esteem and have numerous assets can truly be said to choose a mate.

C. Although many couples are postponing parenthood, most married couples do have one or more children. In contrast to marriage, parenthood is an irrevocable commitment. It is also an ambiguous one--most new parents have little preparation for their roles.

D. The high divorce rate in our society has led to an increase in the number of stepfamilies. Four out of five divorced persons remarry. About 80 percent of remarriages involve children. It is estimated that one-third of all children will participate in a stepfamily before they reach age eighteen. The special characteristics of stepfamilies create special problems that require the stepfamily to go through a period of adjustment. About 60 percent of remarriages end in divorce.

IV. What causes family violence?

Family violence is one of the brutal facts of modern American life. More accurately, physical abuse is one of the facts of family life that came to public attention only in recent years. And the sad fact is that millions of children, wives, and husbands are injured (sometimes quite seriously) by members of their family each year. It is only recently that these facts have become known to the American public, and even more recently that public officials have begun to address the issue of family violence forcefully.

Sociological analysis suggests that the structure of American families tends to encourage violence. Four factors contribute to physical abuse: intimacy (the high level of emotional involvement among family members); privacy (which reduces or shuts out outside controls of violence); social and cultural support for the use of physical force in many situations (such as punishing children); and socialization (it is within their family that most people learn about violence).

In the past decade, the rate of family violence declined somewhat, whereas the numbers of cases reported to authorities and of abusers and victims seeking help increased.

V. Who gets divorced?

Almost half of all first marriages in America end in divorce. Sixty percent of second marriages end in divorce as well. Some people (couples who married young, have no children, have less than a college education) are more vulnerable to divorce than others. Race is another factor in divorce. Black women are twice as likely as white women to be divorced. Religion continues to persist as a major barrier to divorce. The more often a person attends religious services, the less likely he is to be divorced. Divorce rates are higher in urban areas and in the Sun Belt area of the U.S. than in other areas. Presumably, this is because of the greater range of opportunities in urban areas, and the relatively young age and lack of connections of Sun Belt residents. How well children adjust to a divorce seems to depend on whether they maintain good relationships with both parents. In most cases, their parents remarry, with the result that there are many more *stepfamilies* today than ever before.

VI. What is the future of the family in the United States?

There is good evidence that although the institution is changing, the family is here to stay. Although more marriages end in divorce today than fifty years ago, fewer end with the premature death of a spouse. Although more couples are voluntarily childless, fewer couples are involuntarily childless. Although more women are working outside the home, they have fewer children and so may spend more time with each one. In short, there are more choices in family life today than in the past. And the large majority of Americans still choose to have families. However, the nuclear family is largely a phenomenon of the past. The challenge for the future is reconciling traditional images of the family with nontraditional realities.

CONCEPT REVIEW

Match each of the following terms with the correction definition.

a. divorce rate
b. homogamy
c. monogamy
d. polyandry
e. polygyny
f. exchange theory

g. serial monogamy
h. stepfamily
i. polygamy
j. nuclear family
k. modified extended family
l. extended family

1.___   A marriage involving only one man and one woman.
2.___   The number of divorces per 1,000 (married women or men) in a given year.
3.___   A network of nuclear families that establish separate residences but maintain ties with one another.
4.___   Mate selection is the result of a series of calculations.
5.___   A mother, father, and their unmarried children who form an independent household.
6.___   The marriage of one man to two or more women at the same time.
7.___   One exclusive, legally sanctioned, but relatively short-lived marriage after another.
8.___   The tendency to marry someone who is similar to oneself.
9.___   Members of three or more generations, related by marriage, who live together or near one another.
10.___   The marriage of one woman to more than one man at the same time.

11. _H_   A household that includes at least one spouse with children from a previous marriage.

12. _I_   The marriage of one man to two or more women or of one woman to two or more men at the same time.

Answers

1. c	5. j	9. l
2. a	6. e	10. d
3. k	7. g	11. h
4. f	8. b	12. i

REVIEW QUESTIONS

1. The majority of adults in the United States today live:
   a. alone
   b. in nuclear families
   c. with a spouse but no children
   d. with children but no spouse
   e. none of the above

2. Sociological analysis suggests that family violence:
   a. is a symptom of a breakdown in family structure
   b. reflects the structure of American families
   c. is a modern phenomenon
   d. can best be treated by psychotherapy

3. Which of the following illustrates the principle of homogamy?
   a. marrying someone who lives within walking distance
   b. marrying someone with similar marital experience (never married, divorced, or widowed)
   c. opposites attract
   d. marrying for love

4. The major cause of single-parent families is:
   a. divorce
   b. births before marriage
   c. widowhood
   d. delayed marriages
   e. none of the above

5. The term *modified extended family* refers to:
   a. members of three or more generations living in one household
   b. *the classical family of Western nostalgia*

    c. networks of nuclear families who maintain close ties
    d. stepfamilies that include a couple and their children from previous marriages

6. ____% of women ages twenty to twenty-four have never married.
    a. 30
    b. 10
    c. 60
    d. 95

7. One of the new functions of the family is:
    a. the distribution of goods and services
    b. the creation of an intimate environment
    c. socialization of children
    d. regulation of sexual activity

8. Which of the following predictions about the future of the family do the authors of your text endorse?
    a. Divorce rates have peaked and will probably decline in coming years.
    b. The percentage of people who marry will decline.
    c. Sex roles in the family are likely to remain asymmetrical.
    d. People will continue to organize families of one kind or another and society will attempt to adjust to nontraditional families.

9. Many couples view having children as a problem because:
    a. They will not be able to have extra money to save and invest.
    b. They will not be able to maintain a neat, orderly household.
    c. They will experience a drastic change in lifestyle, which may disrupt the wife's career in particular.
    d. None of the above.

10. Which of the following determines how long a marriage will last?
    a. age at first marriage
    b. socioeconomic status
    c. race
    d. all of the above
    e. none of the above

11. Which of the following is *not* characteristic of cohabitation?
    a. Living together is a step toward marriage.
    b. Couples who live together before marriage have higher divorce rates than other couples.
    c. Cohabitation is a substitute for marriage.
    d. None of the above.

12. It is estimated that _____ of all U.S. children will see their parents divorce before they reach age eighteen.
    a. 5%
    b. 75%
    c. 40%
    d. none of the above

13. In most human societies, people believe that:
    a. There is no such thing as *love*.
    b. A marriage will not last unless it is built on love.
    c. Individuals should be free to choose their own mates.
    d. Love is not a solid foundation for marriage.

14. Which of the following is true about couples in which the wife is pregnant?
    a. The husband tends to ignore his wife.
    b. The frequency of sex increases.
    c. The husband does more housework.
    d. The wife feels attractive.
    e. None of the above.

15. Studies comparing full-time homemakers with working mothers find that:
    a. Most housewives are lonely.
    b. Working women have lower self-esteem and less confidence as a result of the stress they encounter on the job.
    c. Most working mothers would give up their jobs if they could afford to.
    d. Working mothers are less likely to say that they are *very happy* with their marriages.
    e. None of the above.

16. The number of cohabitating couples was estimated to be _____ in the mid-1980s.
    a. 25 million
    b. 500,000
    c. 2.5 million
    d. none of the above

17. Which of the following statements about family violence is *false*?
    a. Each year about 2 million children are physically abused by a member of their family.
    b. Almost as many men as women are victims of family violence.
    c. Family violence is most often found in poor, uneducated families.
    d. Neighbors and relatives are usually reluctant to *interfere* by reporting family violence to authorities.

18. Marianne has been divorced for three years. She dated one man for a year and a half, thought about marrying him, but found he had other ideas. She is debating whether moving in with the man she is dating now will lead to marriage. Marianne falls into which category of singlehood?
    a. involuntary but temporary
    b. voluntary but temporary
    c. voluntary and stable
    d. involuntary but stable

19. How much time a father devotes to child care depends on:
    a. the wife's schedule
    b. the number of hours the mother works
    c. whether or not the mother believes the father is competent at child care
    d. none of the above
    e. all of the above

20. Which of the following statements about marriage in the United States today is *false?*
    a. Young people are marrying somewhat later.
    b. Fewer people are marrying today than in the past.
    c. The overwhelming majority of Americans marry at least once.
    d. More people choose to get married than to live together without a marriage license.

21. The most common form of marriage in human societies is:
    a. monogamy
    b. polygamy
    c. polygyny
    d. polyandry

Answers

1. e: There is no one typical American family today. (See section entitled The American Family in Perspective.)
2. b: Some of the best things about families (Intimacy and Privacy) bring out the worst in individuals. Cultural support for the use of physical force and early experiences of hurt in the home make family violence all the more likely. (Behind Closed Doors: Violence in the Family)
3. b: Conforming to the principle of homogamy, a majority of Americans have always chosen to marry someone of their own race, religion, social class, and (approximate) age. With so many divorces and remarriages, martial status has been added to this list. (Courtship, Marriage, and Children)

4. a: Widowhood used to be the major cause of single parent families, but today the major cause is divorce. (One-Parent Families)

5. c: Research shows that actual extended families were not as common in the past, and that isolated nuclear families are not as common today, as many people believe. (The American Family in Perspective)

6. c: Sixty percent of women between the ages of twenty and twenty-four have not yet married. The main reason for this singlehood is that many young adults are choosing to postpone marriage (it is not that many are deciding never to marry). (Courtship, Marriage, and Children)

7. b: Although the family retains some influence on economics, socialization, and sexual activity, it does not control these areas of social life in contemporary societies. The family's main function today is emotional gratification. (Family Functions)

8. d: Your text also suggests that claims that the family is a dying institution are likely to continue. (The American Family in Perspective)

9. c: Most couples rate having children as more important than having extra money or having an orderly household. Their primary worry is that the child may bring about a drastic change in life style, in particular that it would disrupt the wife's career. (Families without Children)

10. d: Socioeconomic status, age at first marriage, and race all help determine whether a marriage will last. Other factors include religion, and whether individuals live in urban areas or the Sun Belt region of the country. (Who Gets Divorced and Why)

11. c: Only a very small percentage of couples see cohabitation as a substitute for marriage. For most it is a stage similar to engagement. (Living Together: A New Stage in Courtship)

12. c: It has been estimated by Glick (1988) that 40% of all U.S. children will witness their parents divorce before they themselves are eighteen. (Children and Divorce)

13. d: The emphasis on romantic love in Western societies is unique. Most societies recognize that two people (especially adolescents) may fall in love, but consider marriage too serious to leave to inexperienced, emotionally volatile young people. (Choosing a Mate)

14. c: In late pregnancy the division of labor in the household (who does laundry, dishes, and so forth) may be more egalitarian than at any other time. During this time the husband feels that his wife is in a *delicate* condition and so he is more willing to help his wife with domestic chores. (Marriage and Children)

15. e: All of the stereotypes appear to be untrue. (Dual-Earner and Dual-Career Families)

16. c: The number of unmarried couples living together tripled during the 1970s and has leveled off to about 2.5 million in the 1980s. (Living Together: A New Stage in Courtship)

17. c: Family violence occurs at all levels of society. The poor and non-whites are overrepresented in official statistics because they are more likely to be given the label *abuser* or *victim*. (Behind Closed Doors: Violence in the Family)

18. a: Most singles in their early twenties fall into category b (voluntary but temporary); many elderly singles into category d (involuntary but stable). Many divorced people, like Marianne, fall into category a (involuntary but temporary) (Singlehood)

19. e: All of these are factors affecting the amount of time fathers devote to child care. In addition, the father's relationship with his own father is important. And, if the child is a boy the father is more likely to be involved in child care. (Dual-Earner and Dual-Career Families)

20. b: Marriage is as popular as ever. Ninety-five percent of all Americans will marry at least once. (Courtship, Marriage, and Children)

21. a: Although 75% of the societies in the World Ethnographic Survey allow polygyny, few men are able to secure or afford more than one wife. Monogamy is the most common form of marriage by default. (Family Structure)

MYTH OR FACT?

1. Most people who physically abuse their children are psychologically disturbed.   t/f
2. Divorce has harmful, long-term effects on children.   t/f
3. An only child is a deprived child.   t/f
4. Second marriages are usually more successful than first.   t/f

Answers

1. *False.* The percentage of people who are mentally ill is no higher among child abusers than it is in the population as a whole.
2. *False.* Divorce seems to have mixed effects on children. After an initial period of upset, some children thrive while others remain disturbed. But the majority do recover.
3. *False.* Research suggests that in some ways only children are advantaged. This should not be surprising: Their parents have more time (and more money) to spend with them.
4. *False.* The divorce rate for second marriages is slightly higher than for first marriages, but only slightly.

CRITICAL THINKING

1. Social scientist Mary Jo Bane writes:[1] "In technology, progress is the

standard. In social institutions, continuity is the standard, and when change occurs it is seen as decline rather than advance." How does this apply to the family?

2. Your text describes a great many different family life styles. What are the advantages and disadvantages of these different arrangements?

3. Citing a study by the Census Bureau, *The New York Times* reports,[2]

> Judging by the ratio of single men to single women, marriage prospects would appear to be better for younger women and older men. The study found that from the age of 15 to 24 there were 112 single men for every 100 single women; from 25 to 34 there were 119 single men for every 100 single women.
>
> After that age, single women outnumbered single men. From the age of 35 to 44, it was 84 men for every 100 women; from 45 to 64, the ratio was 54 for every 100 women, and after the age of 65 there were only 26 single men for every single woman.

Explain this demographic imbalance. Then consider the implications. Remembering that about one in three marriages ends in divorce, draw up a life history for a woman now twenty-two years old and another for a man the same age.

4. Most studies of changing gender roles focus on role conflicts for women, especially working mothers and career women who want to be mothers. Changing gender roles also affect men, as Jerrold Shapiro found.[3]

> Not too long ago, pregnancy was strictly "women's work." An expectant father didn't have much to do until the day of birth. Then his job was to get his wife to the hospital on time, smoke cigarettes and pace a well-worn circle in the hospital waiting room, anxiously awaiting the nurse's report on the sex of the child and on the health of the mother and baby. It was rare for a father to be present at the birth. . . .
>
> Times have changed. Today, it is the rare husband or hospital that expects the father to be absent. Fathers also expect to play a much greater role in child-care than their fathers did. "Help around the house" is no longer limited to keeping the family car in running order and the lawn well-trimmed.
>
> Such major changes in cultural expectations have naturally brought with them new problems for fathers-to-be. From the moment he knows of the pregnancy, a man is thrust into an alien world. He is encouraged, instructed and cajoled to be part of the pregnancy and birth process, something he knows little about. He is expected to become the coach or

supporter for his wife, who has the leading role in the drama. He has no role model, since his own father almost certainly didn't do what he is expected to do.

These difficulties, while troublesome, can. . . be overcome. . . . Another problem is far more serious and confusing. I call it the cultural double bind. Men are encouraged to participate fully in the pregnancy and birth of their children but are simultaneously given to understand, in a multitude of ways, that they are outsiders. Most of all, it is made clear that while their presence is requested, their feelings are not, if those feelings might upset their wives. . . .

A young woman, about to have her first child, is expected to be frightened and ambivalent. Furthermore, her changes and feelings are supported and explained by the biological alterations in her body. The father-to-be has neither the support systems nor the cultural sanctions for what he experiences. [pp. (36-38 passim)]

5. The number of single parents in the United States today includes a growing number of unwed, teenage mothers. One researcher questioned 2,500 young women, most of whom had been pregnant, about their attitudes toward sex, birth control, and pregnancy.[4] She found seven reasons why unwed women get pregnant: (1) I didn't know how to prevent it. (2) How can you plan something that is supposed to be spontaneous? (3) What would he have thought if I'd come prepared the first time? (4) I intended to remain a virgin until I got married. (5) I didn't care, because we were going to get married. (6) I thought it was his responsibility. (7) I didn't think it could happen to me. Most of the young women in the survey were high school students or dropouts. Are attitudes among college students different? On a first sexual encounter are you comfortable asking someone if he or she is *prepared*? Can we reduce the number of unwed pregnancies?

Notes

[1] Mary Jo Bane, *Here to Stay: American Families in the Twentieth Century,* New York: Basic Books, 1976.

[2] More Women Postponing Marriage, *The New York Times*. (December 10, 1986) p. A22. Copyright 1986 by The New York Times Company. Reprinted by permission.

[3] J. L. Shapiro, The Expectant Father, *Psychology Today* (January 1987), pp. 36-42. Reprinted with permission from Psychology Today Magazine.

[4] C. Lindemann, *Birth Control and Unmarried Women*, New York: Springer, 1974.

Chapter Thirteen

EDUCATION

OBJECTIVES

After reading Chapter Thirteen you should be able to give in-depth answers to the following questions:

1. What caused the *schooling revolution* in the United States?
2. Does the school system in the United States reduce or reinforce social inequality?
3. What are the major issues facing American education today?
4. How does the educational system in the United States compare with those in other societies?

CONCEPTS

You should also be familiar with the following sociological concepts:

education
schooling
contest and sponsored mobility
status competition
tracking

CHAPTER REVIEW

I. What caused the schooling revolution in the United States?

Your text examines three explanations for the dramatic expansion of formal education in twentieth-century America: schooling for industrialization, schooling for capitalism, and status competition for a *credential society.*

A. Functionalists hold that mass education serves the needs of an advanced technological society. According to this view, the creation of new occupations in the early twentieth century, the influx of foreign workers to American cities and factories, the knowledge explosion of the mid-twentieth century, and widespread acceptance of egalitarian ideas all contributed to the schooling revolution. Schools serve five basic functions today: instruction; socialization; custody and control of young people; certification; and selection.

B. Conflict theorists view mass education as serving the needs of capitalists. During the early twentieth century, schools were designed to turn immigrant and rural children into obedient workers; later the emphasis shifted to developing white-collar skills and team (or company) loyalty. Far from promoting egalitarian ideals, schools protect the status quo--by using tests and other allegedly objective measures that favor youngsters of upper- and middle-class backgrounds, and by maintaining the illusion of equal opportunity. Schools produce a surplus of qualified personnel--a boon to employers.

C. A third explanation of the schooling revolution stresses status competition. Poor parents believed schooling was a route to social mobility and demanded more education for their children. As more lower-class youngsters began completing high school, more middle-class students went on to college, keeping one educational step ahead. Today, many lower-class students attend college and many desirable jobs require a graduate or professional degree. The result is that educational *credentials* become a form of investment and serve to maintain social inequality.

II. Does the school system in the United States reduce or reinforce social inequality?

Has mass education opened opportunities for social mobility, as many Americans believe? Your text concludes it has not. Any number of studies have shown first, that the higher a student's socioeconomic status, the further up the educational ladder he or she will go; and second, that equal education has not produced equal incomes for blacks, women, and other minorities. Why do youngsters from white middle- and upper-class backgrounds profit more from education than other children? Your test examines four possible explanations.

A. The simplest explanation is that these youngsters are more intelligent. On the average, they do achieve higher scores on IQ and other intelligence tests and receive better grades in school. But does this mean that they are smarter? (Could they perform as well on the streets of a ghetto or on a farm?) IQ tests measure a limited set of cognitive skills. Many critics feel they are biased against creative children as well as minority youngsters.

B. A second possibility is that lower-class and minority parents do not prepare their children for school as well as middle- and upper-class parents do. Most social scientists today reject the theory of cultural deprivation: Cultural differences are not necessarily deficits. But there is evidence that lower- and middle-class parents have different socialization goals for their children. Lower-class parents tend to emphasize neatness, good manners, and also obedience to authority--behavior that is highly valued in elementary school. Middle-class parents tend to emphasize self-direction and curiosity--qualities that are valued in high school and college. All parents want their children to do well in school and go on to college. The critical difference seems to be that where lower-class parents hope their children will continue their education, middle- and upper-class parents know how to help their children achieve their goals.

C. A third possible explanation for unequal performance in school is that middle- and upper-class children attend better schools. The Coleman report, the result of a massive study designed to assess the impact of school integration published in 1966, rejected this view. Coleman found little correlation between school quality and student performance. In 1980 the National Center for Educational Statistics sponsored a large-scale study of America's high school sophomores and seniors. The survey included both private (namely Catholic) and public school students. Coleman, Hoffer, and Kilgora analyzed the results in 1981 and again in 1987. They found that on tests of vocabulary, reading, and mathematics students from private schools performed better than those from public schools. Catholic schools were especially effective with poor and minority students. The study also noted that private school students were much more likely to enroll in college than were graduates of public schools. Coleman and Hoffer concluded that Catholic schools succeed because they are part of a community merging people of different generations and socioeconomic backgrounds.

D. The fourth possibility is that not all students are treated equally in school. Research shows that assignment to college preparatory or *general* tracks in high school is based to some degree on subjective evaluations and social class background. Research also suggests that tracking magnifies differences in motivation and ability among students in our public education system. Overall evidence suggests that tracking may be good for students with high ability, but reinforces social inequality among other students. Here is a classic example where *institutionalized racism*, in regard to minority students, can occur.

III.   What are the major issues facing American education today?

The issues discussed in your text can be rephrased as the following questions:

What is the impact of de facto racial and economic segregation?

Which is better for students, centralization or community control?

How can the quality of education be improved?

How can we make teaching a more attractive occupation?

Why are American students falling behind students in other advanced nations in educational performance?

Does a college education *pay off*?

IV. How does the educational system in the United States compare with those in other societies?

Your text shows that a society's education system reflects its underlying values, by comparing the U.S. school system with those found in the U.S.S.R., China, and Japan. In the United States, students are evaluated in terms of individual performance. Collaborating with classmates on homework or exams is defined as *cheating*. In the Soviet Union and on Israeli kibbutzim, students are evaluated in terms of their contributions to group performance, collaboration is rewarded. In the United States, every child is given an opportunity to compete for a small number of top academic rewards; education is viewed as a contest. Until recently, only a small percentage of students in France and Britain were admitted to programs designed to prepare them for universities; all other students were given a general education. Thus higher education in these countries was sponsored. The combination of individuality and open competition is uniquely American.

CONCEPT REVIEW

Match each of the following terms with the correct definition:

   a. education
   b. schooling
   c. tracking
   d. status competition
   e. contest mobility

   1. _b_   Formal instruction in a classroom setting.
   2. _d_   The quest for prestige and social esteem.
   3. _a_   The formal or informal transmission of knowledge.
   4. _e_   A system in which status is seen as the result of individual talent and effort.
   5. _c_   Assigning students to different classes or programs on the basis of test scores and teacher recommendations.

   Answers

   1. b
   2. d
   3. a
   4. e
   5. c

REVIEW QUESTIONS

1. When the president of a college hands out diplomas on graduation day, which function of education is he or she serving?
   a. instruction
   b. socialization
   c. certification
   d. selection

2. The theory of status competition advanced by Hurn differs from other views of the schooling revolution in that it:
   a. views mass higher education as functional
   b. views mass higher education as dysfunctional
   c. traces the schooling revolution to the vested interests of educators
   d. traces the schooling revolution to the hopes and dreams of parents for their children

3. There are any number of popular misconceptions about the nature of intelligence and IQ. Which of the following beliefs is *true*?
   a. Intelligence is innate: either you have it or you don't.
   b. Intelligence is fixed: If a smart child is doing poorly in school, he or she hasn't *lost* his or her intelligence.
   c. IQ tests are quite accurate in predicting success in school.
   d. Some ethnic groups are smarter than others.

4. In preindustrial America, which of the following institutions was responsible for the education of children?
   a. the family
   b. the church
   c. the school
   d. all of the above

5. In *A Place Called School*, Goodlad reports that the quality of education in America:
   a. increases in high school
   b. decreases in high school
   c. remains about the same over the school years
   d. is rated *poor* by most students

6. Compared to twenty-five years ago, the cash value of a college degree is:
   a. about the same
   b. much higher
   c. slightly higher
   d. somewhat lower

7. Which theoretical view holds that one of the consequences of the school-ing revolution is to create an oversupply of trained personnel?
   a. structural functionalism
   b. conflict theory
   c. status competition
   d. sponsored mobility

8. Which sociologist concluded that *school brings little influence to bear on a child's achievement that is independent of his background and general social context*?
   a. James Coleman
   b. Christopher Hurn
   c. Michael Rutter
   d. Charles Silverman

9. The value of a college degree on the job market declined somewhat in the 1970s because of:
   a. the nationwide decline in SAT scores
   b. an increase in the numbers of students earning college degrees
   c. economic recession
   d. b and c

10. Studies of the impact of school integration show that:
    a. Racial integration has strong, positive effects on minority students.
    b. Racial integration has negative effects on white students.
    c. Economic integration has positive effects on minority students.
    d. Economic integration has no effect on white or minority students.

11. In 1986, the number of females graduating from college:
    a. was much less than males
    b. exceeded that of males
    c. stayed the same
    d. none of the above

12. A college education today:
    a. is essentially worthless
    b. guarantees upper-middle-class prosperity
    c. is considered a minimum and not sufficient for financial success
    d. has changed in value over the years
    e. c and d

13. In the People's Republic of China:
    a. Education planners try to further socialism.
    b. Individuality is emphasized greatly.

   c. Children are taught to place the needs of the state and the group above their own.

   d. a and c.

14. What contributed most to American schools taking on the function of socialization?

   a. industrialization

   b. immigration of foreign workers to American cities

   c. the knowledge revolution

   d. status competition

15. One criticism of Coleman's second report, in which he concluded that academic demands and stricter discipline in Catholic schools have a positive effect on school achievement, is that:

   a. He did not control for differences in student background.

   b. He paid too much attention to expenditures per pupil.

   c. He ignored intangible factors.

   d. He did not allow for the possibility that parents sending children to private school place a higher value on education than other parents.

16. One main difference between the American and Soviet school systems is:

   a. the American emphasis on achievement

   b. the Soviet use of sponsorship

   c. the emphasis on individual achievement in the United States and in group achievement in the U.S.S.R.

   d. the separation of work and study in the United States and the mixture of work and study in the U.S.S.R.

17. After comparing the socialization goals of lower- and middle-class parents, Kohn found that:

   a. Middle-class children are better prepared for advanced education.

   b. Lower-class children are culturally deprived.

   c. Middle-class parents encourage conformity.

   d. Lower-class parents encourage independence.

18. Vocational training in West Germany is considered:

   a. to be a dead end

   b. to be for those who will never be financial successes

   c. highly respected

   d. the domain of many German industries who wish to hire the students they have sponsored

   e. c and d

19. In the U.S. over ____ % of high school students enroll in college. In Great Britain, the number is ____ %.
    a. 40, 12
    b. 12, 40
    c. 90, 10
    d. 2, 4

20. Which of the following is not one of the three features that distinguishes Japanese schooling from American schooling?
    a. Each child is seen as a unique individual and his or her success is attributed to innate or inherited ability.
    b. All children are born equal.
    c. Academic achievement is the result of effort and persistence.
    d. There is no ceiling on achievement.

21. The low level of participation of working-class parents in their children's education demonstrates:
    a. that they don't value education
    b. that they don't attempt to motivate their children
    c. that middle-class parents are better equipped to meet teacher expectations than working-class parents
    d. none of the above

Answers

1. c: One of the functions of education is to verify that individuals have met certain standards. (See section entitled Schooling for Industrial Society.)
2. d: In Hurn's view, education has become a status symbol. Much as Americans used to compete with their neighbors over who owned the biggest car, so they compete over whose children have the most education. (Hurn is neutral on the question of whether the schooling revolution is functional.) (Schooling for Capitalism)
3. c: This is both a strength and a weakness of IQ tests. They are useful in predicting school performance but may obscure creativity, *street smarts,* subcultural knowledge, and other cognitive assets. (Schooling for Capitalism)
4. d: But the family (followed by the church) held primary responsibility for teaching values and skills; school was a luxury. (The Schooling Revolution: Three Interpretations)
5. b: Goodlad found that elementary school teachers are more likely to *humanize* education than are high school teachers (who fall back on lectures and standardized procedures). (Teacher Quality)
6. d: One reason is that the country experienced an economic recession at

about the same time as the huge *baby boom* generation began graduating from college. Thus there were more graduates and fewer jobs. (The Quality of Education)

7. b: According to conflict theory, the *capitalist elite* uses the education system to serve its own interests--in this case, being able to offer lower wages because there are more people seeking jobs than there are jobs available. (Schooling for Industrial Society)

8. a: This view was expressed in Coleman's early (mid-1960s) study; Rutter came to quite different conclusions. Coleman later amended his view, after comparing public and private (mostly Catholic) high school students. (Unequal Schooling)

9. d: The decline in the dollar value of a college degree in the 1970s was due to the *combination* of a boom in college degrees and a bust in new job opportunities. As the number of college graduates declines and employment opportunities in *knowledge* industries increase, this trend is reversing. (Status Competition and Credentials)

10. c: The best evidence indicates that economic integration has more impact than racial integration alone. One reason may be that poor children who attend predominantly white, middle-class schools learn more about educational opportunities and *payoffs* than they would in other schools. (Schooling and Equality)

11. b: There were 486,000 male college graduates in 1986, and 502,000 female college graduates. (Schooling for Industrial Society)

12. e: The value of a college degree has changed over the years so that it may now be considered a minimum requirement and does not insure success. (The Quality of Education)

13. d: China, as does the Soviet Union, attempts to further socialism through education, placing special emphasis on the needs of the group or the state. This is in direct contrast to the American system, which stresses individuality. (Education in the Soviet Union and China)

14. b: The early-twentieth-century movement to enroll all children in school reflected both a concern for immigrant children who roamed the streets while their parents worked and a distaste for foreign customs. (The Quality of Education)

15. d: But this does not detract from the finding that poor and minority students benefit from such schooling. (The Quality of Education)

16. c: *Collective socialization* begins the moment Soviet children enter school and intensifies as they grow older. (Education in the Soviet Union and China)

17. a: The reason, according to Kohn, is that middle-class parents want their children to be self-directed and independent-minded. (Schooling and Equality)

18. e: West Germans attach a great deal of importance to vocational education, and German industries are eager to hire the vocational students

they sponsor in the country's school system. (Education in Western Europe)

19. a: Over 40% of America's high school graduates enroll in college. In Great Britain, where until the late 1960s a system of sponsored mobility existed, only 12% of eighteen-year-olds are enrolled in universities. (Education in Western Europe)

20. a: The Japanese do not stress the unique individuality of children, as Americans do. They believe all children are born equal, and with hard work have no limits on what they may achieve. (Education in Japan)

21. c: In his study Lareau found that parents in the two communities saw education as equally important. Middle-class parents, however, were better equipped to meet teacher expectations because they view teachers as their intellectual equals. (The Home Environment)

MYTH OR FACT?

1. Although most do not graduate from college, a majority of American students today continue their educations beyond high school.   t/f

2. Illiteracy is a serious problem in developing nations but not in the United States.   t/f

3. International comparisons show that Americans are as well educated as any people on earth.   t/f

4. Standardized tests show that student achievement in the United States is declining steadily.   t/f

Answers

1. *True.* At the turn of the century, most American children completed only a few years of schooling. Today most young people have some college or vocational training beyond high school. The *schooling revolution* is an established fact.

2. *False.* Estimates are that 25 million Americans (more than the combined populations of New York City, Chicago, and Los Angeles) are totally illiterate, and 35 million more are functionally illiterate. The United States ranks a low forty-ninth in literacy among member nations of the United Nations.

3. *False.* In a comparison of student achievement in industrial nations, American youth did not rank first or second on any of nineteen measures, and came in last on seven of these measures.

4. *False.* Although achievement scores on a variety of tests did decline in the 1960s and 1970s, in the 1980s they seemed to level off. In particular, SAT scores have shown small but steady increases in the past several years.

CRITICAL THINKING

1. A recent study by the National Assessment of Educational Progress (NAEP) project (funded by Congress and carried out by the Educational Testing Service) found that writing skills decline between the fourth and eleventh grades (reported by Hechinger, 1986[1]). The study also found that interest in writing declines over the school years: 57 percent of fourth-graders but only 39 percent of eleventh-graders say they like to write. The researchers, professors Arthur N. Applebee and Judith A. Langer of Stanford University's School of Education, suggest a number of reasons why this might be so: High school teachers have to cope with as many as 150 students and so rarely have time to discuss writing with individual students; they are more likely to mark mistakes than to demonstrate interest in what students are writing; and school classes are chopped up into periods that are too short for effective writing. Do their conclusions support the ideals for quality education described in your text? From your own experience, can you cite other reasons why interest in writing declines in high school? As a teacher or high school principal, how might you reverse this trend? (If you like to write, can you explain why you *escaped* the usual pattern of decline?)

2. Another study by the NAEP found that, on the average, young adults (ages twenty-one to twenty-five) perform better on standardized reading tests than do seniors in high school! A *New York Times* educational correspondent comments:[2]

    This suggests that whatever happens after the students leave school does more for their reading skills than what happened in school. . . .
    Is it the motivation to learn something that suddenly is recognized as a necessity to getting and keeping a job? Is it on-the-job training? Is it the impact of a new set of peers who, in contrast to the adolescent peer culture that dominates the life in schools, stress the more serious aspects of real life? Is it an awakening of interests that may have been dormant when only grades rather than rewards of the adult world were at stake? (p. C13)

    This study raises interesting questions about education versus formal schooling. Does our society place too much emphasis on formal schooling, ignoring the role of informal education? What other studies in your text support this conclusion? (Hint: Review the discussion on Schooling and Equality)

3. In 1986, the Carnegie Foundation for the Advancement of Teaching issued a very pointed and critical report on higher education in America entitled

College: The Undergraduate Experience in America.[3] The report was based on a three-year study that included surveys of 5,000 college faculty members, 5,000 undergraduates, 1,000 college administrators, 1,000 high school students, and 1,000 parents. Their responses to questions were compared with those in surveys conducted in the late 1960s and the 1970s. Among other findings, the authors report (our own summary):

"Training and skills for an occupation" moved from the bottom to the top of the list of "essential" outcomes of a college education; "learning to get along with people" and "formulating values and goals for life" declined in importance.

In many classes, there is a mismatch between faculty and student goals. Faculty see their job as promoting scholarship, sharing ideas, and gaining appreciation from students for their own activities. Students are concerned primarily with grades, and rarely question a professor's assertions; vigorous discussion and debate are rare. Women outnumber men in many colleges, yet often are overshadowed by men in the classroom. They may turn in brilliant work and get high grades in exams, but seldom speak up in class. Not only do male students talk more, their opinions often carry more weight.

Students tend to see the library as a quiet place to study, not as a resource for independent study. Few students look up an original source cited in their textbooks or do additional reading unless required to do so.

Concern for physical well-being has increased, with many more students enrolling in health courses and fitness programs today than in the past. At the same time, alcohol and drug abuse are problems on most campuses.

Do you believe these findings apply to your college or university? How would you go about testing your perception versus the Carnegie report?

Notes

[1] F.M. Hechinger, Stubborn Pockets of Illiteracy, *The New York Times*: (December 16, 1986), pp. C1, C13.

[2] Hechinger, op. cit. Copyright 1986 by The New York Times Company. Reprinted by permission.

[3] The Carnegie Foundation for the Advancement of Teaching. *College: The Undergraduate Experience in America,* New York: Harper and Row, 1987.

Chapter Fourteen

RELIGION

OBJECTIVES

After reading Chapter Fourteen you should be able to give in-depth answers to the following questions:

1. What are the basic elements of religion?
2. What did Durkheim, Marx, and Weber see as the relationship between religion and society?
3. How are religions organized?
4. What role does religion play in contemporary society?
5. What is the status of religion in America today?
6. How has religion in America been restructured over the past four decades?

CONCEPTS

You should also understand the following sociological concepts:

religion
sacred
profane
belief
ritual
totem
established church
sect
denomination
cult
secularization
civil religion

CHAPTER REVIEW

I. What are the basic elements of religion?

Although the contents vary enormously, all societies have some form of religion--that is, an established set of beliefs and practices dealing with the ultimate meaning of life. Religion fills the gap between human aspirations and abilities; between social expectations and experiences; between the ambiguities of life and the need to understand.

Your text identifies four basic elements of religion. Religious beliefs are ideas about a divine or supernatural order that organize people's perceptions of events. Religious rituals are symbolic representations of beliefs and events that confirm this supernatural order. Subjective experiences are inner feelings that reveal or confirm one's faith. The fourth element of religion is a community of believers who share this faith.

II. What did Durkheim, Marx, and Weber see as the relationship between religion and society?

Durkheim, Marx, and Weber all saw religion as a social phenomenon that both reflects and influences the society in which it is found. But each drew different conclusions about the relationship between religious beliefs and social structure.

A. Durkheim began with the observation that all societies distinguish between the sacred (or holy) and the profane (or ordinary). In the simplest societies, people treat the totem that is associated with their clan with awe. The totem is a personification of the clan; in effect, they are worshipping society itself. Elaborating on this, Durkheim argued that religion gives concrete expression to our unconscious awareness of social forces. He went on to suggest that the function of religion in society is to establish a moral community and to reinforce social solidarity through community rituals. He held that if religions as we know them were to disappear, some *functional equivalent* would arise to replace them.

B. In contrast, Marx stressed the dysfunctions of religion. In an often-quoted passage, he characterized religion as *the opium of the people.* By this he meant that religion lulls the masses into inaction by preaching that existing social conditions are divinely ordained or that suffering in this world will be rewarded in the next. For Marx, religion is the epitome of alienation (or separation from self). Its function is to maintain the economic status quo.

C. Whereas Marx saw religion as an obstacle to social change, Weber saw it as an agent of social change. Weber began with a puzzle: Why were the leading capitalists of the day overwhelmingly Protestant? Why not Catholic (or Buddhist or Muslim)? He found an answer in the Calvinist phase of the Protestant Reformation. Calvin believed that the individual's fate in the hereafter was preordained but he did not advocate passive acceptance of whatever life brought. Rather he preached the redemptive value of work. The Protestant work ethic, with its peculiar combination of hard work and deferred gratification, was ideally suited to capitalism. Under Calvinism, investing in profit-making ventures became a moral duty. In this case, then, religion played a major, active role in social change.

The one point on which all of these theorists would agree is that the structure of religion and that of society are intertwined, even if they disagree on *how.*

III.   How are religions organized?

Religions are organizations as well as sets of beliefs. Your text identifies four distinct types of religious organizations: the established church, the sect, the denomination, and the cult. (Compare how your religious background fits with this particular categorization.)

A. An established church is a state religion. It supports and is supported by the existing social structure; it is accepted by most members of society as *the one true faith.* (Note that the term *church* applies to any state religion, Christian or non-Christian.)

B. A sect also claims to be the one true religion. But unlike an established church, it opposes the existing social structure and may withdraw from society or actively attack established social institutions.

C. A denomination is a religious organization that accepts the social order, and also accepts the existence and legitimacy of other religions. Unlike the established church and sect, it does not claim to hold the only key to salvation.

D. In everyday conversation the terms *sect* and *cult* are used interchangeably. Sociologists use the term *cult* to describe a loosely organized religion that opposes the existing social structure, but focuses on changing the individual rather than on changing society.

As this typology shows, the relationship between religion and social structure in modern societies is variable. The same religion may be a sect in one society, an established church or denomination in another. All religions must at some point face the dilemma of institutionalization. In becoming established (attracting members, creating symbols, developing organization, and so on), it may find that its original values and goals are distorted or abandoned.

IV.   What role does religion play in contemporary society?

Most sociologists agree that the trend in modern societies is toward secularization. But they disagree about what this means.

Some believe that religion is dying, that it has been reduced to the status of a hobby. Weber was one of the strongest critics of secularization. Although he approved of the rationalization of business, he deplored the application of cost-benefit analysis to things such as education and friendship. In his view, the decline of religion produced *specialists without spirit, sensualists without heart.*

Others argue that although religion is changing, it is not disappearing. Bellah, for example, sees the defining characteristic of modern religion as the emphasis on personal autonomy. People are less inclined to accept the teachings of their religion without question or to expect prayer to solve social problems. Bellah sees this as the product of religious evolution (from primitive to archaic, historic, and early modern religion). He also sees civil religion (the belief that a nation has a special relationship to God) as evidence of the continuing need for sacred symbols. Conversely, Robert Wuthnow sees civil religion in America as divided, with conservatives maintaining that the U.S. occupies a special place in the divine order, and liberals focusing more on humanity than the nation itself. Wuthnow contends that the presence of two competing civil religions has allowed the development of two more secular ideologies. These views are that science and technology will solve all social problems, and that the United States is *number one* because it is *great* and wealthy.

V.   What is the status of religion in America today?

For most of this century, participation in organized religion has grown steadily. America is considered one of the most religious nations in the industrial world. Interest in religion, however, is not evenly distributed through the population. Women, blacks, and Americans age fifty or older typically attend church more often than other members of the population. Married and widowed Americans are more active than those who are single or divorced. Catholics attend services more regularly than Protestants and Jews. Those least involved in religion are young adults aged eighteen to twenty-four.

Religion in the U.S. today is characterized by two apparently contradictory trends: A majority of Americans hold traditional religious beliefs, and many are members of churches or synagogues. However, less than 40% of those same persons polled said they attended services weekly. Many sociologists believe this to be the result of privatization of religion. Americans draw a distinction between their personal relationship with God and participation in a religious organization.

VI. How has religion in America been restructured over the past four decades?

Religious life in America has been seen to change since World War II. Robert Wuthnow, a sociologist who surveyed religious life in America over the past four decades, has concluded that the nature of religion has changed *radically.* In the 1940s, religion was primarily centered around neighborhood churches. People achieved a large part of their identities based on their membership in a religious denomination. Church and government had a relaxed, alliance-type relationship. By the 1980s, television ministry had become as important as the neighborhood church; people's identities were derived more from where they stood on social issues rather than their membership in a particular denomination; and religion had become an outspoken voice in American politics.

Religion in America today, according to Wuthnow, is polarized. Boundaries between denominations have been blurred as members of many different religions routinely join forces in opposition or support of social issues.

Religion has become issue-oriented and as a result of is often at the forefront of political debates.

CONCEPT REVIEW

Match each of the following terms with the correct definition:

a. cult
b. ritual
c. secularization
d. totem
e. religion
f. denomination

g. established church
h. belief
i. civil religion
j. profane
k. sect
l. sacred

1.___ A conviction that cannot be proved or disproved by ordinary means.
2.___ A set of beliefs, rituals, and symbols that define a nation's special relationship to God.
3.___ Ordinary, everyday things that may be treated casually.
4.___ That which is holy, inspires awe, and must be treated with respect.
5.___ A religious organization that asserts its unique legitimacy and stands apart from society.
6.___ A set of institutionalized beliefs and practices that deal with the ultimate meaning of life.
7.___ A religious organization that claims unique legitimacy and has a positive relationship to society.
8.___ A sacred emblem that members of a group or clan treat with reverence and awe.
9.___ The removal of religious control over social institutions and individual behavior.
10.___ A religious organization that does not accept the legitimacy of other religions, and, additionally, has a negative relationship to society.
11.___ A formalized, stylized, behavioral enactment of religious beliefs.
12.___ A religious organization that accepts the legitimacy of other

religions and has a positive relationship with the society in which it exists.

Answers

1.	h	7.	g
2.	i	8.	d
3.	j	9.	c
4.	l	10.	a
5.	k	11.	b
6.	e	12.	f

REVIEW QUESTIONS

1. Sociologists who study religion analyze:
   a. the validity of different religious beliefs and practices
   b. the personal benefits individuals derive from religion
   c. the organization of religion and its relationship to society
   d. the history of religion

2. Which of the following theorists saw religion as an agent of social change?
   a. Durkheim
   b. Marx
   c. Weber
   d. none of the above

3. Which of the following religions is gaining members in the U.S. today?
   a. mainline Protestant
   b. fundamentalist and evangelical Protestant
   c. Roman Catholic
   d. all of the above
   e. a and b
   f. b and c

4. Religious beliefs differ from other kinds of beliefs in that they:
   a. deal with intangibles
   b. attempt to explain the meaning of life
   c. influence and are influenced by the society in which the religion is found
   d. are based on faith in things that cannot be proved or disproved by ordinary means

5. In what place and time would the Roman Catholic Church be classified as

a denomination?
a. The Roman Empire
b. medieval Europe
c. the United States today
d. Italy today

6. Durkheim maintained that all societies:
a. have some form of totem
b. distinguish between the sacred and the profane
c. worship in the same ways
d. hold primitive beliefs about social forces

7. The average age at which a person typically joins a cult is _____ and the length of membership is ___.
a. 15, 4 years
b. 35, 2 months
c. 20, 2 years
d. 40, 5 years

8. Weber held that the Protestant work ethic:
a. was responsible for the rise of capitalism
b. contributed to the rise of capitalism
c. was a by-product of the rise of capitalism
d. disproved Marx's economic view of history

9. The main difference between a sect and a cult is that:
a. A sect accepts the existing social order.
b. A cult accepts the existing social order.
c. A sect accepts the legitimacy of other religions.
d. A cult focuses on individual salvation rather than on social change.

10. Robert Wuthnow contends that:
a. Civil religion in America is divided.
b. The U.S. has one unified civil religion.
c. The presence of two competing civil religions has opened the door for other materialistic ideologies.
d. None of the above.
e. a and c.

11. _____ out of 4 Americans is/are members of a church, or have attended services in the last six months.
a. One
b. Two
c. Three

    d. cannot be determined

12. Which of the following theorists saw contemporary religion as the ultimate cause of alienation?
    a. Durkheim
    b. Marx
    c. Weber
    d. Bellah

13. In seeking to establish itself, a religion may admit members with mixed
motivations. This illustrates:
    a. the dilemmas of institutionalization
    b. secularization
    c. the dysfunctions of religion
    d. all of the above

14. Which of the following comes closest to Durkheim's notion of a *functional equivalent* to religion?
    a. archaic religion
    b. fundamentalism
    c. totemic religion
    d. civil religion
    e. denominations

15. During the past few decades, religion:
    a. has become an institution in retreat
    b. has become more active
    c. is often in the forefront of political debates
    d. b and c
    e. none of the above

16. Who called religion *the opium of the people?*
    a. Weber
    b. Marx
    c. Durkheim
    d. Bellah

17. All religions share one of the following characteristics. Which one?
    a. a quest for visions and mystical experiences
    b. rituals that symbolize beliefs
    c. a belief in spirits
    d. a belief in God

18. One example of secularization is:

a. religious sponsorship of political campaigns and social movements (such as the *right-to-life* movement)
b. an ecumenical council whose members are meeting to debate the issue of nuclear freeze
c. the ruling against prayers in public schools
d. TV evangelism

19. When the Puritans rebelled against the pomp and ceremony of the Anglican Church and set sail for the New World to found a *society of saints,* they were:
a. an established church
b. a sect
c. a denomination
d. a cult

20. Although it would be an exaggeration to say that the United States is experiencing a religious revival, the 1980s did see an increase in:
a. church attendance
b. belief in God
c. agreement that religion is very important
d. cult membership

21. Which of the following religions is *not* an established church in the sociological sense of the word?
a. the Anglican Church in Elizabethan England
b. the Anglican Church in Britain today
c. the Shiite Muslims in Iran
d. Judaism in Israel
e. d and c

22. Who saw the spread of rationalization and the decline of religion in modern societies as confining human beings to an *iron cage* and reducing love and marriage to *mundane passions*?
a. Durkheim
b. Marx
c. Weber
d. Bellah

Answers

1. c: Sociologists study the social dynamics of religion.They do not study the psychology or theology. (They may research the history of a religion, but their focus is on social institutions.) (See first page of Chapter 14.)

2. c: Weber's prime example was the Protestant Reformation, as linked to the establishment of the work ethic and the spread of capitalism. (Religion and Society: Three Views)

3. f: The Roman Catholic Church, fundamentalist groups, and *new* religions have gained members. (Religion in the U.S.: An Overview)

4. d: People may believe in God and also in modern medicine, sociological analysis, and the wisdom of Plato. The difference between religious and other beliefs is that the latter can be proved or disproved by observation or logic. Faith is, by definition, belief without question. (The Elements of Religion)

5. c: A denomination is a religious organization that is not affiliated with the state and coexists with other religions. (Although Italy is not a religious state per se, the overwhelming majority of the population is Catholic and the Catholic Church influences most areas of public and private life.) (Types of Religious Organizations)

6. b: Religious beliefs and practices may vary, but the idea that some things (objects, places, people, days) are holy and should be treated with reverence is universal. The question for Durkheim was *why?* The answer was that religion functions to create and maintain a moral community. (The Sacred, the Profane, and the Collective)

7. c: The average age at which a person joins a cult is twenty. The average length of membership is less than two years. Thus, participation in unconventional religions is considered to be a temporary youthful phenomenon. (Box: Cults or Legitimate Religions?)

8. b: Weber saw the Protestant work ethic as one of many factors in the rise of capitalism. His goal was not to prove Marx wrong, but to show that one-dimensional explanations of social change are simplistic. (Religion and Society: Three Views)

9. d: Cults are more loosely organized, more transient, and more individualistic than sects. They focus on the salvation of the individual cult members. (Types of Religious Organizations)

10. e: Wuthnow holds that civil religion in America is divided between conservatives who believe the U.S. occupies a special place in the divine order and emphasize capitalism and the free enterprise system, and liberals who focus less on the nation and more on humanity in general. This division has led to the development of two views: the first, that technology can solve all problems, and the second that America is a *great* nation. (Civil Religion)

11. c: Three out of four Americans report that they are *churched*; that they are members of a church or have attended services in the last six months. (Religion in the U.S.: An Overview)

12. b: Where Durkheim held that religion reduces alienation by linking individuals to a moral community. Marx argued that religion creates alienation by denying that human beings are responsible for social

injustices. (Religion and Society: Three Views)

13. a: The original members of a religion may be wholeheartedly dedicated to its values, beliefs, and practices. If it seeks to expand, however, a religion may have to admit members who are as interested in making social contacts, in gaining prestige, or in some other personal ambition as they are in the religion itself. (The Dilemmas of Institutionalization)

14. d: This term applies to peoples who treat their national heroes and holidays as sacred and believe that their country has a special relationship to God (or the gods). Communism or another political ideology might also serve as a functional equivalent for religion. (Civil Religion)

15. d: During the past few decades, religion has become polarized. As a result, it is often at the forefront of political debates and has become quite active in social issues as well. (Religion in America Today)

16. b: Marx held that religion supports the existing system of social stratification by declaring that all life follows a divine plan, denying the role humans play in social institutions, and thus, lulling the masses into passive acceptance of the status quo. (Religion and Society: Three Views)

17. b: All religions use rituals to recall and reinforce sacred beliefs. The other answers apply to some, but not all, religions. (The Elements of Religion)

18. c: Secularization refers not to the involvement of religion in public affairs, but to the reverse--removing religion from public affairs (in this case, education). (The Dilemmas of Institutionalization)

19. b: In rejecting the Church of England, the Puritans were a sect. Once they arrived in the New World and established their own communities, however, they became a church. (Types of Religious Organizations)

20. c: Oddly, the percentage of people who say religion is very important has increased in recent years, but church attendance has not. (Religion in the U.S.: An Overview)

21. b: The Anglican Church in England today is best described as a denomination. (Recall that the term *church* is not restricted to Christian religious organizations.) (Types of Religious Organizations)

22. c: Durkheim, who believed that religion was functional, might have agreed with Weber; Marx, who saw religion as dysfunctional, would have strongly disagreed. (Religion and Society: Three Views)

MYTH OR FACT?

1. The United States is the only Western nation that has never had a state religion.   t/f

2. Church membership is higher today than ever before in

U.S. history.   t/f

3. Americans are among the most secular people in the
    world.   t/f

Answers

1. *True.* The history of Europe is in large part the history of struggles
    between established state churches and challenging religions, or sects.
2. *True.* The best available statistics indicate that only 16 percent of
    the U.S. population belonged to religious congregations in 1850; 36 per-
    cent in 1900; and 49 percent in 1940 (still a minority of the popula-
    tion). Today over 60 percent of Americans are church or temple members.
3. *False.* Many more Americans than Canadians, Italians, British, French,
    or Japanese say they believe in God. A majority also say that they be-
    lieve in the power of prayer, in a life after death, and in the Bible.
    America thus seems to be among the most religious of the industrial
    nations.

CRITICAL THINKING

1. In *The Secular City,* Harvey Cox argued that religion is disappear-
    ing: "For some, religion provides a hobby, for others a mark of national
    or ethnic identity, for others still an esthetic delight. For fewer and
    fewer does it provide an inclusive and commanding system of personal and
    cosmic values and explanations."[1] Do you agree or disagree with Cox?
    What evidence in your text would you cite to support your view?

2. Reread the description of the rise and fall of the People's Temple in
    Chapter Eight of your text. Would you characterize the People's Temple as
    a church, a denomination, a sect, or a cult? Why? How does the tragic
    story of this religious group illustrate the ways in which the functions
    of religion--consolation, authoritative answers to the meaning of life,
    social control, prophecy, identity, and maturation--can become dysfunc-
    tions?

3. Unconventional religions come in "all shapes and sizes," ranging from the
    Church of Scientology, which claims a world membership of 5.4 million, to
    a group in New Mexico who call themselves Druids and number less than
    forty members. Your text puts these religions in historical perspective.
    But it does not address the question of why people join these groups,
    especially those groups which require individuals to give up former as-
    sociations and activities and to devote themselves entirely to their new
    religion.

The sociologists John Lofland and Rodney Stark have identified seven steps in the conversion process. (1) Preconverts are in a state of tension. The circumstances in which they find themselves do not fit their expectations. They feel that their problems are acute. (2) Those not susceptible to conversion tend to explain their problems in either psychiatric or political terms. When they face seemingly insoluble problems, they see themselves as victims of their psychic backgrounds or as victims of the system. Preconverts, in contrast, tend to impose religious meanings on events. (3) Preconverts come to see themselves as religious seekers. Some go from church to church looking for answers. (4) Preconverts have reached something they see as a turning point in their life. Many have recently moved; lost or quit a job; graduated from, failed in, or dropped out of school (usually college). (5) Most become friends with members of a sect and develop emotional bonds with individuals before they consider conversion. (6) Most have few, if any, intimate friends with whom they might discuss their problems or religious thoughts. Often no one knows they are thinking about conversion. (7) Verbal conversion (outwardly agreeing with what members of the sect say) does not necessarily lead to total conversion. Preconverts become true converts after intense and prolonged interaction with committed members of the sect. Constant exposure to the sect's world-view, plus group support, enable and encourage the preconvert to reorganize his or her thoughts and life.[2]

Try substituting a radical political group for the unconventional religion in the preceding paragraph. Do you see how the seven steps of conversion might lead to political activism? Try substituting psychoanalysis or est. Do you know anyone who is committed to either of these? How is conversion to a political ideology, a group like est, or psychoanalysis like religious conversion? How do they differ?

Notes

[1] Harvey Cox, *The Secular City,* New York: Macmillan, 1966, p. 3.

[2] John Lofland and Rodney Stark, Becoming a World-Saver: A Theory of Conversion to a Deviant Perspective, *American Sociological Review* 30: (1965), pp. 865-875.

Chapter Fifteen

POLITICS

OBJECTIVES

After reading Chapter Fifteen you should be able to give in-depth answers to the following questions:

1. What led to the emergence of states?
2. What is distinctive about modern states?
3. Do political realities in the United States today match our democratic ideals?
4. How has warfare changed?

CONCEPTS
You should also understand the following sociological concepts:

politics
state
power
authority
traditional authority
charismatic authority
rational-legal authority
welfare state
minimal state
democracy
political party
interest group
political action committee (PAC)
protest movement
war
military-industrial complex

CHAPTER REVIEW

I. **What led to the emergence of states?**

Politics exists in every society we have studied, even in *headless* societies without a ruler, like the Tallensi, as unusual as that society may seem. The appearance and emergence of nation-states, with specialized institutions for distributing power, is a relatively recent development. Your text traces the emergence of states, and then looks at the underlying changes in the source of political authority.

A. The first stage in the development of states was the separation of the office of king from the person who was king. But kingdoms were loose alliances of principalities, not nations in the modern sense of the word. The second stage in the development of states involved the drawing of national boundaries and creation of public bureaucracies. In Europe, these developments occurred because the expansion of capitalism made rules based on traditional loyalties obsolete.

B. The development of states depends on the separation of the public and private spheres and the emergence of a new type of authority. Traditional authority (based on custom) and charismatic authority (based on personal leadership qualities) must give way to rational-legal authority (based on loyalty to a political system and a body of laws).

II.   What is distinctive about modern states?

In the Western world, the development of states spanned the sixteenth to nineteenth centuries. During this period, the role of the state was seen as protecting national boundaries and maintaining internal law and order. In the twentieth century, states began to manage a variety of collective goods, leading to the creation of welfare states.

A. In welfare states, the government assumes responsibility for individual well-being (helping those who cannot provide for themselves) and for the economy as a whole (protecting and regulating business). As a result, the size and scope of the government increase dramatically. (The opposite of a welfare state is a minimal state.)

B. Welfare states developed in all Western nations in the twentieth century. But in the United States (and elsewhere), the continued expansion of the welfare state has been challenged (particularly in the 1980s), with the conservatives of the nation gaining control of the White House and, for a period of time, the Senate.

III.   Do political realities in the United States today match our democratic ideals?

Your text compared political ideals and political realities. If you are unsure of the difference, go back to the text for a review.

A. American political institutions are based on an ideal democracy. Americans believe, first, in the rights of the individual. Our Constitution and many of our laws are designed to protect the individual from tyranny or exploitation. Second, we believe that the authority of the government rests on the consent of the governed. The government exists to *serve the people* --not vice versa. Third, we believe in both majority rule and minority rights. The majority does not have the right to oppress minorities. Finally, we believe in equality of opportunity. Each person should have an equal chance in life. The major change in political ideals in this century has been in the expansion of the definition of citizens' rights, not only at the national level, but at other levels as well.

B. Today's political realities depart from political ideals in a number of ways. (1) Voter apathy: One in four Americans who are eligible to vote do not register, and almost half of those who register do not vote, even for a presidential election. (2) Party politics: Political parties in the United States do not have the power, organization, or ideological distinctiveness of those in Europe. Although Americans usually vote along social-class lines, there are many crossovers on the basis of specific issues. (3) Interest groups and PACs: The decline in party politics in the United States has been met by an increase in the number and influence of special-interest groups and PACs (political action committees, committees that raise funds for particular candidates). (4) Protest movements: Since the 1960s, organized civil disobedience has become a common, accepted way of influencing government policies and decisions, at all levels. In 1989, protest movements became a major force in the world's communist countries, beginning in China (although unsuccessful there) and spreading with great success throughout Eastern Europe, as a reading of a daily newspaper would demonstrate. In fact, events moved at such a rapid pace that most of the country's leading political analysts were baffled.

IV. How has warfare changed?

Your text shows how the history of the state and the history of war are intertwined. This should assist you in placing conflict within a context you may not have considered previously.

A. In tribal societies, comparative research has shown that war is unknown; conflict is limited to *showdowns* and feuds. Agrarian states were the first societies we know of to use violence to conquer new territories and populations.

B. The first wars were quarrels among rulers and were fought by professional soldiers; ordinary citizens were mere observers. The rise of modern national states (plus new technologies for killing) led to new, more *popular* and more deadly forms of war. In revolutions, patriots use guerilla tactics against the state army. A series of largely bloodless revolutions occurred in Eastern Europe during 1989. They accomplished sweeping political change. In total wars, the entire citizen bodies of opposing nations are mobilized.

C. Although World War II was the last total war, many of the military institutions created during that war remain intact. The major issues for the military today are leadership, motivation, and discipline; the major issues for the public are the cost of the continuing arms race and the threat of nuclear war.

CONCEPT REVIEW

Match each of the following terms with the correct definition.

a. political party
b. authority ✓
c. minimal state
d. war
e. state
f. democracy
g. interest group
h. welfare state ✓
i. political action committee (PAC) ✓
j. rational-legal authority ✓
k. power ✓
l. protest movement
m. charismatic authority
n. politics
o. military-industrial complex ✓
p. traditional authority

1.___ The ability to control what other individuals and groups do, regardless of their wishes.
2.___ A collectivity organized to gain and hold legitimate control of government.
3.___ Authority that is based on and limited by custom, rather than on formalized sets of rules which are written.
4.___ The institutions and organizations that have a monopoly over the use of force in a given territory.
5._i_ An organization formed to collect small contributions from large numbers of people for a political candidate or cause in order to promote an issue.
6._d_ The use of killing by one community to force another community to do its bidding.
7._o_ The web of common interests among high officials in the Pentagon and defense industries.
8.___ Authority based on exceptional personal qualities.
9.___ A political system based on popular participation in the decision-making process, or rule by the people.
10.___ The process whereby people gain, use, or lose power.
11.___ A state in which the government tries to ensure the well-being of citizens by taking over activities once considered the responsibility of the family and the local community.
12.___ A state in which the government does no more than is absolutely necessary to maintain national autonomy and internal order.

13.___ Power that depends on the recognition that a person has a legitimate right to make certain types of decisions for others.

14.___ A group organized to pressure public officials to make decisions that will benefit its members or promote a cause.

15.___ A grass-roots effort to change established policies and practices.

16.___ Authority that is based on and limited by a formal system of rules or laws.

Answers

1. k	7. o	13. b
2. a	8. m	14. g
3. p	9. f	15. l
4. e	10. n	16. j
5. i	11. h	
6. d	12. c	

REVIEW QUESTIONS

1. Which of the following illustrates the exercise of authority as your text defines the term?
   a. A father gives his son a sound beating when he learns the boy stole candy from a local store
   b. A group of protestors holds a sit-in to block construction of a nuclear power plant.
   c. The Vietnamese army assists the government of Cambodia in suppressing rebellions.
   d. The president of a company fires an employee whom he dislikes.

2. Which of the following have Americans added to their list of democratic ideals in recent years?
   a. the pursuit of life, liberty, and happiness
   b. equality of opportunity
   c. the right of minorities to be protected from the majority
   d. the right to Social Security
   e. all of the above

3. The lobbyist's main weapon is:
   a. bribes
   b. illegal campaign contributions
   c. expert information
   d. false information
   e. all of the above

4. The Americans who have demonstrated against the construction of nuclear power plants are best described as:
   a. a political party
   b. an interest group
   c. a protest movement
   d. a strategic elite

5. Which of the following forms of political participation has increased the most in recent years?
   a. voting
   b. membership in political parties
   c. lobbying
   d. protest movements

6. About what percentage of registered voters went to the polls in the 1988 presidential election?
   a. 40 percent
   b. 50 percent
   c. 60 percent
   d. 70 percent
   e. 80 percent

7. One of the differences between political parties in Western Europe and the Democratic and Republican parties in the United States is that:
   a. European parties tend to avoid taking strong ideological positions.
   b. The Republican and Democratic parties are aligned with social classes.
   c. The Republican and Democratic parties exercise strict control over members' votes in Congress.
   d. In Western Europe, the *party* selects the head of state.

8. Mahatma Gandhi never held political office in India. But he led that nation's struggle against British colonial control of that country and is widely regarded as the father of modern India. Which type of authority did Gandhi exercise?
   a. traditional
   b. rational-legal
   c. charismatic
   d. religious
   e. political

9. The phrase *headless society* refers to:
   a. a society in which there are no politics
   b. a society in which there are no specialized political institutions
   c. a society in which leadership is based on rational-legal authority

    d. a society without a king

10. Studies of American voters indicate that they:
    a. do not vote along social-class lines
    b. do not vote along party lines
    c. cross party and social-class lines on particular issues
    d. are more likely to vote in local than in presidential elections

11. The difference between protest movements and PACs is that protest movements:
    a. challenge existing policies
    b. mobilize previously uncommitted citizens
    c. raise funds for a candidate or cause
    d. employ civil disobedience to further their goals

12. The major difference between total wars and other forms of warfare is:
    a. mass mobilization
    b. the use of guerilla tactics (especially troop dispersal)
    c. high rates of civilian casualties
    d. all of the above

13. A key factor in the rise of nation-states was:
    a. the decline of kingships
    b. the concept of citizens' rights
    c. the creation of public bureaucracies
    d. total wars

14. Which of the following was *not* a tenet of Reagan's economic policy, supply-side economics?
    a. Tax cuts free up private wealth for investment.
    b. Government should make it attractive for businesses to expand.
    c. Raising taxes provides more money to the poor, thus lowering unemployment.
    d. Government spending should be reduced.

15. Television reports about whether a candidate is doing poorly or well:
    a. have little effect on the candidate's campaign
    b. affect the candidate's ability to attract campaign funds
    c. affect the candidate's ability to put ideals before the public through television advertisements
    d. none of the above
    e. b and c

16. The rise of nation-states in Europe took place in:

a. the sixteenth century
b. the seventeenth century
c. the eighteenth century
d. the sixteenth through the eighteenth centuries

17. The state has a monopoly over the legitimate use of force in a territory. This monopoly depends on:
a. acceptance by citizens
b. acceptance by citizens and other states
c. rational-legal authority
d. coercion

18. In modern wars, troops are dispersed. Studies of soldiers in combat situations show that a major problem is:
a. desertion
b. disobeying orders
c. lack of training for sophisticated equipment
d. unwillingness to kill

19. Which of the following is *not* an Eastern European nation which recently had a revolution overthrowing its communist government?
a. Albania
b. Poland
c. Hungary
d. Czechoslovakia

20. Since World War II, the U.S. has spent ___ dollars on the arms race.
a. 3 million
b. 5 billion
c. 25 billion
d. 17 trillion

Answers

1. d: Authority is not confined to the political arena. In our economic system, a boss has the legitimate right to hire and fire employees (unless there is a union contract or the decision is based on race, sex, or age). (See section entitled Power, Authority, and Legitimacy.)
2. d: The idea that the federal government bears some responsibility for the physical and mental well-being of citizens is a comparatively new one. (The Modern State)
3. c: Although some political persuaders undoubtedly do attempt (sometimes successfully) to bribe public officials, make illegal or quasi-legal

campaign contributions, and plant false information, in the long run, these actions can hurt the lobbyist as well as the officials. (Interest Groups and PACs)

4. c: The difference between an interest group and a protest movement is that the former is an organized group designed to promote special interests and the latter is a grass-roots movement aimed at challenging existing politics and practices. (Protest Movements)

5. d: Voting and membership in political parties have declined in recent years; lobbies have long been unofficial participants in the political scene. (American Democracy)

6. b: About 25 percent of eligible Americans register to vote. A third of eligible voters vote in nonpresidential elections. The 1988 presidential election in which George Bush defeated Michael Dukakis had the lowest voter turnout in sixty-four years. (American Democracy)

7. d: Under parliamentary systems, the party that wins a majority in an election chooses the prime minister. There are no primary elections as in the United States, and the people do not vote directly for their head of state. (Party Politics)

8. c: Like other charismatic leaders, from Jesus to Mao, Gandhi was regarded as a saint by many of his followers. (Power, Authority, and Legitimacy)

9. b: In *headless societies,* there is no formal government and the public and private spheres of life are merged. (Headless societies do not have kings, but neither do democracies or workers' states). (Introduction)

10. c: Party loyalties based on social class have weakened, but they have not disappeared. Working-class Americans usually vote for Democrats and upper-class Americans for Republicans, but many cross these lines to vote for a particular candidate or for a particular issue. (See first page of Chapter 15)

11. d: All of the other answers apply to both protest movements and PACs. (Interest Groups and PACs)

12. c: World Wars I and II are called *total wars* because killing was not confined to professional soldiers on the battlefield. Civilians produced the means of war, and died when cities, factories, and supply routes were bombed. (Modern Warfare and the Nation-State)

13. c: The creation of public bureaucracies was a necessary ingredient in the rise of nation-states; the concepts of citizens' rights, decline of monarchies, and total wars were more a consequence than a cause of the emergence of nation-states. (The Rise of the State)

14. c: Supply-side economics calls for tax cuts only. By cutting taxes, it is believed that businesses will expand, more jobs will be created, and unemployment will drop. (Beyond the Welfare State)

15. e: A candidate's positions are in effect reduced to slogans by the media.

The media's perception of a candidate's campaign seriously affects that candidate's ability to attract campaign funds and successfully advertise. (Media Politics)

16. d: We included this question to remind you that the history of nation-states in your text is a condensed version, summarizing developments that spanned centuries. (The Rise of the State)

17. b: A state cannot maintain itself through coercion alone; all states depend on some degree of consent by the governed, however grudgingly. The continued existence of a state also depends on recognition by other nations. Westerners tend to see a rational-legal system of government as the only legitimate source of authority; other peoples see tradition and/or charisma as a legitimate source of authority. (Power)

18. d: According to one study, 85 percent of infantrymen do not shoot, even when their own position is under attack. This surprising finding led to Marine Corps programs designed to overcome the inhibition against killing--in effect, *desocialization* programs. (War and Revolution Since World War II)

19. a: Although revolutions spread rapidly throughout Eastern Europe after events in Poland and Hungary, some communist countries remained isolated and have not experienced any dramatic change. Albania was successful in preventing revolution by strictly monitoring its mass media and persons entering the country. (Box on Eastern Europe)

20. d: The U.S. has spent over $17 trillion on the global arms race. That's about 1.9 million dollars every minute. (The Nuclear Arms Race)

MYTH OR FACT?

1. Many fewer Americans than Western Europeans exercise their right to vote. t/f
2. It is illegal for a lobbyist to draft a speech for a senator or to offer the head of a government agency a free ride on a private plane. t/f
3. The United States, the Soviet Union, and their NATO and Warsaw Pact allies have accounted for 25 percent of global military expenditures since 1960. t/f
4. Those who benefit most from a welfare state are the poor. t/f

Answers

1. *True.* Approximately 80-90 percent of Western Europeans regularly turn out for elections. Only about 50 percent of registered voters turned out for the 1988 presidential election in the United States, and only about a

third of eligible voters turn out for other nonpresidential elections.

2. *False.* The freedom to petition the government is guaranteed in the Constitution. There is nothing illegal about any citizen offering an official information or personal favors. Professional lobbyists are required to register with Congress. (Few do register; the law is full of loopholes.)

3. *False.* The United States, the Soviet Union, and their respective *allies* have accounted for more than 82 percent of global military expenditures since 1960.

4. *False.* The welfare state is designed to protect businesses as well as individuals. Moreover, most recipients of social welfare programs are middle class (especially Social Security recipients and veterans).

CRITICAL THINKING

1. The purpose of terrorism is to perpetrate acts so heinous as to instill in others a feeling of profound terror. This terror then is intended to intimidate and influence others to cause some action or take new action. It is critical to note that terrorism should be defined by the nature of the act rather than by the identity of the perpetrators. Studying terrorism objectively is difficult simply because one person's terrorist is another's hero. For example, based on the preceding definition, both the Boston Tea Party and United State's act of shooting down an Iranian Airlines passenger jet (in July 1988) may be considered terrorist acts. In *Theater of Terror,*[1] social scientists Jeffery Rubin and Nehemia Friedland analyze the media's role in international politics.

> Down go the house lights, up goes the curtain, and then--BANG. The stage becomes alive with the sounds, the lights and the characters of a highly dramatic performance. The actors are political terrorists. They are the protagonists of much modern tragedy, and their theater is the globe.
> Terrorists may explode on the scene in Teheran, Beirut or Latin American (more recently, even in Scotland), but they soon take the show on the road via television or transport technology [i.e. hijacking a jet]. . . . For today's terrorists, all the world is indeed a stage. And that may be an apt metaphor to help us come to grips with and perhaps devise methods of dealing with political terrorism. (p.18)

Terrorist attacks are not random. The drama begins with an act designed to capture the attention of the audience (for example, a hijacking). Having gained center stage, the terrorists must develop a dramatic theme or message (communicate their political goals via a set of demands). They must also deliver a convincing performance (too often, killing one hostage to prove they "mean business"). This drama is not performed for the benefit of the hostages, or even the government of the target country; terrorists seek a world audience. To reach this large, diverse public, they need the mass media. Rubin and Friedland state:

> In terrorist situations, media personnel are a bit like drama critics who convey information to a group much larger than the immediate theater audience. Terrorists usually do all they can to make sure television, radio and newspaper people tell about the event in sufficient detail, emphasis and color to attract and hold the audience's attention.
> The media are important to terrorists because they not only relay information, but like good drama critics, interpret it as well. The slant they give--by deciding which events to report and which to ignore, by intentionally or unintentionally expressing approval or disapproval--can create a climate of public support, apathy or anger. (p. 24)

Meanwhile, the other actor in the drama, the government of the target country, responds by stalling, to test the credibility of terrorist threats. If the threats seem credible, the target government will attempt behind-the-scenes negotiations, explore the feasibility of using force, or both. In act three, the target government either concedes to one or more terrorist demands or counterattacks. The danger with either move is that the target government will lose face.

Rubin and Friedland hold that the terrorist theater metaphor suggests constructive ways of handling such situations. Terrorist demands are taken too literally. Terrorists seek "influence beyond their actual means or strength" (p. 18). Underlying specific demands is a cry for recognition. If target governments and world organizations would acknowledge the legitimacy of their claims, terrorism might be reduced. The media could assist by granting such groups prime-time coverage, appearances on *Meet the Press*, and the like. Target governments seek security. Often this can be accomplished only through behind-the-scenes negotiations (as when Syrian President Assad arranged a face-saving formula whereby Israel released political prisoners after hostages on a TWA jet were set free). Here, too, the media can help by not exposing negotiations. When a terrorist drama has begun, the media might act as go-betweens, extracting concessions in exchange for air time. (Rubin and Friedland hold that banning coverage of terrorist incidents might backfire, provoking deadlier acts, such as poisoning a city's water supply, to attract attention.)

206 PART FOUR: THE CHANGING SHAPE OF SOCIETY

Do you agree with Rubin and Friedland's analysis? Can you suggest other ways to make the terrorist drama more predictable and less deadly?

2. In December 1986, thousands of Chinese university students took to the streets protesting bad food, poor housing, rising fees, and bureaucracy, and calling for greater freedom of expression. Mass demonstrations took place again in the spring of 1989. This second wave of protests began on April 16 when students gathered to mourn the death of Former Communist Party General Secretary, Hu Yaobung. At their height in June, over a million persons (students and civilians) were participating. The demonstrations were abruptly halted when Chinese army troops, under the direction of leader Xia Deng, opened fire on the protestors, killing an estimated 5,000. Tiannemen Square, where the protest movement and subsequent massacre took place, was closed off and martial law was imposed on the country. We tend to associate student protest with Western democracies. In fact, this form of political activism has a long history in China as well. Although not successful in that country, student protest movements for democracy in Eastern Europe have had amazing results. How do the protests in China and Eastern Europe compare with those in the U.S. in regard to their political scope, i.e., objectives?

Notes

[1] J. Z. Rubin and N. Friedland, Theater of Terror, *Psychology Today* (March 1986), pp. 18-28. Reprinted with permission from Psychology Today, Magazine. Copyright 1986 (APA).

Chapter Sixteen

TECHNOLOGY, WORK, AND THE ECONOMY

OBJECTIVES

After reading Chapter Sixteen you should be able to give in-depth answers to the following questions:

1. What are the distinguishing features of a capitalist economy?
2. How has the social structure of capitalism in the U.S. changed?
3. How have the nature and meaning of work changed?
4. How has the computer facilitated U.S. evolvement into an *information society*?
5. What is the nature of today's global economy?

CONCEPTS

You should also understand the following sociological concepts:

capitalist economy
command economy
corporation
monopoly
oligopoly
conglomerate
multinational corporation
infrastructure
service economy
productivity
automation

CHAPTER REVIEW

I. What are the distinguishing features of a capitalist economy?

In a capitalist economy, private ownership of property is viewed as a sacred right. The means of production--mines, farms, factories, investment capital--are controlled by individuals. Moreover, personal success is defined largely in terms of property or wealth. The driving force in a capitalist economy is the profit motive. To increase their personal wealth, business owners strive to identify what consumers need and want and to produce better products at lower prices. Capitalist ideology holds that this benefits not only successful entrepreneurs, but also society as a whole. The restraining force in a capitalist economy is free competition on an open market. Production is governed by the laws of supply and demand.

The opposite of a capitalist economy is the command economy found in socialist and communist nations, in which the means of production are owned by the state, economic activities are centrally planned, and the state guarantees that individuals' needs will be met.

In practice, no economy is purely capitalistic or communistic, but contains elements of both types.

II. How has the social structure of capitalism in the United States changed?

Your text explains how increases in the scale and complexity of production (illustrated by railroads) led to changes in economic institutions, including: the rise of corporations, increased government regulation, and the emergence of multinational corporations.

A. Corporations differ from privately owned businesses in three ways: the individuals who own or work for a corporation are not legally responsible for its actions; ownership is dispersed through the sale of stocks and ownership, and management is separate. (Whether managers act in ways that benefit the company and stockholders or concentrate on protecting their own interests is the subject of much debate.) Control of corporations assumes several forms. These include owner control, in which a dominant stockholder serves as the corporation's CEO (retaining control over operations); strategic control, in which someone who is not a member of the executive board or management controls the corporation from the outside by issuing directives to the CEO; or intercorporate control, where a CEO must acquiesce to the demands or agenda of other corporations, banks and financial institutions in particular. Today's giant corporations evade free market forces in two ways. (1) Many industries (from soap to automobiles) are oligopolies, in which *competition* is limited to a small number of large corporations. (2) Conglomerates have interests in many different industries, which protect them from losses in one area. The result is an *asymmetrical economy,* in which private entrepreneurs must compete against economic Goliaths.

B. The growth of the federal government can be seen in part as a response to the growth of big business. The government plays a dual role in the economy; it provides goods and services that enable companies to do business, and it regulates business activities to protect the public interest. Since the 1930s, federal government policies have been governed by Keynesian (pronounced Cainzian) economics. According to this view, the government must spend to boost the economy during economic depressions, and cut back to rein in the economy during periods of inflation. In recent years, however, this approach has been challenged by monetarists who argue that limiting the growth of the money supply is the best way to control the economy, and supply -side economists who purport that Keynesians place too much emphasis on consumer demand and advocate cutting taxes to free up private wealth for investment.

III.   How have the nature and meaning of work changed?

Your text considers how the structure of business and the economy shapes the experience of working.

A. Industrialization had a profound impact on the nature of work. When craftspeople and farmers became factory workers, they lost bargaining power, opportunities for creativity, and control over their own activities-- trends that continue today.

B. The current shift from an industrial to a service economy has contributed to the development of two separate worlds of work: a primary labor market that offers high wages and promotion opportunities, and a secondary labor market composed of low-skill, low-paying, dead-end jobs.

C. Even so, the work ethic remains strong.

IV. Is the United States becoming an information society?

The replacement of human workers with machines is no longer science fiction. Already, automation (the use of technological control to minimize the need for human workers) is moving from the factory to the office. At the forefront of the U.S. surge toward an *information society* is the computer.

Computers are machines for processing information. Their primary advantage is that they augment human brain power by expanding memory capacity and speeding up data retrieval and calculations at a dazzling rate that, perhaps, even their developers could not have imagined. In most settings, the introduction of computers (and recently, minicomputers) has not led to dramatic changes in the way people work, although computers have increased the ability of organizations and society to monitor and control both material and human resources. But, the full impact of the computer revolution is yet to be felt, as more types of hardware and software become affordable.

The most controversial use of the computer is in the area of automation. Whereas previously tools complemented the human laborer in the workplace, today human beings are more frequently becoming accessories to machines. More recently, use of automation (and in particular the computer) has begun to move out of the manufacturing sector of the economy into the service sector. The result has been, in many instances, to eliminate human judgment, as computer programs make decisions for both worker and client. Thus, office automation has changed the nature and experience of work, reducing the workers' autonomy and discretion, deskilling the job requirements, and in many cases alienating the worker, as Karl Marx predicted.

V.   What is the nature of today's global economy?

Our world is no longer composed of separate autonomous national economies. Today global oligopolies determine the business opportunities, employment patterns, and standard of living of everyone on earth. The European Economic Community (an agreement among European nations to remove physical, technical, and financial barriers in order to more efficiently manage and coordinate economic and social policies) will take full effect in 1992 and bring radical economic changes in Eastern Europe and the Soviet Union. The serious financial problems of Third World Nations due to lack of development will ultimately affect the economic agenda of all the world.

CONCEPT REVIEW

Match each of the following terms with the correct definition:

a. monopoly ✓
b. automation ✓
c. infrastructure
d. capitalist economy ✓
e. service economy ✓
f. conglomerate

g. corporation
h. multinational corporation
i.   command economy
j.   productivity
k. oligopoly ✓

1. ___   An economy in which most workers are not directly involved with the production of goods.

2. _b_   The use of computers or other high-tech devices in order to control production, reducing the need for human workers to a minimum.

3. _f_   A corporation with holdings and subsidiaries in a number of different industries.

4. _k_   The domination of an entire industrial sector by a relatively small number of large companies; specifically in a capitalist economy.

5. _d_   An economic system in which (ideally) the means of production are privately owned, economic activities are based on free enterprise and the profit motive, and the distribution of wealth is determined by the market.

6. _g_   An organization, created by law, whose existence, operation, and liabilities are independent of particular owners and managers.

7. ___   The means for moving raw materials, goods, people, and ideas

from one place to another in a society or region.

8.___ The ratio of goods produced to human effort.

9.*A* A firm that controls an entire industry, eliminating competition.

10. *i* An economic system in which (ideally) the means of production are owned by the state, economic activities are centrally planned, social welfare is a state responsibility, and the distribution of wealth is more or less even.

11.___ A corporation with holdings and subsidiaries in several different nations.

Answers

1.	e	7.	c
2.	b	8.	j
3.	f	9.	a
4.	k	10.	i
5.	d	11.	h
6.	g		

REVIEW QUESTIONS

1. Which of the following does *not* fit with capitalist ideals?
   a. free and open competition
   b. centralized planning by the government
   c. consumer sovereignty
   d. the profit motive
   e. none of the above

2. Which sector of the economy has grown at an accelerated rate in recent years?
   a. the primary labor market
   b. the secondary labor market
   c. information industries
   d. manufacturing
   e. all of the above

3. A major tire company buys a supermarket chain, timberland, and a movie production company. The company is building:
   a. a monopoly
   b. a corporation
   c. a conglomerate
   d. a multinational corporation
   e. all of the above

4. Economic competition within the U.S. television industry has led to:
   a. diversification
   b. increased quality
   c. cutbacks and consolidation
   d. none of the above

5. The board of directors of a corporation is responsible for:
   a. selecting top management
   b. protecting the public interest
   c. the sale of shares
   d. managing daily operations
   e. a and b

6. Which of the following economists has stressed the role of the government as an enabler for big business?
   a. Adam Smith
   b. John Maynard Keynes
   c. John Galbraith
   d. Milton Friedman

7. Today, white-collar work includes:
   a. high-prestige, high-paid jobs
   b. highly skilled jobs
   c. low-skilled jobs
   d. a mixture of high-paid, low-paid, high-prestige, low-prestige, highly skilled and low-skilled jobs

8. Which of the following is *not* part of the traditional American work ethic?
   a. standing on one's own two feet
   b. the belief that work confers dignity
   c. self-fulfillment
   d. viewing financial success as a major source of status

9. Which of the following is *not* a form that corporate control may assume?
   a. stockholder control
   b. owner control
   c. intercorporate control
   d. strategic control

10. *Infrastructure technology* refers to:
    a. techniques for automating work
    b. techniques for moving goods and services, and people and ideas, from

     place to place
  c. techniques for increasing management control
  d. golden parachutes

11. Which of the following economic theories holds that the government should adopt a laissez-faire posture toward the economy?
  a. Keynesian economics
  b. monetarism
  c. supply-side economics

12. The major difference between a service economy and an industrial economy is that in a service economy:
  a. Automation of the textile and other industries is involved.
  b. Government regulation is increased.
  c. A majority of the population is involved in the production of goods.
  d. A majority of the population is *not* involved in the production of goods.

13. One of the following groups equated hard work with virtue. Which one?
  a. the Greeks
  b. the Hebrews
  c. the early Christians
  d. the early Protestants

14. Maximizing managerial power has resulted in:
  a. increased productivity
  b. increased worker autonomy
  c. increased worker creativity
  d. decreased autonomy and productivity

15. During the 1980s the economic crisis in the Third World became more severe, so that per capita income in black Africa dropped to:
  a. $12,000
  b. $4,000
  c. $450
  d. $2,000

16. Which of the following occupations is *not* in the secondary labor market?
  a. dishwasher
  b. travel agent
  c. garment industry worker
  d. taxicab driver
  e. all of the above

17. Antitrust laws prohibit the formation of:
   a. monopolies
   b. oligopolies
   c. conglomerates
   d. multinationals

18. Which of the following is a reason why Western manufacturers are attracted to the newly opened Eastern bloc?
   a. engineering and manufacturing skills plus low wages
   b. a reputation for producing high-quality products
   c. extremely high worker productivity
   d. none of the above

19. The description of a corporation as a *person under the law* calls attention to:
   a. the limited liability of corporations
   b. the separation of ownership and management
   c. the diffusion of ownership through the sale of shares
   d. corporate asymmetry

20. The idea that industrialization dehumanizes work and alienates workers originated with
   a. Adam Smith
   b. Karl Marx
   c. Emile Durkheim
   d. Richard Edwards

Answers

1. b: According to capitalist ideology, central planning interferes with the laws of supply and demand. (See section entitled Capitalist Ideals.)
2. b: The shift from an industrial to a service economy is sometimes interpreted as increasing the need for highly skilled *intellectual* workers; in fact, the greatest increase has been in low-skill, low-paying jobs. (The Social Organization of Work)
3. c: The term *conglomerate* refers to a large corporation with investments in a number of different industries. In recent years, corporate growth has been due more to diversification than to expansion. (Corporate Capitalism)
4. c: Television, like any other business, makes changes designed to achieve the maximum amount of profit. Increased competition among the major TV networks has unfortunately led them to implement budget cutbacks rather than improve their quality to attract more viewers. (TV as Big Business)

5. e: The board of directors is responsible for establishing general policy and selecting top personnel; management is responsible for implementing policy. (Corporate Capitalism)

6. c: Galbraith was one of the first economists to oppose the conventional wisdom that government is the enemy of big business, by pointing out the role of government as an enabler. (Government and the Economy: Issues and Policies)

7. d: White-collar work today is different than in the past. It now consists of a variety of salary, prestige, and skill levels. Even the more professional white-collar jobs require less training and offer fewer opportunities for advancement. (The World of Work)

8. c: The idea that leading an independent, creative, and satisfying life is as important as supporting one's family, holding a steady job, or getting ahead is one of the *new rules* that emerged from the counterculture of the 1960s. (The Meaning of Work; see also Chapter Three)

9. a: Ordinary stockholders generally do not interfere with management. A major or dominant stockholder may exercise owner control, someone from outside the corporation may exercise strategic control, or other institutions (principally financial institutions) may utilize intercorporate control. (Who Controls Corporations?)

10. b: Infrastructure plays a key role in economic development. Railroads led to the first burst of industrialization in the United States; telecommunications led to another expansion. (Big Business: Some Historical Background)

11. b: Of the three economic approaches discussed in your text, monetarism is closest to the ideals of capitalism set down by Adam Smith. (Government and the Economy: Issues and Policies)

12. d: The term *service* is used loosely to describe any work not directly related to the production of goods, from the job of janitor to that of financial analyst. (The Social Organization of Work)

13. d: Unlike the other groups listed, the early Protestants saw idleness as sin--including the *idleness* of philosophers, whom the Greeks revered, and the *idleness* of priests and nuns, whom the early Christians revered. (The Meaning of Work)

14. d: Allowing managers more power has resulted in less autonomy for workers and decreased productivity overall. (The Technology of Management)

15. c: Per capita income in black Africa dropped from $560 to $450. This change involved a great deal of human suffering--starvation, chronic malnutrition, etc. (The Economic Crisis in the Third World)

16. e: *Travel agent* may seem a glamorous occupation, but it offers little job security, few chances for promotion, and low wages--characteristics of the secondary labor market. (The Social Organization of Work)

17. a: Control of an industry is against the law in the United States; domination of a market (through oligopolies) is not. (Market Dominance)

18. a: Western countries are interested in pursuing business opportunities in Eastern Europe because of the labor pool there. Workers are highly trained, but accustomed to very low wages, thus allowing Western industries to capitalize on brain power while spending little of their profits for employee salaries. (The World System)
19. a: One of the reasons why relatively small companies incorporate is to protect the owners from personal liability. If a corporation becomes bankrupt, its factories and inventory may be sold to pay off debts, but the owner's house and car are *safe.* (Corporate Capitalism)
20. b: Karl Marx predicted that workers in capitalist, industrial societies would become alienated from their work for two primary reasons: First they would work and sell their labor to someone else rather than for their own gain, and second they would produce only parts of a product and not the finished good. (The Impact on Workers)

MYTH OR FACT?

1. Computers change the way people work.   t/f
2. The future of the global economy depends upon closing the gap between Japan, the U.S., and Europe.   t/f
3. Most American workers say they are satisfied with their jobs.   t/f

Answers

1. *False.* Most studies show that rather than change their behavior to adapt to computers, most people make computers conform to their usual work patterns. However, the text does indicate that computers have an effect in the workplace in regard to reducing the human element in a job and scaling down job requirements.
2. *False.* The future of the global economy depends on closing the gap between the rich nations of the world and the Third World Nations.
3. *True.* However, most also say that if they had their lives to live over, they would go into a different line of work. Thus, most Americans could be described as resigned to their jobs, but not satisfied.

CRITICAL THINKING

1. S. C. Allyn, a retired chairman of the board of the National Cash Register Company (NCR), likes to tell the following story. Allyn was one of the first American civilians to enter Germany after World War II, in August 1945. He made his way through burnt-out buildings and rubble to what had been a thriving NCR factory before the war. The factory lay in ruins. Allyn saw two men in rags working on the wreckage. As he approach-

ed, one of the men looked up. "We knew you'd come!" Both were NCR employees Allyn hadn't seen for years. The three of them went to work, doing what they could to clean up. A few days later an American tank pulled up. The GI at the helm waved. "Hi, I'm NCR, Omaha. Did you guys make your quota this month?" The factory had been destroyed in the war, but the company, with its hard-driving, sales-oriented culture, had survived.

In *Corporate Cultures,* Terrence Deal and Allan Kennedy argue that the most successful companies in the United States are those that have a strong corporate culture. Corporate culture consists of a shared philosophy, often captured in a slogan ("IBM means service"; "At GE progress is our most important product"); heroes who personify these values and serve as role models (the man who invented the motor for an electric toothbrush, or the international manager who exorcized ghosts from a factory in Singapore); rites and rituals (everyday rules about "the way we do things around here" and special occasions, such as company picnics and Christmas parties); and an organizational structure that makes people feel important. At one computer company, even stock clerks are put through four intensive hiring interviews. They feel special, even before they get the job. The founder of the company personally welcomes all new employees. Loyalty to the company and productivity are both high. As one worker put it, "My job is important, and if I don't do it, Tandem [the company] doesn't make a buck."

In summarizing their study of the best American corporations, Deal and Kennedy conclude: "These corporations have values and beliefs to pass along--not just products. They have stories to tell--not just profits to make. They have heroes whom managers and workers can emulate--not just faceless bureaucrats. In short, they are human institutions that provide practical meaning for people, both on and off the job."[1]

Think about places you have worked--a summer camp, a department store, a law firm, whatever business it was. Did the company have a strong corporate culture? Did employees have a positive identification with the company, or were they negative and cynical? How did this affect their work? Ask yourself the same questions about your college or university. Does it have a distinct identity, heroes, and rites and rituals? How does the university culture affect students' attitudes toward classwork and extracurricular activities? Are most students "loyal" and "productive?" How do you think this culture affects faculty and other employees?

2. Daniel Bell's vision of the information society is optimistic about the future; other social thinkers (as your text suggests) are skeptical, even

pessimistic. Economists Barry Bluestone and Bennett Harrison[2] are among the pessimists. The decline of old-line industries, they argue, threatens our future.

> Underlying the high rates of unemployment, the sluggish growth in the domestic economy, and the failure to successfully compete in the international market is the deindustrialization of America. By *deindustrialization* is meant a widespread, systematic, disinvestment in the nation's basic productive capacity. Controversial as it may be, the essential problem in the U.S. economy can be traced to the way capital--in the forms of financial resources and of real plans and equipment--has been diverted from productive investment in our basic national industries into unproductive speculation, mergers and acquisitions, and foreign investment. Left behind are shuttered factories, displaced workers, and a newly emerging group of ghost towns. (p. 6)

Bluestone and Harrison look at the consequences of deindustrialization, first, from the point of view of the economy as a whole.

> Our share of the world's manufacturing exports has fallen from more than 25 percent to less than 17 percent in the last twenty years, and relative to our strongest competitors, it could easily be argued that we are being rapidly pushed to the sidelines. It is disturbing to learn, for example, that the 1980 trade deficit with Japan reached over $10 billion. Even more shocking is a listing of the two countries' major exports. In terms of dollar value, the number one Japanese product sold to America was passenger motor vehicles, followed by iron and steel plates, truck and tractor chassis, radios, motorbikes, and audio and video tape recorders. America's seven exports to Japan, in order of dollar value, were soybeans, corn, fir logs, coal, wheat, and cotton. . . . [A]t least with respect to our most important competitor, the United States has been reduced to an agricultural nation trying desperately to compete with the manufacturer of the world's most sophisticated capital and consumer goods. (p. 5)

Bluestone and Harrison also look at the human and social costs of deindustrialization.

> The costs . . . go well beyond lost wages and foregone productivity. Workers and their families suffer serious physical and emotional health problems when employers suddenly shut down operations, and the community as a whole experiences a loss of reve-

nue needed for supporting police and fire protection, school, and parks. Entire cities and towns can be brought to the brink of bankruptcy, as has happened in Detroit, Chicago, and a host of smaller municipalities throughout the industrial Midwest. (p. 11)

The authors calculate that a 1 percent rise in unemployment can be linked to 37,000 additional deaths, including 920 suicides and 630 homicides, as well as 4,000 more admissions to state mental hospitals, and 3,000 to state prisons. These estimates may be an exaggeration, but even if the authors are off by half, the human cost of deindustrialization is high.

Bell's optimism and Bluestone and Harrison's pessimism can be seen as extremes, and the truth assumed to lie between the two. Read the economic sections in your paper for the next several weeks; review the descriptions of the U.S. economy in the text. Which view of the future seems closer to the facts you find in these sources?

3.   In *Working*, Studs Terkel[3] interviewed a firefighter who is clearly an exception to the norm of "blue-collar blues." His work is dangerous, but he loves it.

> When you get smoke in your lungs, these guys are spittin' out this shit for two days. A fireman's life is nine years shorter than the average workingman because of the beating they take on their lungs and their heart. More hazardous than a coal miner. The guy don't think nothing's wrong with him. You don't think until you get an x-ray and your name's on it . . . .
> You get a fire at two, three in the morning. . .Guys are yellin', "Come on, we go. First Due." That means you gotta be the first engine company there. You really gotta move. It's a pride. You gotta show you're the best. But what they're fighting' over is good. What they're fightin' over is savin' lives.
>
> . . .
>
> Last month there was a second alarm. I was off duty. I ran over there. I'm a bystander. I see these firemen on the roof, with the smoke pouring out around them, and the flames, and they go in. It fascinated me. Jesus Christ, that's what I do! . . . The firemen, you actually see them produce. You see them put out a fire. You see them come out with babies in their hands. You see them give mouth-to-mouth when a guy's dying. You can't get around that shit. That's real. To me, that's what I want to be.
> I worked in a bank. You know, it's just paper. It's not real. Nine

to five and it's shit. You're lookin' at numbers. But I can look back and say, "I helped put out a fire, I helped save somebody." It shows something I did on this earth.

Another interview, with a staff writer for an institution that publishes health-care literature, revealed a different pattern. Nora Watson told Terkel, "As I work in the business world, I am more and more shocked. You throw yourself into things because you feel that important questions--self-discipline, goals, a meaning in your life--are carried out in your work." When she started working for the institution, she came in early and left late. She read everything she could about the subject she was working on. But she soon found she was "wrecking the curve." No one else was working hard and no one wanted her to. She could do everything she was assigned and more in two hours and spend the rest of the day reading, shopping, daydreaming. Was she happy? No. "It's so demeaning to be there and not be challenged. It's humiliation, because I feel I'm being forced into doing something I would never do of my own free will--which is simply waste itself. . . . It is possible for me to sit here and read my books. But then you walk out with no sense of satis-faction, with no sense of legitimacy! . . . It's like being on welfare. . . . It's the surprise of enforced idleness. It makes you feel not at home with yourself. I'm furious. It's a feeling that I will not be humiliated. I will not be dis-used."[3]

Compare this staff writer with the fire fighter. Do they have the same values? The same needs? Why is one content and the other not?

4. One of the answers to the question, "Why study sociology?" is, "To get a job." We thought you might like some practical information on how socio-logists earn a living.[4]

At some time in their careers, almost all of the 15,000 sociologists in the United States teach at a college or university. Although most pro-fessors teach only two or three classes a semester, most work forty-five to sixty hours a week--preparing for classes, writing books and scholarly papers, doing research, training graduate students, and serving on uni-versity committees or in regional or national associations or the Ameri-can Sociological Association. In 1980 full professors earned between $20,000 and $35,000 for a nine- to ten-month academic year. There is also the "psychic income" of academic freedom, being able to indulge one's curiosity, teaching the courses you want to teach, and introducing stu-dents to knowledge that may change their view of the world.

About a quarter of all sociologists hold positions outside universities, in government agencies, nonprofit organizations, and the business world. They can be found in the Bureau of the Census, the Societal Analysis Department of General Motors Research laboratories, or health centers and hospitals that are developing programs for delivering medical services-- to name a few. These sociologists devote most of their time to writing and editing, developing projects or formulating policy, administering projects, doing research, and supervising personnel. In 1975, half had incomes between $25,000 and $50,000.

By "sociologists," we mean individuals who have earned a doctorate in sociology. Job opportunities for individuals with a master's degree or B.A. in sociology range from personnel manager in a small firm to staff member in a research institute to traveling representative for a publishing company. Students who wish further information should consult a pamphlet called *Careers in Sociology,* published by the American Sociological Association.

Notes

[1] Terrence E. Deal and Allan A. Kennedy, *Corporate Culture: The Rites and Rituals of Corporate Life*, Reading MA: Addison-Wesley; 1982, p. 15.

[2] B. Bluestone and B. Harrison, *The Deindustrialization of America: Plant Closings, Community Abandonment, and the Dismantling of Basic Industry*. New York: Basic Books, 1982. Copyright 1982 by Barry Bluestone and Bennett Harrison. Reprinted by permission of Basic Books, Inc.

[3] Studs Terkel, *Working: People Talk About What They Do All Day and How They Feel About What They Do*, New York: Avon, 1974: pp. 586-589; 676-678. Copyright 1974 by Studs Terkel. Reprinted by permission of Pantheon Books, a Division of Random House, Inc.

[4] This is based on Everett K. Wilson and Hanan Selvin, *Why Study Sociology?* Belmont, CA: Wadsworth, 1980, pp. 9-15.

Chapter Seventeen

POPULATION, GLOBAL ECOLOGY, AND URBANIZATION

OBJECTIVES

After reading Chapter Seventeen you should be able to give in-depth answers to the following questions:

1. How rapidly is the world population expanding?
2. How is the population of the United States changing?
3. How will population growth affect global ecology?
4. What is the impact of urbanization on social life?

CONCEPTS

You should also understand the following sociological concepts:

demography
birth rate
fertility rate
death rate
net growth rate
life expectancy
demographic transition
momentum factor
zero population growth
urbanization
census
green revolution
greenhouse effect

CHAPTER REVIEW

I. How rapidly is the world population expanding?

The world population is expanding at the rate of about 237,000 people a *day*, and will very likely top 6.3 billion before the year 2000. But population growth is distributed unevenly. Your text uses demography (the scientific study of population) to contrast patterns of population growth in Western nations and in the Third World.

A. Western nations have completed what social scientists call the *demographic transition.* This term refers to a pattern of three distinct stages in population growth. In Stage I, birth rates are high, but death rates are also high and population growth is slow. In Stage II, birth rates remain high but death rates decline because of improved agricultural technology, transportation, sanitation, and other factors. Population growth soars. In Stage III, birth rates decline and the balance between births and deaths is restored. The *population explosion* is over.

B. Most Third World nations are in Stage II of the demographic transition: death rates have fallen but birth rates remain high. Because the populations of these countries are young, population growth has a built-in *momentum factor*. Even if couples limit themselves to one or two children, it will be decades before zero population growth is achieved. Although there is no simple solution to the problem of population growth in the Third World, analysis of the demographic transition in Western nations suggests that economic development is *the best contraceptive*. When people enjoy a high standard of living and social security they are more likely to limit family size. Also, raising the status of women has been linked to smaller families.

II.   How is the population of the United States changing?

The fact that a nation is in Stage III of the demographic transition (as the United States is) does not mean that there are no changes in its population profile. The 1980 census revealed two major changes in the U.S. population. The first is a decline in fertility. Americans have fewer children today than they did twenty-five or fifty years ago. One reason for this is the increased availability and use of contraceptives in this country. The second is a trend among women to postpone marriage and childbirth while they pursue a career or a higher level of education. At present, the overall fertility rate in the United States is one of the lowest in the world. Whether this pattern will continue is difficult to say: economic conditions may have delayed effects on attitudes. The second change is in the age structure. The population of the United States is growing older (that is, the proportion of middle-aged and other Americans has increased while the proportion of young people has declined). The median age of the population has risen from twenty in 1970 to thirty-two in 1989. In 2011, the baby boom generation will begin turning sixty-five. By 2030 almost 25 percent of the United States' population will be sixty-five or older.

III.   How will population growth affect global ecology?

In the late eighteenth century, Thomas Malthus argued that humanity is condemned to cycles of feast and famine. When food supplies are abundant, the population will grow until eventually it outstrips available resources, leading to hunger and war. Was Malthus correct? Your text considers two views of the future, analyzes current patterns of supply and distribution, examines technological solutions to short supplies, then summarizes the current state of affairs.

A. Predicting the future is not a simple matter of arithmetic. Social patterns of supply, distribution, and consumption must also be taken into account. Knowing how many people will be on the earth in the year 2000, how many bushels of wheat will be produced, how many barrels of oil available, and the like, does not tell you how many people will be hungry or cold or unemployed. Worldwide food production has increased dramatically within the past two decades. Enough food is produced now to feed 6 billion people, 1 billion more than exist on the earth. The hunger in the world today is the result of distribution, not supply. The commercialization of agriculture has undermined food self-sufficiency in much of the Third World. Energy shortages are also the result of *distribution, not supply*. Keep that in mind as you evaluate policies you will be asked to support as a taxpayer.

B. Technology can produce *miracles*, but also entails environmental risks. The Green Revolution, for example, greatly expanded the amount of food produced per acre. But it also increased vulnerability and displaced agricultural workers. The increased food production brought about by the Green Revolution has resulted in lower grain prices, causing Third World nations to go further into debt. The problems of production and displacement related to the Green Revolution are further aggravated by overpopulation which has reduced the amount of available land and deteriorated that land which is available.

C. One of the major problems facing the world today is its consumption patterns. Overpopulation alone is not a problem. The impact of people on ecosystems and nonrenewable resources is, however, a major problem. Consumption patterns for food and fuel are grossly disproportionate, so that industrial nations (and the United States, in particular) are much more extravagant in their use of natural resources. Future supplies of fuel and food are dependent on current patterns of consumption. Continued population growth means that the absolute amounts of energy and fuel needed will continue to increase. In regard to this, the depletion of one major renewable resource, trees, needs to be corrected, presumably, by the use of reforestation programs (oil, gas, coal, etc., are not renewable). This will not be an easy problem to fix.

D. Environmental risks are also becoming more prevalent in the world today. Oil spills (The Exxon *Valdez*) nuclear power accidents (Chernobyl) and air pollution are the biggest threats. But these are only the tip of the iceberg. The greenhouse effect, which is the buildup of carbon dioxide, methane and other gases in the earth's atmosphere allowing heat to enter the atmosphere but not to escape, may cause the earth's climate to grow warmer and the earth's farmland to become dry and unusable, and as a result of the melting of polar icecaps, sea level may rise and flood many of the world's major cities.

IV. What is the impact of urbanization on social life?

Sociologists have long viewed the big city as modern society in microcosm. Tonnies, Durkheim, and Marx all were concerned about the alienating effects of urban living. Your text looks, first, at patterns of urbanization in the United States, and then at world patterns.

A. The urbanization of the United States can be divided into three stages: the emergence of big cities (compact centers of manufacturing and population that developed as a result of industrialization and immigration); the growth of metropolitan regions (geographical expansion made possible by new technologies of transportation and communication, exemplified by the suburban shopping mall); and deconcentration (recent population shifts from the Snow Belt to the Sun Belt and from metropolitan to rural areas). More recently, big cities have reversed this trend to a degree. For example, Los Angeles has experienced a 17 percent growth in population. Deconcentration has changed the function and demographics of older cities: Once the centers of manufacturing and affluence in the nation, these cities are now centers for specialized services and *warehouses* for large segments of the nation's poor.

Among American sociologists, the view that cities promote depersonalization, alienation, and social disruption has been challenged by research that illuminates the role of ethnic and other subcultures in creating urban communities.

B. The rich nations of the world seem to be entering a period of deurbanization. In contrast, the populations of Third World cities are exploding. Drawn to the city by lack of opportunities in the rural areas, many such migrants are forced into the *informal sector* of the economy.

CONCEPT REVIEW

Match each of the following terms with the correct definition.

a. census
b. demographic transition
c. fertility rate
d. life expectancy
e. net growth rate
f. zero population growth
g. urbanization

h. momentum factor
i. Green Revolution
j. birth rate
k. death rate
l. demography
m. greenhouse effect

1.___ The number of births per 1,000 people in a population in any given year.

2.___ The percentage increase in a population, in a given period, taking into account immigration and emigration as well as birth and death rates.

3.___ The scientific study of population.

4.___ Population growth that will occur because a large percentage of the population is in or about to enter its childbearing years.

5.___ A systematic count of an entire population.

6.___ The three-stage pattern of population change that accompanied the transformation of Western nations from agricultural to industrial societies.

7.___ The number of deaths per 1,000 people in a population in a given year.

8.___ The average life span of individuals in a population.

9.___ The number of births per 1,000 women in a given population in their childbearing years (ages fifteen to forty-four) in a year.

10.___ The point where birth and death rates are roughly equal, so that a population is stable, that is, it neither increases nor decreases.

11.___ The invention of new strains of wheat, rice, and beans that greatly increase the yield per acre.

12.___ An increase in the percentage of a population living in urban settlements and a resulting increase in the influence of urban culture and life styles.

13.___ A buildup of carbon dioxide, methane, and other gases in the atmosphere which will act as a shield, allowing heat from the sun to enter the earth's atmosphere, but not escape.

Answers

1. j	7. k	13. m
2. e	8. d	
3. l	9. c	
4. h	10. f	
5. a	11. i	
6. b	12. g	

REVIEW QUESTIONS

1. The human population of the earth presently stands at about 4.4 billion. Estimates are that by the year 2000 it will reach:

    a. 5 billion
    b. 6.3 billion
    c. 10 billion
    d. 15 billion

2. Which of the following sociologists believed that the city has a dehuman-izing effect on residents?
    a. Herbert Gans
    b. Claude Fischer
    c. Louis Wirth
    d. Allan Schnaiberg

3. Which of the following may be a result of the greenhouse effect?
    a. Polar ice caps would melt.
    b. Sea level would rise.
    c. Land would become arid and unusable.
    d. All of the above.
    e. None of the above.

4. Which of the following sociologists sees cities as *promoting* the de-velopment of subcultures and the individual's involvement in social groups?
    a. Herbert Gans
    b. Claude Fischer
    c. Emile Durkheim
    d. Louis Wirth

5. The fertility rate of a nation is a measure of:
    a. the number of women of childbearing age
    b. the number of babies born per 1,000 population
    c. the number of babies born per 1,000 women ages fifteen to forty-four
    d. the momentum factor

6. The major difference between nineteenth-century European sociologists and twentieth-century American sociologists is:
    a. European sociologists associated urbanization with social change.
    b. European sociologists saw urbanization as leading to alienation and anomie.
    c. American sociologists saw urbanization as a cause (rather than a con-sequence) of modernization.
    d. American sociologists see cities as providing new opportunities for sociability.

7. Third World cities continue to grow, for a variety of reasons. Which of

the following does *not* contribute to urban growth in the Third World?
a. lack of national infrastructure
b. diminishing economic opportunities in the countryside
c. lack of alternatives
d. job opportunities in capital cities

8. The largest city (that with the greatest population) in the U.S. today is:
a. Chicago
b. New York
c. Los Angeles
d. Washington, D.C.

9. A nation enters Stage III of the demographic transition when birth rates decline to replacement levels and the population growth rate slows down. Which of the following has helped to slow population growth in Western nations?
a. economic development
b. modern birth-control methods
c. Social Security programs
d. the decline in infant mortality
e. all of the above
f. a-c

10. In Kerala, India, the relatively low birth rate may be attributed to:
a. the high status of men
b. the high status of women
c. an increased age at first marriage for women
d. none of the above
e. b and c

11. Which of the following is not an environmental problem associated with the green revolution?
a. irrigation depletes the soil of vital nutrients
b. chemical fertilizers and pesticides pollute the water supply
c. insects develop an immunity to chemical pesticides
d. air pollution is increased

12. The population of the _____ area(s) of the U.S. experienced an increase during the late 1970s and early 1980s.
a. Midwest/North central
b. South and Southwest
c. Northeast
d. None of the above

13. Changes in population growth patterns in the Third World differ from those that occurred in Western nations in that:
    a. In the Third World, death rates have fallen but birth rates remain high.
    b. The decline in death rates in the Third World is due in large part to imported technology, medicine, and food.
    c. Changes that took several hundred years in Western nations have occurred in a matter of decades in the Third World.
    d. All of the above.
    e. b and c.

14. Which of the following represents a recent change in social patterns in the United States, one revealed by the 1980 census, which continued throughout most of the 1980s?
    a. Fertility rates declined.
    b. More people moved out of cities than into them.
    c. Most Americans now live in metropolitan regions.
    d. More and more industries are locating in the suburbs.

15. Malthus' *Essay on the Principles of Population* (1798) is a classic, but Malthus did not anticipate:
    a. improvements in agricultural productivity
    b. widespread use of birth control
    c. changing attitudes toward family size
    d. the effects of wars and famines
    e. all of the above
    f. a-c

16. The problem of world hunger is primarily one of
    a. food production
    b. food distribution
    c. food consumption
    d. none of the above

17. Which of the following social phenomena is *not* a result of the demographic episode known as the baby boom?
    a. the growth of child-centered industries in the 1950s and 1960s
    b. the oversupply of schools and teachers in the late 1970s
    c. the undersupply of men of marriageable age in the 1960s and 1970s
    d. the growth of the retirement industry

18. An elderly gentleman from Calcutta comments that the biggest change in his lifetime is that, *We have learned how to keep from dying.* This observation illustrates that India is in which stage of the demographic

transition?
a. Stage I
b. Stage II
c. Stage III
d. This observation does not apply to the demographic transition.

Answers

1. b: This may not sound like a huge increase (from 4 to 6), but we are talking about billions! Two billion is equal to the entire population of the world in 1930, or almost 1,000 times the population of the United States today. (Imagine what would happen if 1,000 nations the size of the United States were added to the world tomorrow.) (See first page of Chapter 17.)
2. c: Wirth agreed with Tonnies that cities create a depersonalized social order, in which people are motivated by self-interest and intimate relationships are rare. (Urban Studies in the U.S.)
3. d: The greenhouse effect results from a buildup of gases in the atmosphere which allow heat to enter the atmosphere but not to escape. This increases the temperature of the earth over time, causing land to become arid and sea level to rise. (Environmental Risks)
4. b: Where else, Fischer asks, can chess fanatics or Pacific islanders or homosexuals find so many people who share their norms, values, and interests? (Urban Studies in the U.S.)
5. c: The birth rate only measures babies born. The fertility rate gives demographers a measure of average family size. (World Patterns)
6. c: Both European and American sociologists associate urbanization with social change and both have debated the impact of urban living on social relationships. However, American sociologists have given urbanization a greater causal role in modernization. (Urban Studies in the U.S.)
7. d: The populations of Third World cities are growing much faster than are jobs, housing, or social services. As a result, large numbers of urban immigrants are forced into marginal occupations. (Urbanization in Global Perspective)
8. c: During the 1980s, Los Angeles led the trend among big cities replacing their population. It grew by 17% and replaced New York as the country's most populated city. (The Urbanization of the United States)
9. e: You probably recognized answers a through c. One would think that a decline in infant mortality would increase, not decrease, population growth. In fact, it seems that people have more children when there is a risk that some will not survive childhood than when they can expect most offspring to live. (World Patterns)
10. e: Kerala, India, has the lowest birth rate in India, in large part due

to a tradition of respect for women which is followed there. Women's improved status has allowed them to become literate, to work to earn income, and to defer marriage until a later age (twenty-two). (World Patterns)

11. d: Air pollution is not a direct consequence of the green revolution. Its primary negative effects involve soil and the water supply. (Food Supplies and Distribution)

12. b: The population of the south and southwest grew at twice the national rate. (The Urbanization of the United States)

13. e: Western nations did go through a period when death rates fell but birth rates remained high. In the West, this stage was followed by a period of industrial expansion and economic growth. In the Third World, economic growth is not catching up with population growth. (World Patterns)

14. b: This is new: For the first time in this century, more people left the city for suburban and rural homes than left farms and suburbs for the city. All of the other answers refer to ongoing trends. This trend began to reverse itself in the late 1980s. (Urbanization)

15. f: Malthus saw war and famine as natural controls on human population growth; he did not foresee that people could or would reduce family size. (Population and Global Ecology)

16. b: Worldwide food production has increased dramatically, and even though consumption patterns are unequal, distribution is the underlying issue in world hunger. (Food Supplies and Distribution)

17. d: The baby boom generation is now in its thirties and forties and has yet to reach retirement age. The growth of the retirement industry is due to increases in longevity, not the baby boom. All of the other answers describe changes resulting from the large difference in generation size--the pig-in-a-python effect. (The Changing Age Structure)

18. b: The population explosion in Stage II of the demographic transition is due more to a decline in death rates than to an increase in birth rates. (World Patterns)

MYTH OR FACT?

1. There is enough food being produced in the world today to feed 6 billion people, 1 billion more than the total population of the earth.   t/f
2. Birth rates tend to rise in times of economic prosperity.   t/f

Answers

1. *True.* Much of the hunger in today's world is the result of distribution, not supply.

2. *False.* The relationship between economics and fertility is a complex one. The declining birth rates in Western nations during Stage III of the demographic transition are linked to industrial and economic development. In this country, birth rates dropped in the roaring twenties and prosperous sixties. Exactly why they did is not clear, but your text provides suggestions.

CRITICAL THINKING

1. Nowhere are the interrelated problems of population growth, environmental deterioration, and urban sprawl more visible than in the cities of the Third World. Mexico City is an example.[1] The population of Mexico City has doubled in the past decade alone, reducing the quality of living for all of the city's 16 million inhabitants. Nearly 2 1/2 million automobiles, 35,000 factories, and the smoke from garbage dumps pour 11,000 tons of waste materials into the air everyday. Doctors around the world come to the city to study new respiratory diseases. All major cities have slums, but those in Mexico City house an estimated 5 million people. New squatter settlements, called "lost cities," appear almost weekly. The average Mexican family includes six or seven people; 51 percent of the families in Mexico City live in one room. Middle- and upper-class Mexicans who have moved to the outskirts of the city spend an average of three hours a day commuting through toxic fumes to work. Laborers often spend five hours a day standing in lines or crushed into buses and subways. Despite these conditions, the mass movement of population from the countryside to Mexico City continues. Estimates are that the population will reach 30 or 35 million by the turn of the century.

    How does urbanization in the Third World differ from urbanization in more developed nations? What social changes or public policies might prevent Mexico City from becoming more crowded, congested, and polluted in the future?

2. In *The Urban Experience,*[2] Claude Fischer (whose view of urban living is described in your text) speculates about the future of cities. Where do we go from here? Fischer suggests four possible directions. The first is the emergence of the Supercity, which long ago captured the imagination of science fiction writers. According to this scenario, most of the world will come to resemble Manhattan. Every family on earth will be crowded into tiny apartments in giant skyscrapers. At the opposite extreme is *total dispersal*, or what has been called the postcity age. According to this scenario, modern communications technology will render cities obsolete. It will soon be possible for the president of a major

corporation to conduct all business from a remote mountain cabin; or a student to attend classes, do research, turn in papers, and take exams without ever leaving home. An "electronic web" of households and small settlements would replace urban living altogether. A third possibility is *more of the same:* Cities will continue to spread geographically, gradually melding into one another. A fourth possible future is *dispersed towns.* In this scenario, the spreading metropolis breaks up into medium-sized cities and towns, perhaps divided by parklands and linked by high-speed highways and railways.

After reading Chapter Seventeen in your text, which of these four urban futures would you consider most likely? Which would you consider most desirable? Why?

3. Discussions of modern societies often ignore the continued existence of rural communities. In his study of the survivors of the flood in Buffalo Creek (the small town in West Virginia described in Chapter One of your text), Kai Erikson showed that the flood had destroyed not only a town, but also a community, or *Gemeinschaft.*

> [T]he neighborhoods strung out along Buffalo Creek . . . were like the air people breathed--sometimes harsh, sometimes chilly, but always a basic fact of life. For better or worse, the people of the hollow were enmeshed in the fabric of their community; they drew their being from it. When that fabric was torn away by the disaster, people found themselves exposed and alone, suddenly dependent on their own personal resources.
> And the cruel fact of the matter is that many survivors, when left to their own mettle, proved to have meager resources, not because they lacked the heart or the competence, certainly, but because they had always put their abilities in the service of the larger community and did not know how to recall them for their own individual purposes. A good part of their personal strength turned out to be the reflected strength of the collectivity--on loan from the communal store--and they discovered that they were not good at making decisions, not very good at getting along with others, not very good at maintaining themselves as separate persons in the absence of neighborly support.[3]

On the basis of this description, what would you say are the advantages of belonging to a close-knit community? the disadvantages?

Notes

1 *The New York Times*: (May 15, 1983), pp. 1 and 12.

2 Claude S. Fischer, *The Urban Experience,* New York: Harcourt Brace Jovanovich, 1976.

3 Kai T. Erikson, *Everything in Its Path*, New York: Simon and Schuster, 1976, pp. 214-215. Copyright 1976 by Kai Erikson. Reprinted by permission of Simon and Schuster, Inc.